MONEY TO
BURN

Peter + Barbara,

All ROADS lead to
Ricklands.

B I L L   B R O W N

Editors:
Lesley Dahl
Sandra Pace

ISBN: 1540610780
ISBN 13: 9781540610782
Library of Congress Control Number: 2016919814
CreateSpace Independent Publishing Platform
North Charleston, South Carolina

FOREWORD

Money to Burn is a fictionalized account of actual events that occurred in a very small rural community in one of the more progressive southern states in the country. It's a story with many twists and turns and different characters, some real, others the product of my imagination. Names have all been changed and are not related to any person involved in any of the actual situations in an effort to protect the innocent – and the guilty.

Telling this story presented me with a serious challenge in tying together all the events that happened from the 1940s forward in these villages and in surrounding counties. It has been a formidable task, but worth the effort to bring this incredible tale involving murder, sex, counterfeit money, the Mafia, bank fraud, and bootlegging to the page.

It has been a decades long task gathering and organizing this information. A verbal synopsis of this material was presented to a number of focus groups over the years to determine the story's interest-generating ability and/or its publishing viability. It passed muster in each case.

This is a story of two parallel universes. One that chronicles the choices one criminal and his "boys" made in their search for their pots of gold and how their story intertwined with the second, the long and winding road the "Bank" followed in its quest to reach the pinnacle of its industry, and in doing so, became "too big to fail."

ACKNOWLEDGEMENTS

I owe a debt of gratitude to EC's daughter, Elaine Cain, and to Bobby Hanes, both of whom met with me on their own time and spoke candidly about this incredible story and their roles in it. They validated many parts of this story, but both agreed that much of the story should be fiction, as it now is. They filled in blanks and provided important details about aspects of this story. Without their participation, there would be no *Money to Burn*.

Additionally, there are many other unnamed persons who deserve my appreciation for the bits and pieces they contributed to the overall story. Their information was most helpful in pulling the stories and events together in a meaningful way. So "Thanks" to you folks as well. You know who you are.

To my wife, Sandra, my daughter, Melissa, and my Catman, as always.....

"First you get the facts straight, then you distort them at your leisure!"

Mark Twain

TABLE OF CONTENTS

PART ONE

Chapter 1
THE ABDUCTION

On a cool spring night in May 1952, EC and his young wife Clara drove down the rain slick highway in his shiny brown Packard. They had just left their house at the Fork, and it was pouring. The wipers could barely keep the windshield clear enough to see even a few feet beyond the fancy hood ornament.

Clara screamed, "Why the hell don't you slow down before you kill us both? If I can't see anything, how the hell can you?"

"I'm doin' just fine, just shut the hell up," EC spit out. "Goddamn women," he muttered.

Clara bristled. "You're a sexist pig. Always puttin' women down. You've never known how to treat a lady. No respect at all. None at all."

EC clammed up, letting her think he agreed with her.

It was an ordinary Sunday night for EC and Clara, his second wife, and they were making their usual weekly revenue run to EC's cash cows, drive-in movies in three different communities. They had been making the same run every week for years. In the beginning it was a cozy "let's go collect the money together" type of a deal. However, by now their Sunday night run had become a grind. Tonight they were not speaking, at least not civilly.

Clara cleared her throat and said in a cold, hard voice, "EC, you gotta quit screwing around with Katy. *Now*. We've had this friggin' conversation before, but I assure you, we are not gonna have it again."

EC slammed on the brakes and jerked the car onto the shoulder of the road. "What the hell you talking 'bout?" He wheeled around in his seat and shouted, "Katy's just the damn babysitter."

"You gonna hit me again?" Clara asked, raising her arms in self-defense. She collected herself and said, "EC, everyone in town knows you're screwing her. Everyone has seen the two of you together. Even your own daughter knows something's going on."

At the mention of Elaine, EC's five year old daughter, he winced.

Clara was still talking. "If you don't quit seeing her, I swear I'm going to tell every goddamn thing I know about all of your crooked business deals. All of them. Do you hear me? Even the plates. And you know there's a lot to tell. You'll be damn sorry, I can promise you that."

Smoldering, EC snorted under his breath, "I'll take care of it."

Outside, the rain continued to fall.

Inside, silence fell.

EC, not the type to take too kindly to such threats from his wife, had already considered this nagging problem. They had argued about Katy before, and he had already started weighing possible solutions. He could simply cut off the affair with Katy, never call her again. Just like that. But could he do that? Did he *want* to do that?

As he steered the car back onto the road, the wipers flapped trying to keep the water off of the windshield. It was a losing battle. The rain was ferocious.

EC thought back five years to when he and Clara first met and started dating. It was about that same time he found out he had knocked-up another local girlfriend. He thought he had learned his lesson once before, with his first wife Brenda, but damned if he hadn't made the same mistake again. He didn't have to marry that second girl, though, because she died giving birth to Elaine. For $1,000 cash, he'd gotten the top county lawyer, Ed Pascal, to arrange for Elaine's adoption. Now he and Clara were raising Elaine together. A lot of water had gone over the dam since they'd married; socially, business-wise, and criminally. A very great deal of water had flowed over that dam for sure.

After EC collected the funds from his drive-in theater on the river in New Ferry, he got back in the Packard with Clara to head home to the Fork. In a sarcastic, mockingly sweet voice, EC asked Clara, "You ready to go home now, dear?"

"Certainly," Clara replied. "Where the hell else is there to go on a night like tonight? Anyway, I need to get back home so I can take my bath and wash my hair before midnight." She was still being very cool to EC and it was a long silent trip back to the Fork.

When they pulled up to the house, they went inside without speaking and there was no more conversation between them for the rest of the evening. EC paid Katy, the babysitter, and closed the door behind her as she left. Then, very quietly, EC lay down on the bed in their bedroom and fell asleep, fully clothed. Clara went into the bathroom to bathe and wash her hair. Elaine slept in her back bedroom.

Outside, gravel crunched under the weight of car wheels pulling into the yard. Then came the sound of an engine being turned off. If Clara had not turned on the water in the tub, she might have heard first one car door shutting, and then another, muffled clunks. Then a key turning in the front door lock. Quiet steps from two sets of feet moved carefully through the house toward the bathroom.

One intruder tapped lightly on the bathroom door. Clara, still fully clothed and expecting to see EC, or maybe Elaine, cracked the door open. The man grabbed Clara by the neck and forcefully placed an ether-laced gauze pad over her nose and mouth. Her eyes swelled in shock and fear. In seconds her body went completely limp. The second man taped the ether pad to her face to make sure she did not wake anytime soon.

There were no screams, no yells, no turned-over furniture, and no signs of a struggle left anywhere. The stronger man flung Clara over his shoulder like a sack of feed while the other quietly raised the bathroom window, tore the lacy curtains from the rod, and pulled down the roll-up shade. As all three exited through the front door, one of the men picked up the keys to the Packard from hall table, along with a money bag lying next to them.

They placed Clara on the back seat of the Packard. One man got into the driver's seat and started the engine. The other got into the second car and they headed east.

Later that night Elaine called out, "Mama, I want a glass of water." When she got no response, she got out of bed and went to her parents' room to wake her daddy. "Daddy, can I have some water? Where is Mama hiding?" EC got Elaine a glass of water but he couldn't answer her question. The two of them went into every room looking for Clara. They saw the torn curtains in the bathroom. Then they went outside and around the house searching and calling for her, but Clara was nowhere to be found and the Packard was gone. EC called the Sheriff's Department to report his wife's abduction and his missing car.

The way EC coolly conveyed it to the cops when they arrived was, "Someone musta come in through the bathroom window and grabbed Clara. They stopped long enough to pick up the money bag with $9,800 inside, plus the keys to the Packard. They went out through the front door, which they left open." EC continued, "I didn't hear a sound, no screams, nothin', and I was only ten feet away. Elaine woke me up from a deep sleep wanting some water. That's when I realized Clara and my car were gone. That's all I know."

One of the lawmen said, "Mr. Cain, you say you were on the bed asleep less than ten feet away from the bathroom where Clara was taking a bath, and you didn't hear a thing? No screams, no yelling, no cussing, no sounds of someone struggling? That just don't sound right."

With contempt in his voice, EC replied, "Deputy, that is what I just told you. Believe me, if I said that's what happened, that's exactly what happened. Don't question my integrity again. Understand?"

"Hey, I'm just trying to do my job, Mr. Cain. Just trying to gather all the preliminary information possible. I don't mean to imply anything. I just want to get the facts as they happened. That's all."

EC turned away, lit his cigar, and walked outside. He was noticeably upset – with Clara's abduction, with the officer's line of questions.

There was no sign of any scuffle. There was no turned over furniture, no broken glass. There were no signs of forced entry. All of this happened while EC was sleeping. An unbelievable set of events that EC, Elaine, and the law officers were trying to sort out in the middle of the night at the Fork. Everyone was totally mystified.

Elaine kept asking EC, "Where did Mama go?" Clara was only twenty-seven years old, and little Elaine was afraid for her Mama, the only mother she had ever known.

While EC, Elaine, and several lawmen were trying to sort out what had just happened to Clara, EC's brown Packard rolled through the streets of Groveland and turned onto Branch Road headed toward New Ferry. The town was asleep and there were no other cars on the road. Clara lay unconscious in the back seat. The driver headed to a pre-determined location just off Branch Road, about halfway to New Ferry, and turned into the Pocosin, a thick, swamp-like forest that was part and parcel to the Hofmann Forest 76,000 acre tract owned by the North Carolina State University Endowment Fund. The second car followed the Packard into the forest.

Both cars stopped when they reached their designated spot. They left their lights on so they could see what they were doing. The second driver got out of his car and approached the Packard. He opened the rear door and looked at Clara.

"Do we need to get her out of the car?"

The Packard driver got out and said, "Yeah, give me a hand. We need to lean her body up against the side of the car."

They struggled to get Clara out of the car. Once her unconscious body was outside the Packard, the driver, who seemed to be in charge, said, "Remove all her clothes, including her stockings."

The second man said, "Okay. Hold her up and I'll rip her clothes off." Once he'd done that he handed Clara's stockings to the first man. "Here, wrap these tightly around her neck."

Once in place, he tightened the stockings. Clara made an awful noise and her eyes bulged; her neck and face began to turn red. The Packard driver said, "Make sure it's so tight you cut off her airway. You gotta stop the oxygen supply to her lungs. She should be dead in a couple of minutes." Slowly Clara went totally limp. Her eyes rolled back in her head and she stopped breathing.

The second driver looked up and said, "She's dead. Now what?"

The Packard driver spoke very calmly, as if they were discussing where to set up a picnic instead of what to do with a woman they had just strangled to death. "Help me get her body in the front passenger side seat. Throw her clothes in the back seat. Hurry up. We need to get her to the dump site before the sun comes up." Together they placed Clara in the front seat of the Packard.

"Now, get in your car and follow me. Don't lose sight of my car because I'm not stopping until we get there. And do not speed. You hear me?"

"Yeah," the second man muttered.

Both men jumped into their respective cars and drove out of the Pocosin; the Packard leading the way. Once they reached Branch Road they turned left and headed toward New Ferry. They took Highway 17 toward Wilmington.

Forty-five minutes later both cars turned off the highway and took a southeastern route that led directly to the ocean. When they reached a deserted area of Carolina Beach, the driver of the Packard sped up and drove the car right up onto a sand dune until it mired down and became stuck. He got out of the car and yelled to the other man, "Come over here and help me get her body arranged in the car."

They arranged Clara's body so that one of her legs was sticking through the steering wheel and the other was draped over the front seat backrest in a glaring sexual position. It was a horrible, degrading sight for anyone to see.

The Packard driver handed the other man some clean rags and said, "Wipe down the outside of the car. Get the door handles and the windows. Clean them good. I'll do the inside. We can't leave any prints anywhere. Now, get busy."

After they finished the wipe down, they got into the second car and sped away. Their job was over. They had done what they had been paid to do. They had kidnapped Clara and killed her. They had driven her dead body through three counties and left her in the front seat of the Packard on a seldom used deserted beach. Clara was no longer a problem to anyone who had considered her a problem.

———

The local media had a field day with the story. Nothing like this had ever happened in Groveland or at the Fork. The word spread to larger papers in nearby cities and onto TV stations all over North Carolina. Speculation about where Clara was, who kidnapped her, and who might be involved ran wild. Had EC had anything to do with this? And if he did, how was he able to react to Clara's threats so soon? He must have had a plan already in place. But how had he set it in motion? Did he make a phone call? And when had he made the decision – *if* he'd made the decision – to take Clara out of the picture and get rid of his wife of just five years? And how could he take away his little girl's mother?

But the real question was why? The newspapers reported that no one had seen anything, no one had heard anything, and no one knew anything.

Elaine remembers the sheriff's deputies in her house, and the way her dad looked and acted. He was calm and collected; every hair in place, immaculately dressed, and definitely in charge. She was terrified that her mama would never be coming back.

In the next few days after Clara was kidnapped, EC's small house was overcrowded with family members, friends, neighbors, and law officers. The two small bedrooms and the tiny living room were running over with people. It was confusing and disruptive. Some people were crying, others asked question after question. Too many aunts were trying to look after Elaine. There was more food than all of these visitors could possibly eat.

Elaine loved seeing the sun go down each day because that was when most of those well-meaning folks went home.

As the days passed, there was no news about where Clara was or whether she was dead or alive. This lack of information was making lots of the families in the county nervous. EC put up a good front, not only for the law, but for Elaine, for his family, and for his "special friends." An undercurrent of suspicion was starting to surface around the county. How could all this have happened in their small house with EC on the bed right next to the bathroom from which Clara was allegedly taken? No noise, no screams, no commotion, no scuffle – none of it made sense if a young woman was fighting for her life.

The story was headline news all over the southeast. One headline in a major state newspaper read "WHO KIDNAPPED CLARA?" For days it was the lead story in most papers and on most TV news shows. Pressure was growing on the authorities to produce answers to a multitude of unanswered questions.

Chapter 2
THE CRIME SCENE

Early in the morning, three days after Clara went missing, a lonely angler spotted a fancy brown car parked up on the sand dunes about a hundred yards away from where he was surf casting. He trudged over the dunes toward the dead calm ocean. There was no activity around the car, and the fisherman assumed it was two love birds enjoying themselves after a night of partying.

He returned to where he'd left his gear and prepared to get at least three baited lines in the ocean before he sat down in his beach chair. As he was pouring a cup of hot coffee from his thermos, he noticed lots of little sand fiddlers and crabs crawling all around in the water looking for something hidden in the sand to eat. But the fisherman was more interested in catching lots of black drum than thinking about those little sand critters.

He was thinking what a great day it was for surf fishing. Not too hot, very little wind; and the ocean as calm as a lake. If there were any hungry drum out there this morning looking for breakfast, they wouldn't have any problem eyeing his bait. He was feeling very optimistic that he'd catch a "mess of fish" to take home to his family. He could already taste the fried drum, coleslaw, and hush puppies his wife would prepare that night.

After he had reeled in seven of those nice-sized black drum, the fish stopped jumping on his live bait. This didn't concern the fisherman one bit as he was satisfied with his success. Once again, his interest returned to the brown car. Still seeing no visible signs of activity around the car, he rounded up all his fishing gear and decided to go check it out.

As the fisherman climbed up the sand dunes and approached the rain-spattered Packard, he realized there was someone inside. He was shocked to see that it was a lifeless nude woman. One of her legs was sticking through the steering wheel; the other leg was draped over the seat. Her stockings were tied tightly around her neck. He knew at once she was dead. Her body had already started to decompose in the spring sunshine, and the stench was godawful.

The fisherman dropped his gear and his catch and fell to his knees, retching. His heart raced. Panic set in and he didn't know what to do. He was scared to death. Should he just leave and let someone else find her? No, he decided. Her family deserved better than that.

He left his gear and his catch right where he'd dropped them and ran like hell for his car. He raced at top speed down the beach for several miles until he reached Joe's Fishing Pier. He ran inside the battered, weather-worn wood building and frantically screamed at the man behind the counter, "There's a dead woman in a car up the beach. She's been murdered. It's awful! Help me, *please*."

The pier operator said, "Hold it, man. Slow down. Tell me where you saw this dead woman. Where on the beach? How far from here?"

The fisherman, overwhelmed and in shock, stammered, "A few miles south of here. I can take you there."

The pier operator called the County Sheriff's Department, hung a Closed sign in the window, locked the doors, and he and the fisherman rushed back to the Packard.

Within a short time several law enforcement officers began arriving at the scene. It took little time for the deputies to figure out that the murdered woman was Clara Cain, Edward Cain's missing wife.

EC was notified and summoned to the site at Carolina Beach to identify her body. He didn't fail to realize the irony of Clara's body being found in the same area where they'd spent the first night of their honeymoon.

EC arrived with some family members and, unbelievably, his small daughter. With Elaine perched on his shoulders, he approached the Packard where Clara lay spread eagle in the front seat. No one could possibly imagine what he was thinking by bringing his five year old daughter to see such a gruesome sight.

A blue tarp covered the car windshield shielding the body from onlookers, but Clara was easily visible through the driver's side window. One of EC's sisters yelled at EC, "You can't let Elaine see her mother like that, you damn fool!" EC didn't respond. His sister grabbed Eileen from EC's shoulders and fled from the scene, but not before Elaine had seen her mother, dead and naked, stretched out in that horrible, compromising pose – and she never forgot it.

The county coroner and his young assistant arrived. The coroner was a short little man wearing an NC State baseball cap. His face was very red – from too much sun or too much drinking or both. His face matched the red in the State logo on his cap. He walked straight to the Packard, took a look around at the crowd that had gathered, and asked in a hushed voice, "Next of kin?"

EC half raised his hand and responded, "I'm her husband."

The coroner said, "Sorry for your loss, sir. Step over here please. I want you to steady yourself, because I am going to ask you to look at the body inside the car. After you've looked at her, I want you to turn to me and tell me the name of the person inside the car."

EC stepped forward, both hands in his pants pockets, and said, "Okay, sir, I'll do that."

The coroner grabbed one end of the heavy blue tarp and his assistant grabbed the other. They rolled the tarp back in one motion.

EC's hands went straight to his face. He covered his eyes and nose and cried out, "Oh my God! Clara, my dear Clara. Who could have done this to you?" The onlookers gasped.

The coroner looked around and motioned Jack, one of EC's brothers, to step forward and physically support EC who looked as if he might collapse. His whole body was shaking.

After a few moments, the coroner leaned over to EC and asked very quietly, "Can you please tell me who this woman is and how you are related? Take your time, son, there's no reason to hurry."

EC, leaning heavy on his brother's shoulder, cleared his throat and spoke directly to the coroner, "Sir, this dead woman is Clara Mercer Cain. She is my beloved wife of just five years.

This is also my car."

The coroner said, "It's obvious to me that her death was caused by strangulation. It will be officially listed as the cause of death. Her death will also be classified as a homicide."

EC nodded and asked quietly, "Will there be an autopsy?"

The coroner answered firmly, "No reason to have one. Everyone can see how your wife died."

EC turned around looking for support from his family. They surrounded him and held him tight.

The coroner turned to his assistant and said, "Son, gather up all of the material evidence and box it up tightly. Then let's get the body in the body bag so we can get her back to the morgue before dark."

"What about the stockings tied around her neck? What do you want me to do with them?" He asked. He kept staring at Clara's dead, naked body. He was staring way too long, as if he had never seen a naked woman before.

"For the time being, nothing," the coroner said. "We'll handle that later. Hurry! We need to get the hell out of here. Come on, let's go."

EC and his family slowly made their way back to their cars and started the long trip back to the Fork. EC cried all the way home, which just made it harder for Elaine. She sobbed all the way home too. She could not forget the screams of disbelief, the sheriff's deputies, the red lights flashing on so many patrol cars, and the sirens shrieking as more deputy cars arrived. It was an overwhelming nightmare for a five year old child, and a day that would torment her for the rest of her life.

The coroner turned to the deputy sheriff and said, "You may want to call a tow truck and impound this car. I don't know about it, because it's not my department, but you never know what you might find in there after you dust it for prints."

The deputy nodded.

The coroner's decision to forego an autopsy removed forever the opportunity to determine whether there were any sedatives or sleep inducing drugs in Clara's blood system. That was likely a major mistake in the overall investigation.

Because the body was found in a different county than where the deceased lived, it took several days of red tape and paperwork before the body could be released to the local authorities. Clara's parents demanded that they get Clara's body so they could properly bury their daughter and put her soul to rest. They were adamant that their daughter's funeral would be handled by her family at a place and time they alone chose.

EC, Elaine, and some of EC's relatives did not understand, much less agree, to this demand. They thought it was only right and legal that a wife's funeral should be the business of her husband. But EC never pushed back, not even once. This only increased the town's speculation about his possible guilt.

Clara was buried in her hometown cemetery in her family's plot, one county over. A young, beautiful woman who had so much promise was now gone forever. She left behind little five year old Elaine, now twice orphaned and alone with her father, and not a single clue as to why Clara was murdered.

EC and Elaine attended Clara's funeral, but the tension in the air was thick enough to cut with a knife. According to witnesses, it was a most unpleasant ceremony, especially for Elaine because she was caught in the middle between EC and her mother's family; a tough place to be.

Clara's parents believed EC had their daughter murdered and they never forgave him, nor did they ever change their minds. But their love and care for Elaine never faltered and years later Elaine inherited money from their estate.

When EC, Elaine, and EC's brothers and sisters got back to the Fork after the funeral, Aunt Sadie made Elaine a toasted pimento cheese sandwich, poured her a glass of milk, and fetched her a couple of chocolate-chip cookies. Elaine gobbled it all down, and then came her questions.

"Why is Mama dead?"

"Mama is in heaven now," EC told her.

"But what happened to her? Where did she go?"

"Mama passed away. She's with God now," EC answered.

"Why did she die?"

EC shook his head. "I don't know."

"Who will take care of me now?"

"All of us will always take care of you," EC promised Elaine.

While EC was trying to answer Elaine's questions and calm her down, his brother Jack made coffee. Finally, Elaine wore down and EC put her to bed. The adults sat around the kitchen table and talked among themselves, drinking their coffee. Everyone was tired and sleepy and very weary after such an emotional day.

Chapter 3
THE INVESTIGATION

Local, state, and federal agencies wasted little time in launching an all-out investigation to find the parties responsible for Clara's kidnapping and brutal murder. Officers branched out in all directions in many North Carolina towns to question an ever-growing list of people who might have some idea of what happened, and why. Clues were coming in at an amazing rate, as well as accusations and allegations about who was involved. Speculation was at a fever pitch. EC and Elaine were questioned extensively, and so were their neighbors. So were EC's two brothers, Jack and Gerald, as well as some of EC's rowdy business partners.

There were reports that the murderers took Clara to a remote forest near New Ferry where they murdered her. There were early reports that the authorities had located and actually identified a specific area in the forest as the crime scene. A local resident living near the access road to the forest told the sheriff, "I was on my tractor plowing some of my land and I saw lots of traffic in and out of the forest on the days prior to the discovery of Clara's body. There's never been that much traffic in and out of that road since I've owned this farm."

The sheriff responded, "Thanks for coming forward with this information. I'll see that we investigate that area carefully. You might have just identified the murder scene."

It appeared one party drove her dead body in the Packard to the beach location where she was found, while an accessory followed in another car so they'd have a way back home. It was fairly obvious that there were at least two people involved in Clara's abduction and murder.

Other reports said the murder was done by EC's friends in the Miami mafia. There were all kinds of stories about trips EC made to Melbourne, Miami, and Cuba. When and why he may have gone to these places was never determined. There was little or no evidence that ever contributed to this theory. But it certainly caused a great deal of conversation as to exactly what types of operations EC was actually involved with at the time. Speculation continued to swell.

Everyone in the county, in every little town and crossroad, was talking about Clara's murder. At school, at the barber shop, at the grocery store, at the feed mill, at the cafe, you could not go anywhere where Clara's murder was not the topic of conversation. People were hanging out at the barbershop just to see what they might hear about the murder. But as the days passed and no one was charged with the murder, and indeed no suspect was even named, people began to come to their own conclusions.

Weeks into the investigation, no answers were coming to the many questions surrounding Clara's murder. Lots of reports had been put out by the law enforcement agencies, some true, some false, in an effort to trap the killer or killers. Nobody bit and no one was ever listed as a suspect. To this day, Clara's death remains one of North Carolina's most gruesome unsolved murders.

There were lots of people in the Fork, in Groveland, in New Ferry, and in the surrounding counties that were certain EC had Clara killed. Many thought they knew why. People began to remember the controversy about EC's first wife, Brenda. They wondered what ever happened to her. Did she leave with EC's first baby, or was she murdered? Her sudden disappearance was still suspicious to many people.

There were tales beginning to circulate about EC. After he was orphaned at 17, he went to live with his aunt, Emily Richards, in neighboring Kingstown. She operated an infamous whore house named Sugar Hill. It was perfectly situated at the intersection of two major highways on the east side of Kingstown, a vibrant tobacco market town. In season, when farmers brought their tobacco to the market and sold it, their pockets were lined with cash. After another very long and tiring work season ended, many of these men felt the need for wine and women. They became annual patrons at Sugar Hill.

EC became the bouncer at an early age. He was rumored to be responsible for a dead patron that showed up in the Neuse River one morning while EC was working there. Only a few people knew or talked about EC's early record of doing hard time for assault, battery, and robbery.

The authorities, not necessarily the local ones, spent a lot of time talking with EC's brothers, Jack and Gerald, about EC's and Clara's relationship. Two agents from the State Bureau of Investigation (SBI) questioned the brothers intensely for two days straight at the sheriff's office in New Ferry.

The SBI agent asked Jack, "Where were you at the time of the abduction?"

"In my damn bed. Where the hell do you think I was?"

"How about you, Gerald, where were you last night?"

Gerald replied calmly, "I was at home with my wife, my dog, and my whiskey." The SBI guy could believe that answer because he could smell the bourbon coming out of Gerald's pores from across the room.

The other agent chimed in, "Where were both of you the twenty four hours before and the twenty four hours following Clara's abduction?"

Jack looked at Gerald and said, "I was at work until I went home for supper the day before Clara was kidnapped. The same answer applies for the day after she was taken, as well. Of course, I went to EC's house as soon as I heard about Clara."

Gerald said very quietly, "Same here for both days. Nothing unusual about that. I also went to EC's to see if I could help in any way."

The two agents looked at each other, then one asked Jack, "Who did you talk to before and after Clara was forcefully taken from her home?"

Jack squirmed a bit, scratched his three day old beard, and said, "Let's see now. I talked to all my customers that day. Maybe twenty different guys. I talked to my wife. I talked to my employees at the station. I talked with EC and Elaine. I talked to Gerald. That's about it, I guess."

The other SBI guy turned to Gerald and asked, "How did you hear about the incident, and from whom did you hear it?"

Gerald said, "Jack called me with the bad news. It was some shockin' shit to say the least. It's absolutely horrible."

"What were you told?"

Gerald, looking disgusted at such a silly question mumbled, "Jack told me somebody had kidnapped Clara right out the window. Plain and simple."

The other agent asked Jack, "How would you explain how this could have happened with EC literally only ten feet away from Clara in the bathroom?"

Jack, with a look of disbelief on his face, responded, "I have no idea. You're the damn super sleuth, you figure it out."

The agent said, "We're not looking for smart-ass answers. So, no more of that, please."

"That's not smart-ass," Jack replied. "That's the fuckin' truth."

The two agents huddled in the corner for a couple of minutes whispering to one another. Jack and Gerald just sat there and stared at each other.

"Do either one of you have anyone in mind that may have done this?" asked one of the agents.

Jack answered immediately, "Neither one of us knows nobody that would do a thing like this. I mean nobody. What kind of sick bastard goes into someone's house in the middle of the night and kidnaps a man's wife, with her baby in the back bedroom? Nobody we know."

Then a bunch of questions were directed at Gerald. "What did you think of Clara? Were you friends? Did your wives like Clara? What is the story about EC's first wife?"

Gerald stood up and said, "Slow down, goddammit! What's the rush? How about one question at a time? We all liked Clara very much. She was good to EC. Certainly, we were friends as far as I know. Yeah, our wives thought Clara was a nice and pretty lady. Hell, she treated Elaine like she was her own daughter. EC's first wife situation was just your average old "knocked her up" story. He screwed up. No pun intended."

The brothers were pressed hard for information and their answers were short, mostly one or two sentence answers. They were as nervous as two whores in church. That concerned some of the investigators.

The brothers did fairly well until the agents divided them and interviewed them separately on the second day. They began to really bear down on Jack because he seemed to be the most vulnerable. They put a tail on Jack for several days to see where he went, who he saw, and who he talked to in the days right after Clara's body was found. There were some curious findings, but nothing like a smoking gun. Both Jack and Gerald were drinking a lot, seemingly more than usual.

Within a few months, Jack became ill with cancer. His condition deteriorated rapidly, and he was hospitalized in New Ferry Hospital. The unusual thing was that a county sheriff's deputy was stationed at the door to Jack's hospital room twenty four hours a day. No one was ever given a logical explanation for this protection, much less who ordered it, or why.

The word on the street surrounding Jack's total isolation was that he knew he was close to death. Knowing this, Jack wanted to "get right with God" and confess his involvement in Clara's murder. And then there were others who did not want Jack to talk to anyone about anything while he was alive. And he didn't.

Less than a year after Jack died, Gerald passed away. Folks said he drank himself to death.

But despite what Jack and Gerald knew or didn't know about Clara's kidnapping and murder, and regardless of whether one or both were involved in the crime, the local authorities never revealed anything that would point to their involvement in any way whatsoever. Over and done. No harm, no foul with these two fellows. The SBI authorities were really surprised at this outcome. So were the people in the county.

Even later in life Elaine said, "I have never been able to answer that about my Daddy. I have always loved him dearly and thought that he loved me as well. But I have had my suspicions that Daddy may have been involved in Mama's death. But I don't know for certain."

Chapter 4
THE MAN

Edward Earl Cain's troubles started much earlier in his life – about the time he came kicking and screaming into the world in August of 1917.

EC, as he was known to his friends, was born into a poor farming family near the Fork, a rural community in southeastern North Carolina. The Fork was just another country junction, where one NC highway formed a fork in the road intersecting with a US highway. It was surrounded by thousands and thousands of acres of farmland. The land was flat, for sure, but it was also a very productive type of soil that yielded abundant harvests of corn, tobacco, soybeans, and cotton. These crops were the lifeblood for hundreds of farmers who lived there. The Fork was almost exclusively a farming community.

Times were very tough. EC's father and mother struggled to feed and clothe their nine children. EC had no idea what was in store for him or his future. If he had known, he probably would have crawled back into the womb. It was as if he'd been dropped into a third world country. There was no running water, no indoor plumbing, no electric or gas stove, and no refrigerator. That meant the family had to use an outhouse. They had to get their water from a well pump. They had to cut wood for the kitchen stove to cook their meals, and their house was heated by a wood burning fireplace. Living there was not easy. In fact, if the world ever needed an enema, there's a good chance this is where it would go.

The problems in EC's early life were not all self-imposed. It's not as if he chose these people for his parents, much less this desolate backwoods area as a place to grow up. EC's parents died of pneumonia within a month of each other when EC was just seventeen. But EC and his siblings had survived the Great Depression of the 1930s, and that was a real big deal, a least to them.

Soon after his parents died, he went to live with his Aunt Emily in her big house on the hill just east of Kingstown. It was a stately old white frame house with giant columns flanking the front entrance. Beyond the front door, a giant red carpeted stairway rose to the second floor hall that was lined with bedrooms. To the right of the staircase was a large parlor that invited guests to relax on one of several settees or settle down on one of the rich, dark brown, soft leather sofas. Wing-back chairs in front of a giant crackling fireplace blended in well with many of the period antique pieces that filled the room. The wide plank hardwood floor hosted a very expensive Oriental rug. Lamps sprinkled about the room had red shades with white fringe and low lights. Above the fireplace hung an ornate framed oil painting of a beautiful young woman dressed only in a pink satin kimono. The kimono was loosely open on the left side exposing an inviting, creamy white breast. Men could barely take their eyes away from the painting – until the young women of the house filed into the room.

Across the back of the house was a large veranda that extended out over the Neuse River. The covered space was populated with many seating areas that provided "couples" a great place to get acquainted before going upstairs for some serious interaction and cash exchange. Hidden at one end of the veranda was a trap door that led to the river. Patrons who became unruly with the girls, or refused to pay for services rendered, often disappeared through the trap door into the Neuse River.

Besides a home, Aunt Emily provided EC with a job – in her brothel stocked with a stable full of willing young women. They were just what EC was looking for at his young age. As most red-blooded males would have done, he took full advantage of his situation, maybe too much of an advantage. One day after he'd been working at Sugar Hill for about six weeks, Aunt Emily called EC into her office and shut the door. She told EC, "Sit down and listen very carefully to what I have to say. First of all, I didn't invite you here. I only agreed to give you room and board because your folks died, and all children deserve that much, at least. Furthermore, I agreed to give you a paying job so you could maybe get on your feet. It was never my intention to provide you with a house full of young hookers to fuck every day until your dick falls off. So you need to understand one thing, it's my way or the highway. Leave the whores alone. They belong to the paying customers only, not to some young, sex-starved, horny prick. Understand? Do you get it?"

EC, surprised, responded, "Whoa, Aunt Emily, I've never heard you talk so nasty."

Aunt Emily laughed. "This ain't Bible study, son. You're a bouncer in a goddamn whorehouse, choir boy. Grow up."

Frowning and looking guilty, EC responded, "I never thought I was doing anything wrong. The girls I screwed basically begged to have sex with me. Hell, those women know more about screwing than Eve, and she begot the whole damn world. How could I turn them down anyway? It was like I was doing them a favor. Nobody told me to leave them alone."

Aunt Emily sighed, "Look EC, with an attitude like that, you'll never hold a job anywhere. I'll give you a second chance, but if you screw up, shit, that was a bad choice of words . . . if you don't do as I say I'll fire you in a goddamn heartbeat. Now, get back to work."

Aunt Emily was good on her word. A few weeks later in the early morning, a patron, or "John," from the night before was found floating face down in the river behind Sugar Hill. EC, the bouncer, had been seen having a heated argument with the deceased. As often happened in places like Sugar Hill, somebody had too much to drink and started bragging about his manhood or about what he was going to sexually do to a certain girl, and EC intervened. That happened to be the wrong thing to do that night. EC and the client got into a knock down brawl. EC, being younger, stronger, and sober, beat the hell out of the man. He knocked him unconscious, dragged him out to the veranda, and shoved him down through the trap door. EC thought the cold river water would bring the man back to consciousness, but he was wrong. The John's death brought way too much bad publicity to Sugar Hill. Once the police arrived to investigate, EC was on the hot seat for several days. Finally, with some undue influence from some of Aunt Emily's best clients, the police ruled the death an accidental drowning. EC avoided prosecution. But a black cloud continued to follow him around, so Aunt Emily fired him the following week.

Working in the whorehouse was the origin of EC's affinity for women, especially young women who would accept his advances. From an early age, EC never really experienced any female rejection at all. The mindset he adopted and developed early in life had a great deal to do with how he viewed women, and how he treated them both in public and in the bedroom. Sugar Hill was where he got started off on the wrong side of the law, and it was where he lost his moral compass.

EC was a small man in stature with a receding hairline. By his early twenties, he had begun to lose lots of hair. Never considered handsome, even as a young man, he was nevertheless very engaging and had a forceful personality. He was not the slightest bit shy, and he seemed to never meet a stranger. He had just enough bullshit about him to make him charming, particularly to young women. The other thing about him that attracted young women was that he was pretty much a hell raiser. His signature item was his half cigar, always hanging from his lips, usually unlit. He had the unusual habit of chewing those stogies until they were no more. He thought this made him look tough.

EC exhibited a strong desire to get ahead. He was fanatical about doing better than his father had done, and he was not at all opposed to hard work or long hours. Once he got involved in a project, he was hands on and full throttle until things were the way he wanted them.

Self-confidence, ambition, and a horny propensity for pretty women were traits EC possessed in spades. He loved making money because it gave him the freedom to do as he pleased. He was well known in several towns in the surrounding counties for his sexual exploits. He was a kiss and tell kind of guy.

After graduating from high school, EC decided that making a living doing manual labor like cropping tobacco, picking cotton, shucking corn, or plowing the back forty at the south end of a north bound mule all day was not his idea of getting ahead. He decided to see if he could take money from others on a regular basis without working. He started by shoplifting small items and selling or trading them.

Before long, EC stepped up his criminal activity by breaking into houses. He would take anything of value he could find. He'd look for cash hidden under mattresses or in coffee tins in pantries. He loved to steal silverware and nice China. He'd freak out over Oriental rugs and crystal glasses. He always chose the nicer houses. He was a country bandit with an eye for fancy things, and a pretty damn good one at that. He got away with this criminal behavior for almost a year, in part because he chose houses in different towns across several different counties.

Around 1937, EC and a buddy decided to try their hand at outright robbery. They staked out a busy country store several counties over where nobody knew either of them. After casing the target for a couple of days, they moved in for the kill late on a Friday afternoon right before the store closed.

Wearing a mask, EC took the lead and marched into the store and right up to the counter. He demanded of the store clerk, "Open the god-damn cash register and hand me all of the cash! *Now!* Hurry up. Quick, put it in this bag. Do it now. Hurry! Hurry!"

The clerk was more scared than shocked when he saw the gun EC's buddy was bandying about. The clerk begged, "Please don't shoot me. I'll give you the damn money." He grabbed the bag and filled it full of cash. It was a pretty good amount of cash, because the store had been very busy all day. The clerk handed the bag to EC and said, "Here! Take it and leave! Go! Get out!"

EC grabbed the money stuffed bag and turned to his armed partner. "Let's get the hell out of here!" They ran out of the store, got in his old pickup truck, and sped away. They stopped the truck when they got close to home. They opened the bag and started counting the money. They had stolen $1,175. That was more money than either one of them had seen in the last six months.

Two days later a sheriff's car stopped in front of EC's trailer. When EC answered, the deputy asked, "Son, is that your old pickup truck sitting there in the yard?"

EC answered nervously, "Yes sir, that's my pickup."

The deputy said, "That truck was seen leaving the scene of an armed robbery two days ago in the next county. Where were you last Friday afternoon?"

"I was right here. All day and night," EC replied immediately. "I let a buddy of mine borrow my truck 'cause he had a hot date. It wasn't me, no way."

The deputy didn't believe a word EC told him. "The store clerk gave a damn good description of the two robbers and the gun. You look just like one of the two men he described. Come on now, tell me who your buddy is, the buddy you let borrow your truck."

EC said, "Deputy, sir, you know I can't do that." His refusal to answer got him a ride to the sheriff's office for more questioning.

At the sheriff's department, EC was finger printed. Then came his mug shot. EC was getting nervous. He was led down the hall into the interrogation room with four very gray walls, no windows, one table, and two chairs. Then to EC's surprise, the High Sheriff himself walked in and sat down. EC figured he was in deep shit now.

The sheriff started in on EC, "Son, do you have any idea how much trouble you're in?"

"No sir."

"Do you know what kind of penalty you are going to pay for this crime?"

"I'm real sorry that I robbed that store," EC said.

"How did you think you'd ever get away with robbery in plain daylight?"

"But I didn't hurt that man behind the counter."

"Are you just stupid?" the sheriff asked.

"People do that every day. Why am I in so much trouble?"

"But EC, it was not just robbery, it was *armed* robbery. Man, that's some serious shit."

EC was feeling nauseous.

All he could do was repeat himself. "I'm real sorry I robbed that store, but I didn't hurt that man behind the counter. I just stole some money, and I didn't have the gun. People do that every day. Why am I in so much trouble?"

Once the sheriff told EC how serious an offense armed robbery was, it only took a few hours before EC decided he'd better come clean. He gave the deputy all the details about his foray into the world of armed robbery. EC was indicted and jailed. He was placed in a small one man cell. Hardly room to turn around. The conditions were so bad EC was actually looking forward to getting moved to the prison. He felt like he'd fare much better there. His buddy, the other guy involved in the robbery, the one with the pistol, got a free pass.

Two months later EC was tried, convicted, and sentenced to the county work prison farm for nine months. He received such a light sentence because he'd come clean with the sheriff. EC was beginning to feel the touch of the long arm of the law again. But this time things hadn't worked out so easily for him. He found out first hand that being on the wrong side of the law had serious consequences.

While he was in prison, EC decided that when he was released he'd try getting a real job as a means of making a living. When he got out, he returned to the Fork to look for a way to re-start his life.

But first things first. The electricity had been cut off to his trailer. He was months behind on the rent. His brother Jack had his pick-up truck, and he had no money. EC was more than a bit depressed, he was scared. *What the hell can I do*, he thought?

EC walked to Jack's house to see if his brother could help him. Maybe he could get his truck back. Maybe Jack would let him have some gas and food money so he could at least look for a job. Like a good brother, Jack helped EC with a little cash.

EC told Jack, "I've been in hell for nine months. Never want to go back there again. It was an awful place. The food, the living conditions were shitty, and the guards were mean as hell. It was all horrible."

"Get over it, EC. You're home now. You know what not to do to stay out of that hellhole. Get on with your life. Get a job and stick with it," Jack told him.

"Jack, I really appreciate your help with money and advice, but where the hell am I going to find a job now? I'm willing to work, but somebody has to give me a chance and hire me for something."

Jack smiled at EC and said, "How would you feel about a job with a pulpwood crew? It's hard work, but you get paid every Friday. You're strong enough to use a chain saw all day, right?"

"I'd start tomorrow if I knew where to go. Do you know who I need to see?"

"Yeah, Raymond Goodson is the man. He and his boys control the pulpwood business in this county. Maybe you could start out as a logger and work your way up to driving one of his trucks. I'll be glad to take you over there tomorrow so you can ask him for a job."

EC's whole demeanor changed. He was being treated like a real human again. Someone was actually trying to help him. He smiled at Jack and said, "I'll be ready at six o'clock."

EC got the job and spent his days cutting down pulpwood-sized trees with a chainsaw. It was tough work. It was dangerous work as well. But the Goodsons were nice to EC and helped him get started with his new life. They did EC a big favor because he required a great deal of on-the- job training before they felt that he was capable of doing the job he had been hired to do. At least he was getting paid.

EC was on the job for about six months when he lost his footing, and the chainsaw he was using sliced into his arm just above the wrist. Lucky for EC, there were other loggers close by who heard his yells for help and ran to assist him. One tied a belt tightly around his wrist above the cut to slow down the blood loss. EC, squinting from pain, asked, "How bad is it cut? Is it to the bone? Can you stop the bleeding? Can you get me out of here and to the hospital before I bleed to death?"

One of the Goodson boys answered, "Calm down, EC. You'll live. Here, press this towel on the cut and hold it there. We'll get you in my pickup truck and take you to the doc and get this cut disinfected, sewn up, and bandaged. You'll be good as new and back out here in no time."

"I'm not too sure about that," EC muttered.

He was right. The doctor fixed his arm, but EC had no intention of going back in the woods with a chainsaw anytime soon. He thanked the Goodsons and told them he was going to look for a less dangerous job. After a couple of weeks of recovery, he did just that. EC got a job as a truck driver, driving a flatbed for a fertilizer company. He hauled fertilizer bags all over three counties. Often he had to help a customer unload those two hundred pound bags, and that was not an easy task.

The trouble with his truck driving job was it was over as soon as the season was over. So EC had to hit the streets again looking for another paying job. EC found that a pretty difficult task. Jobs, other than farm related jobs, were not too plentiful around the county back then. So for a couple of years, EC continued to stumble from one poor job to another.

EC would work until he saved up a little money, then he would resume his passion for chasing women. This was EC's lifestyle for months on end.

One Saturday night at a square dance in Faison, EC met Brenda Davis. She was attractive, had a great body, and more than that, she was a fabulous dancer. She had lots of rhythm and knew all the dance steps. When she was on the floor she was sexy and attracted lots of attention. EC had to wait in line just to get a dance with her. Immediately, he knew Brenda was worth pursuing. They dated off and on for several months. Then things started getting real cozy, and their relationship became quite intense.

One night when EC went to pick her up to go square dancing, Brenda broke the news, "EC, I'm pregnant."

"What the hell are you talking about? How long?" he yelled as he erupted in a state of rage.

Brenda, in a very shy and timid voice declared, "Three months, I think."

"You think?" EC continued his rant. "Does that mean you don't know how goddamn long you've been pregnant? Does that mean you don't know who the goddamn father might be? I know goddamn well I'm not the only one gettin' in your pants."

Everything went downhill from there as EC tried to make Brenda feel as if it was all her fault. After several days of constant bickering, EC agreed to "do the right thing" and step up as the father. He also agreed to marry her.

EC married Brenda in 1940 at age 23, but it was not what he wanted to do, nor what he had planned to do. Brenda was just a pretty country girl who got caught up in EC's charisma. She was not the first young girl to fall prey to his demands, nor would she be the last.

Once he'd agreed to marry her, EC dropped the bomb. "I want you gone as soon as possible, after the kid arrives. I'll have the damn marriage annulled immediately."

Brenda, broken-hearted and scared to death, begged EC, "Can you please give me a month after the baby is born before I have to leave?"

EC said, "Thirty days. That's it. Period. Got it?"

Brenda was devastated, she had been too afraid to stand up to EC, but when the time came, she and her daughter, Anna Cain, left. Based on EC's demands, they were divorced in no time. Brenda took Anna and moved to Tennessee. It was quite strange. No one heard an explanation, only that Brenda and the child were gone. Some people even thought she was dead or possibly even murdered.

In the mid-40s, once he was clear of any wives or children, cigar chomping EC decided that he would open a country store at the Fork. He knew it would take more money than what he had saved, so he hit up a few of his friends and associates for some financial help. His first stop was the Ford place in Groveland to see Vinny Moser.

Vinny came out of the back office and shook EC's hand. "EC, what brings you to town? Can I help you with something?"

"Yeah, Vinny," EC replied. "I need to talk to you about some business."

"Come on back to my office, so we can talk privately." EC followed Vinny into his office.

As soon as they were alone, EC started talking, "Vinny, I've decided to open a small country store – right in the middle of the Fork, where the two roads intersect. It's a great location, and I think a store there will do great."

"What are you going to sell in the store? Give me an example."

Waving his arms around, EC said, "Some of everything. Groceries, notions, farm clothes, stove wood, kerosene, soft drinks, gas, appliances, just to name a few."

"What can I do to help?" Vinny asked. "You need some money?"

"Vinny, you're too smart. Yes, money is exactly what I need."

"How about me loaning you $10,000 for a year? Will that help?"

EC jumped up out of his chair and yelled, "Hell yes, that will help!"

"Wait right here while I go to my safe and get you the cash."

EC was about to flip out from excitement. He figured he could get the same amount of money out of his buddy, Ralph Thompson. EC felt comfortable that he could open his store on twenty thousand dollars. He knew with that amount, he could fix up the building, add some refrigerated cases, fix his parking lot, put a sign on the building, and stock the store with lots of different kinds of inventory. EC was getting really excited.

Vinny returned to his office and handed EC an envelope with ten thousand dollars inside. He told EC, "I'll get my lawyer to mail you a note to sign, and you can bring it back to me when you can."

EC stuck out his free hand and shook Vinny's hand very firmly, "Thank you so much, Vinny. You'll never know how much I appreciate your help." EC almost floated out of the building.

The next day EC went to see Ralph Thompson with the same proposal. It took Ralph less than ten minutes to lend EC ten thousand dollars.

In just one week EC had raised the necessary money from a couple of his well-heeled friends and opened a country store at the Fork. It looked like many other small supermarkets that sprung up over the coming years. It had a brick facade on the front with two large plate glass windows on either side of the double glass entrance doors. Inside the many shelves and racks held all kinds of products: grocery items, notions, furniture, appliances, and even clothing. There was a small checkout counter in the middle of the store that customers had to pass on their way out. Behind the counter was a short dunce-type stool that EC sat on many hours each day. He knew exactly what was going on in his store every minute.

He was so proud of his store when he first opened. He hung multi-colored banners from the roof out to the gas pump islands. The flags attracted drivers passing by on both highways. Many first time visitors to EC's store were greeted by EC and offered a free Pepsi and a Moon Pie as grand opening celebration giveaways.

Anything in the store could be purchased or charged and put on the ledger. This practice became a popular feature in the years right after the war. So as EC's business prospered, his store became the center of activity at the Fork. It was where all different types of folks went for a variety of reasons. Besides being able to get all kinds of items in the store, they could get a cash loan from EC.

Cain's Supermarket was where EC got his start, and it's where he gained his early success. Cain's is where he found the confidence to expand his business base, and exercise his entrepreneurial acumen. The Fork was where he lived and where he worked. It was where many of his family and friends lived. The Fork was where EC called home.

Over the next several years, many other small businesses began to open in and around the area. The Fork began to grow its own little business community. In one way or another, EC helped many people get started. And because of that, most folks there were very loyal to him. He had become the big fish in the little pond of the Fork, and he liked it that way.

EC backed a local guy that opened a 1950s vintage motel across from his store. The hotel was often referred to as the "The No Tell Motel" and was frequented by many less than desirable patrons. Even some of EC's out of town business associates stayed there from time to time.

Then his brother Gerald, with the help of EC, opened a gas station, garage, and truck stop combination across the highway from Cain's. There was always some type of commotion going on there including drinking, gambling, and fighting. It was a rough and tumble place. In spite of all that, Gerald did well.

One morning EC walked into his store at the Fork and told everyone inside, "I'm going to open a drive-in movie here at the Fork. It's going to be built right over there in that open field across from my house," he said, as he pointed to the spot through his storefront window. "It'll be ready before the summer gets here."

One customer, sitting on a Pepsi crate back by the potbellied stove said, "What the hell is a drive-in movie? I never heard of such a thing. Are there others around here anywhere?"

EC walked over and put some more coal in the stove, laughing when he said, "It's just like a regular movie except you drive your car into the theater parking lot. You and your family watch the movie on a giant screen in the privacy of your car. A speaker that hangs on your car window provides sound from the movie. There is a canteen in the projection building where viewers can buy sodas, popcorn, and candy. That's it. So simple. No, my drive-in movie will be the first one in eastern North Carolina."

One of EC's store employees raised his hand and asked, "Boss, can I run the projector for you? I have one at home, and I have a lot of experience with home movies."

"Why not? You'd be a great projector man."

So a drive-in movie theater opened in the Fork across from EC's country store and home. It seemed a bit foolish at first, as there were not that many households in the community. But EC had more vision than most folks. He believed his drive-in movie would attract movie-goers from miles around, not just the people in the Fork. He was absolutely right. It turned out to be a smart move. Drive-in movies became the rage that swept the country, mainly because it gave couples a place to go and make out, or go all the way, while supposedly watching the latest film from Hollywood. EC was on a roll.

A gentleman farmer and good friend of EC's who lived nearby wanted to be the owner/operator of a feed and grain facility at the Fork. To help his farmer friend achieve his goal, EC went to see his wealthy friend Vinny Moser again. Vinny was the Ford dealer in Groveland, who had given EC his first loan. EC met Vinny in his small, sparsely furnished private office at the dealership. It was just a small little space with a single metal desk with a phone on top, three metal straight back chairs, one heavy duty file cabinet with a big fat lock, and one framed picture of his father on the wall behind his desk. The resemblance between Vinny and his father was incredible.

EC told Vinny the deal about a proposed milling business at the Fork.

After listening to EC describe how honest his friend was, and what a hard worker he was, Vinny asked EC, "Why does your friend need me in the deal? It seems pretty viable to me. Why can't he do it by himself? What does he want from me?"

EC leaned back in his chair, stretched his arms above his head, and replied, "Vinny, don't be so damn hard to get. As is always the case, he needs your money, or credit, or both! It'll take about $200,000 for the land, building, milling equipment, and the grain elevator and storage bins. That's the deal."

Vinny leaned across his desk and said, "EC, what's in it for me?"

EC grinned. "About fifty percent of the deal!"

Vinny stood up and pointed his finger at EC and said, "You damn well better be right about this. Count me in. Tell your friend to come meet me here tomorrow so we can get started with the paperwork and go to the bank."

EC, delighted and smiling, said, "Thanks so much, Vinny. You will not be disappointed, I promise."

"I'm going to hold you to that promise," Vinny said.

The two men shook hands and EC left.

The Fork got a feed mill across the other highway. The new mill facility filled a definite need because all the corn and soybeans that were harvested each fall in and around this community needed a place to be bought or stored. The feed mill too became very successful.

It wasn't long before two enterprising young men decided to open a retail furniture store at the Fork. This surprised many of the people who lived there because they did not think there was a large enough market in the community to support a store that only sold furniture. EC advised the young men that they were making a mistake. He told them they would be better off to open their store in a larger community, like Groveland or New Ferry. They didn't pay EC any damn mind and opened their store at the Fork anyway. Their store struggled from the very beginning.

Before EC and too many other people could protest, an abattoir, a regular old slaughterhouse, was built at the Fork right behind EC's storage warehouse. EC would tell his customers, "The only thing wrong with that business is that on the days the animals are slaughtered, the odors emanating from that facility are disgusting!"

But the owner of this slaughterhouse would always say, "EC, I got all of the necessary permits. We even had to post notices. So don't give me any more crap."

It was true, on slaughter days, fresh air disappeared. As there were a lot of livestock producers in the area, this facility became their closest market place. The slaughterhouse prospered and EC never stopped complaining about how this business slipped into his community under the cover of darkness.

In just a few short years, EC had opened his country store and his first drive-in movie at the Fork, a second drive-in movie in Groveland, and a furniture and appliance store and a third drive-in movie in New Ferry. He now had some serious cash flow for the first time in his life, and he knew how to take advantage of being prosperous.

With businesses in all three communities, EC was seen daily in all three towns. On almost any day you could catch him at Kellam's Drug Store in New Ferry. Most often he'd drop in and visit Vinny Moser at the Ford place two or three times a week. He'd also stop by Ralph Thompson's heavy equipment place and bring him up to speed on how he was doing with all of his business ventures. EC was always stopping in other stores in these towns and buying items that he had for sale at his own store at the Fork. It was just an excuse to go in and chat with the owners. He'd do this at the grocery store and the feed mill, or he'd be seen eating a fried bologna sandwich at The Spot Drive-In in Groveland. Not many days went by that EC didn't stop by Jack's gas station in Groveland and Gerald's truck stop at the Fork to see how they were both doing. EC was a dynamo. He was in constant motion.

Once EC had become somewhat established, he began to enjoy some of his early success. He was crazy about fishing and had been since his early childhood days when he used a cane pole in the nearest pond or lake. As was the custom, during the summer EC would close his store at noon on Wednesdays. Then he'd get a couple of his "boys" and head to the coast for an afternoon of fishing from a pier.

It was not long before EC bought his first motorboat. It was a fifteen foot runabout with a twenty-five horsepower Evinrude outboard motor attached to the stern. On many Wednesday afternoons, plus some Saturdays, EC hauled his boat down to the coast and put in at Brown's Inlet or Bear Creek. He had good luck fishing at both places. He'd always invite one or two others along to accompany him on these trips. It was something he really enjoyed, and he was pretty good at it, too.

EC had a very unusual side – probably more than one. It was not uncommon at all for people to ask EC to lend them a $100. He'd simply open the cash register or pull the money out of his pocket and hand it over to the person asking for his help. Just like that. He helped hundreds of people, some customers, some not, with personal loans. He also made business loans. One thing was well understood, when the loan was due to be repaid, EC was expecting it to be returned with whatever interest was due. If the loan was not repaid on time, the debtor would get a call or most often a visit from EC. You did not have to ask why EC was calling you or why he had dropped by to see you. It was never a pleasant situation for the debtor.

One day, John T, one of EC's regular customers walked into his store at the Fork and said, "EC, I really need $1500 to get by until I can sell my hogs. Things are a little too tight for me right now."

EC looked up from the newspaper he was reading, took the unlit cigar out of his mouth, and asked, "John T, how many hogs you got?"

"I bought them thirty hogs as feeder pigs, ranging from fifty to seventy-five pounds."

"How much longer you got to feed them before they're ready for market?"

"I've fed them for the last couple of months and probably will have to feed them another ninety days or so."

EC loaned John T $1500 until he sold his hogs. The problem was, when the hogs got sold, the debt to EC went unpaid. John T woke up early one Wednesday morning to EC knocking on his front door. EC locked his steel blue eyes on John T's face and said very coldly, "You better bring me my damn money or bring me them damn hogs by Saturday noon! No damn excuses will be accepted. And you damn sure don't want to know the consequences if you fail."

John T only had to look into EC's piercing steel blue eyes to know he wasn't kidding. EC's eyes could bore a hole right through you in an instant.

"I swear I'll get it to you by Saturday."

EC did not lose many of the loans he placed, including John T's.

There was kind of a secret code of silence among those who dealt with EC. Any two of EC's debtors could be eating lunch together and neither one would know that the other had borrowed money from EC. They all seemed to know that EC was strictly business – that he could enforce collection from most any debtor if he had to. One would think only fools would try to screw over EC but, incredibly, some did.

Many people thought of EC as a kind of modern day Robin Hood. He seemed to be a softhearted, compassionate, country gentleman, who was also a successful businessman. This was how his Robin Hood reputation started with many of his early "not so well off" customers.

The Fork was also the place where an over-abundance of many unusual, illegal, and deadly things happened over a short period of years. A bizarre array of criminal activities originated at the Fork, among them murder, arson, moonshine, and funny money. Most of them could be (and were) traced back to EC.

Although EC seemed to have a good number of male and female friends, associates, and family, there is no mistake about it, EC was damned tough. He was mean as hell, and he was unbelievably greedy. But more than anything else, he was street smart. EC was not your average garden variety fool. He was keen and savvy and a great salesman – a combination of traits that proved to be extremely dangerous.

Chapter 5
THE COURTSHIP

Although by the age of twenty-three he had already fathered a child and been married and divorced, EC jumped right back into dating and chasing women. He did his fair share of "getting around." EC thought he had learned his lesson. He was very careful as he played the field over the next several years.

Around the time EC was opening his store and his drive-in movie at the Fork, he started dating a young woman from the next county over. Clara Mercer was eight years younger than EC. She had been born into a successful farming family. Her father had a stellar reputation as a tobacco farmer and a superb game hunter. Her mother's apple pie was renowned around the county. Clara had one older brother and one younger sister, but Clara was the one with the good looks. Most people said her beauty came from her mother. Clara learned early on about helping to do her part with the cooking and household chores. She was keenly interested in horses and became an excellent rider. Her dad gave Clara her first horse on her tenth birthday, and she rode Charlie almost every day.

As Clara grew into her teens, she became very popular with both boys and girls from her school and church. She found school to her liking, and she was a very good student. By the time she reached her late teens, her parents were monitoring too many dating requests. Clara was a special young girl and had the personality to go with her extraordinary good looks. During high school and after she graduated, she dated many different guys, but she never got too serious with any one man until she started dating EC.

Then, much to her parents' chagrin, it was love at first sight. EC's reputation preceded him and Clara's parents were horrified.

One evening, while EC was calling on Clara at her parents' home, a scary incident occurred. Jesse, a young man who lived down the road and still had a crush on Clara from their earlier dating days, decided EC had to go. While EC, Clara, and her parents were chatting inside the house, Jesse parked his pickup truck down the road out of sight. In the dark he worked his way into Clara's yard where EC had parked his car. Jesse slashed all four of EC's tires. He must have lost his mind. He clearly had no idea what EC would do when he found out who slashed his tires, and why.

When EC and Clara walked outside to get into his car and leave and EC saw his four flattened tires, he went ballistic. He immediately figured out it must have been one of Clara's jilted admirers – an obviously young and immature one. He knew he'd find out soon enough.

Luckily, EC only suspected who cut his tires, so without proof he chose to let it go. Another reason he did not try to retaliate was because he didn't want Clara or her parents to know how tough and mean he could be. Jesse caught a huge break.

The irony is that Jesse, the jilted suitor, continued his criminal behavior as he grew into manhood. Over the next few years, he became involved in many illegal activities. He was always looking for trouble and he almost always found it. Actually, his father and brothers were all a bunch of bad asses.

Eventually he got into a knockdown, drag out fight with another thug over some woman. Shots rang out and at the age of twenty-two, Jesse fell dead.

Jesse was buried in Clara's hometown cemetery. His mother insisted that this epithet be placed on his tombstone: Much too Sweet to Linger Long.

To those who knew Jesse as the hell-raiser that he was, her sentiment was amusing. His tombstone with that inscription is still there today.

As EC's and Clara's romance grew into a strong relationship, it became obvious to many observers that this couple would probably get married. Before her parents could do anything to change the situation, Clara and EC began seeing each other several times a week.

One Friday night, EC picked Clara up and drove straight to New Ferry, stopping at the Howard Johnson Inn on Highway 17. Clara's first thought was EC was going to try to take her to bed right there at that motel, that night. She was feeling most uncomfortable and began to say, "EC, this ain't right. I ain't going into any motel with you tonight!"

EC, laughing out loud, said, "Relax, Clara. I'm taking you out to dinner here at the Howard Johnson restaurant. They have the best fried clams you've ever eaten. Shame on you, girl. You got to know that I think more of you than that."

Clara, embarrassed but relieved, said, "EC, you are full of surprises. I never know what to expect from you."

Grinning from ear to ear, EC said, "You ain't seen nothing yet."

They went inside and were seated in a booth by the window. A nice young waitress brought them water and menus. They looked to see if the fried clams were still the main special. They were in luck.

EC said, "Let's order. Are you ready? I'm hungry."

"Yes. I'm starved. I haven't had fried clams since last summer at the beach. Call the waitress."

After the waitress had taken their order and brought them some sweet iced tea, EC started fumbling around in his jacket pocket. Finally, he very carefully removed a little box, opened it, and placed it on the table in front of Clara. Clara looked at the box in amazement.

Before Clara could speak, EC leaned over the table, grabbed Clara's hand and blurted loud enough for most everyone in the restaurant to hear, "Clara, will you marry me?"

Clara did not miss a beat. She grabbed EC's arm and screamed, "Yes, Yes, I will."

Cheers and whistles echoed throughout the restaurant.

The fried clams were delicious.

In a blink, EC and Clara were engaged and on their way to getting married. Clara was all of twenty-two years old and beyond excited. She truly loved EC and could not wait until they tied the knot.

Along with her family and some input from EC, Clara made her wedding plans. Although he knew her parents could afford the wedding expenses, EC wanted to be sure Clara got everything she wanted or needed for their wedding, so he told Clara he would pay for everything but the dresses for her and her bridesmaids. "I don't know anything at all about that stuff," he told her.

Clara said, "I didn't know I was marrying a rich man, but I'll take your offer. You are really too sweet. I may have to add some more things. So it's okay to get them?"

EC smiled and said, "Anything for my beautiful bride. Anything at all."

It was supposed to be a small wedding, just family and a few friends, but before long almost everyone in the Fork got an invitation. In fact, almost everyone EC knew received one, too.

When the day finally came, EC had made good on his promise and everything Clara wanted for their wedding was in place. The wedding chapel was a small white clapboard country church with a steeple on top. It sat on a cleared area surrounded by a plowed-under corn field. Inside there were only forty pews that sat on a highly waxed, shiny hardwood floor. The walls were soft white. There were four stained glass windows, two on either side. It was the perfect setting for a small country wedding.

The inside of the church looked like a florist shop, and the small chapel overflowed with wedding guests. Most were EC's friends. It was standing room only.

The community building where the reception was held was a white-framed one story building. Inside was a giant room with a small kitchen and restrooms tucked off to the side. The walls, ceiling, and exposed beams were all knotty-pine. There were two wagon wheel light fixtures hanging at each end of the room, which was decorated to the nines. Food, beverages, music, and gifts were everywhere. It too was overrun with wedding guests that wanted to be part of the festivities. Clara was ecstatic. She could not have asked for anything more. By country standards, it was a lavish wedding and reception.

When the reception ended, the newlyweds jumped into EC's shiny new brown Packard and headed off to Miami for their honeymoon.

Clara slid into the car, and as soon as they were out of sight of the guests, she moved closer to EC and tucked herself under his arm. "If I get too close, just let me know," she said.

EC smiled. "Clara, you can't ever get too close to me. I love you so much."

Clara teasingly asked, "How much longer before we get to Miami?"

"Too damn long for me," he said. He pulled the car onto the shoulder of the road, put it in park, grabbed Clara and gave her a long kiss. Clara responded with a kiss like EC had not had from her before. EC thought *how the hell did she know how to do that?*

He pulled back and placed his hand softly over Clara's. "We better stop now or we'll never get to Florida."

"The hell with Florida," she said. "Let's get a room."

"Yes ma'am. We can sure do that."

They made it as far as Carolina Beach, near Wilmington, where they checked into a roadside motel. Their hormones took over as they fell into bed. It was a wild and crazy night that kept them awake until early dawn.

Several times during the night, Clara said, "I never knew it would feel that good."

Each time EC replied, "I tried to tell you what you've been missing." They spent the night trying to make up for lost time.

The next day they could barely wait until they found a local breakfast cafe where they re-fortified their bodies with scrambled eggs, bacon, grits, and made-from-scratch biscuits. All that, plus coffee and orange juice, raised their energy level enough to get them back on the road and headed for Florida. Their married life was off to a great start.

Chapter 6
THE TOWN

Much to the delight of dating age couples, EC opened his second drive-in movie in Groveland. He figured that with several hundred more folks living there, his drive-in movie business would do even better. He was right again.

Groveland was located three miles east of the Fork. This rural community also sat amid thousands of acres of some of the flattest land imaginable. The rich soil in the area was great for farming. During the growing season, rows and rows of corn, acres upon acres of tobacco, and fields of soybeans and cotton stretched in every direction. Many of these acres were inside the city limits. Most of the three mile stretch of land between Groveland and the Fork was occupied by a black community. It was one of two black enclaves in Groveland.

It was a nice little farm community of about 700 people, if you counted the folks just across the town limit signs. Until 1950, not all the streets were paved. The town had a mayor – the same one forever – and elected aldermen. Back then there were no term limits.

Groveland was the kind of town where the delightful fragrance of freshly cut grass filled the air on summer afternoons, and where in early September, a smoky haze with its comforting acrid smell, rose from piles of just raked burning leaves. Groveland was a warm and friendly place to live and work.

This was a community with one bank, three churches, one and a half grocery stores, two feed mills with grain elevators, a couple of car dealers, a heavy equipment dealer, two doctors, no dentist, and one white school with dedicated teachers, who cared about providing their students with a sound education. There was also one black school, one traffic light, one hardware store, one mercantile store, one drug store with a soda fountain, one pool hall, a couple of gas stations, one walk-in movie with great popcorn, one fire truck, and one policeman. In those days, it had the best drinking water any thirsty person would ever taste, and there was a very good reason for that. The town's deep well water supply came from the Black Creek aquifer. It was one of three aquifers in the state that had never had anything removed or added to it since first tested by the state Agricultural Department in the early 1940s. For years, the town's water tank bore the slogan, "The Town of Perfect Water," and because it was true, the coffee and iced tea were always excellent.

The town had its share of unusual characters. There was more than one town drunk, one very intelligent alcoholic painter, and Stark Bodie. Bodie owned a downtown store and he commuted to Groveland from Kingstown, 30 miles to the west, every business day. He arrived in his twenty year old black and tan Cadillac every morning at 9 a.m. sharp. How he ever made a dime was a mystery to most folks. One day he walked into the Chevy dealership and bought a brand new Chevy Super Sport, which he paid for with cash he pulled from a paper bag – four thousand dollars. The money smelled as if it had been buried in his back yard for years.

There were two doctors in town. No two folks could be any more different. Dr. Cook was known as the poor man's doctor. No appointment necessary. Just walk into his run-down remodeled gas station office and hope he had time to see you. There were only two metal folding chairs in his waiting room. Sometimes he was glad to see patients. Sometimes he refused to administer service to sick people who stopped by. Sometimes he charged a modest fee, sometimes he refused to accept payment. He was a strange duck.

The other physician, Dr. Marks, had a new, well-furnished office. He was better known as the rich man's doctor. His airplane contributed to that designation. He initiated an appointment system for his practice, and he saw few people without one. He also was not bashful about charging a pretty penny for his medical assistance, and he would and did make house calls.

Three different churches in Groveland mirrored the class structure of the town. The Methodist church attracted the more affluent residents. The four wealthier families in town were Methodists, as were many of the upper middle class folk. These followers of John Wesley didn't exude any kind of attitude, but they were definitely proud of their church.

The Baptist church was home to most of the non-drinking, non-smoking, and non-dancing churchgoers in town. These were the middle class residents who took their religion and Bible belt traditions very seriously. They hosted church activities several nights a week, and the church boasted a very talented choir.

The Christian church was more closely identified with the Evangelical folks in the community. This was where you'd be more likely see an example of "slain in the spirit" and hear a lot more "amens." They made up most of the lower middle class section of town. Their baptismal ceremonies were a sight to behold.

Despite the differences in their styles and methods of worship, many members from each of these congregations were friends, neighbors, and even family with all the others. They were equal opportunity worshipers.

During the war years, there were sirens blasting town-wide blackouts in Groveland and men running through the streets yelling for all lights to be turned off. The blackouts were very common and scary, especially to children. Homes had black shades. Food, tires, gas, and car parts were rationed. Many local men were drafted for the war effort. Local women manned the local fire towers to watch out for enemy planes or attacks. German U Boats were sinking US warships near the North Carolina coast only 45 minutes away. You could actually drive to the coast and see burning ships sinking at sea. There were cement rocket bunkers along the coastal islands, built as fortifications against the enemy. It was a frightening time.

Groveland prospered after the war, and many of its residents worked hard, raised their families, and went to church. Parents saw to it that their children went to school and that they worked during the summers. Many parents helped their kids go to college. Everyone knew everyone.

It truly was a quiet, one-horse town – except for the underground activities going on there. The mix of powerful, greedy men and the criminal element of wannabes made for an amazing emerging business arrangement. They were brazen and totally unafraid of anything or anyone in law enforcement and with good reason. They felt free to do whatever was necessary to bring their illegal acts to fruition.

The criminal element was a collection of a few men, maybe ten in all, scattered about the county. They had known each other from childhood or as early business associates and were close knit. EC was the group's leader. He was ambitious, liked to cut corners, took incredible risks, and violated many state and federal laws. You name the crime and EC and his group did most of them.

Chapter 7
THE OTHER WOMAN

Katy Hoover was born in Groveland to a hard-working tenant family that lived on a wealthy landlord's farm just outside of town. They were a large family, three brothers and three sisters. All the children were expected to do their share of the home chores and later the farm work. The working farm was busy year round with crops of tobacco, corn, soy beans, cotton, winter wheat, as well as raising hogs and chickens. There was plenty of work for everyone.

As Katy grew into an attractive young woman, she and her sweet smile began to be noticed about town. In her early teens she began babysitting for families who knew her and her family through connections with her daddy's landlord. This babysitting job became a very good outlet for Katy and allowed her to grow and meet new and different people. She learned a great deal from these new acquaintances, and her self-confidence and sense of style improved. She was very good with children, but she also interacted quite easily with adults.

After finishing high school, Katy, at the suggestion of some of her friends, applied for a cashier's position at Cain's Supermarket. As soon as she left, the store manager called EC at home and told him, "Katy Hoover just applied for a job."

EC told the store manager, "Call Katy tomorrow and tell her to come back for an interview at one o'clock on Wednesday. I'll interview her myself." EC could hardly wait for Wednesday to come. He decided to get a bit spruced up for the interview.

Finally the time arrived and in walked Katy Hoover. She was wearing a tight blue skirt with a fitted white sweater and she looked damn good. She was a sensuous young lady in a respectable kind of way, but she got her message across quite well. She had grown into a very attractive young woman.

"Hello, Mr. Cain," she said.

EC was surprised at her formality. "Good afternoon, Katy," he responded, prancing around in his new sports jacket like a bantam rooster. Then the electricity began to fly; Katy flirting with EC and EC fawning over her every word. EC hadn't failed to notice how nicely she had grown into an attractive young woman with a beautiful smile – among other things. It took little time for EC to let Katy know she was hired.

"I'm expecting a lot of great things from you," EC told her.

Katy answered, "I know, and you won't be disappointed." EC got her drift.

Because Katy had grown up as one of six children, she had never been the recipient of too much attention. Now all of a sudden this slightly older and successful businessman was following her around like a puppy dog. And she liked being noticed. All of his compliments, plus his kind remarks, sounded good to her. She was old enough, but not experienced enough, to know that fooling around with your boss, who also happened to be married and have a child, was not exactly an approved code of conduct for a nice young woman, particularly in this small rural community. But Katy was smitten with the idea of being with EC. So the relationship continued to grow.

The fact that EC was married to Clara who was helping raise Elaine as if she were her own, did not get in the way of his budding friendship with his new young and sexy employee. EC had always been very nice to Clara ever since they first met. He truly loved her and he was very touched and pleased that she was willing to take Elaine on as her own daughter after they married. Even so, EC had always been a lady's man. He had never met a woman he didn't want to screw. It was no different now, and it would never be any different. So, over the next few months, this employee friendship became more involved and finally became a full blown sexual relationship, a real affair.

The problem was EC and Katy were not discreet enough with their affair to keep it from the prying eyes that followed EC around most days. Clara, his five year old daughter Elaine, other employees, and business partners all noticed. It was no surprise when one day in late 1951, Clara confronted EC and said, "I'm very suspicious about your relationship with Katy. It's a bit too cozy for me. What's your deal with her? Are you screwing her yet?"

EC recoiled. He screamed at Clara, "I'm totally innocent, goddammit. It's just a working relationship. She does work for me, you know."

"That's what the hell I'm worried about."

Then came EC's rage at even being accused. EC demanded, "Clara, you damn well better apologize to me for such a ridiculous accusation. Don't ever falsely accuse me another goddamn time of any wrong doing. I will not put up with your fuckin' bullshit. You got that, bitch?"

Clara turned red with anger and shouted back at EC, "Don't call me a bitch, you goddamn wife beater. Who the hell do you think you are? You just think you can run over every woman you see, but I'm here to tell you, you can't run me into the ground and talk to me like I'm a dog. I will not stand for it."

"You better calm your ass down, woman. Like, right now."

EC's marriage was on the rocks, and he was beginning to realize it.

As he tried to go along to get along with his family, EC's extra marital love life calmed down for the next several months. He was involved with many new business interests that kept him on the move from morning to night. Even so, many of those day trips ended in a nightly hookup with Katy.

To ease the tension and suspicion, Katy found a clerk's position at a new Piggly Wiggly that had just opened in Groveland. One of her older brothers had already landed a job there. The store was owned by the oldest son of her father's landlord. Rendezvous with EC continued. They had a powerful relationship in spite of their age difference. They even talked about the possibility of getting married, if and when EC and Clara divorced.

Chapter 8
THE NEW FAMILY

Several months later, after Clara had been murdered, buried, and all leads had grown cold, the murder investigation slowed almost to a stop. There were still many unanswered questions about her abduction and murder. The hitmen were still at large, and that bothered many town folk. It seemed impossible that the authorities could not catch who murdered Clara.

Elaine was still sleeping in EC's bed because she was scared. She was having the same nightmare every night. She told EC, "Daddy, every night I dream Mama's coffin is in the bed with me. Her arm is reaching out of the coffin trying to touch me. I think she wants me to go with her. Please make her quit and go away. Please make her leave me alone."

EC whispered, "Baby, I'll take care of it. I'll make sure Mama leaves you alone from now on. Don't you worry anymore, I promise." Elaine expected him to keep that promise.

Thankfully, Elaine was of school age, which got her out of the house every day. It was the therapy she needed, and it kept her moving forward with her young life. Elaine liked school, and she was a good student who worked hard to get good grades and EC's approval.

However, it was only a few months before EC and Katy were spending time together again, albeit in private and out of sight of curious eyes. But Elaine knew what was going on. She confronted her father one morning and asked, "Can I go live with one of my aunts?"

EC was surprised at her request and asked, "Why?"

"Figure it out. You're so damn smart."

"Give me a reason."

"Katy," Elaine shouted and then she started crying and stormed out of the house.

Elaine had a choice of more than one aunt to live with as EC came from a large family of five sisters and three brothers. Some were better suited to take care of Elaine than others. Even Elaine's step-grandparents offered to raise her in their home. EC arranged for Elaine to move in with his sister, Sadie. As soon as Elaine went to live with her Aunt Sadie, Katy moved in with EC and just like that, they were together again.

Things were moving at a very fast pace. EC had lots going on, and his relationship with Katy was at full throttle. But that arrangement did not last long. After EC and Katy got married, Elaine came back home to live with them. That's right, EC made a third trip to the alter.

Elaine began calling Katy, Mother. Then things changed quickly. In 1954 a bouncing baby boy joined the family. They named him Edward Earl Cain, Jr.

Katy told EC, "I gave you what you've always wanted, a namesake to carry your name forward."

EC crowed with pride. "This is the happiest day of my life." Katy took little time in taking full credit.

Nothing seemed to bother Katy. It seemed as if she had intended all of this to happen. First came a short courtship, followed by marriage to her former boss and lover, then an instant role as stepmother, crowned by real motherhood with the birth of their son, EC Jr.

What most people didn't understand was how this young attractive woman could overlook the facts surrounding EC. Besides their age difference, the known facts included EC's first shotgun marriage and baby, along with the subsequent disappearance of that family. Then there was the second wife, who was abducted from their home and murdered. Her murderer had never been found. Most importantly, many of the folks in the county believed EC had arranged Clara's death. Most people would have been a bit fearful about getting involved with a person having such a checkered past. It didn't seem to bother Katy at all, but her parents were horrified.

As Elaine grew older, she and Katy became close and began behaving like the mother/daughter combination they had become. Katy became as much a mother to Elaine as she was to her own son, Edward Earl Cain, Jr., whom they called Will. There was an outward expression of love between the two of them for many years to come, and Elaine adored her half-brother Will.

By the time Elaine turned nine, EC and Katy's marriage was still strong and growing. EC was very busy with all his legal and illegal ventures, and he was making a lot of money.

Will grew up at the Fork with a doting mother and a proud father. He got all the attention a little tot could want. EC absolutely adored Will and until Will was about four years old, EC took him with him on his travels around the county.

It was about that time that EC got so busy with other deals and obligations that he began to spend less time at home. His time with Will was becoming non-existent. Will was devastated, but as he grew older, he gradually realized he had to move on with his life.

Chapter 9
THE OTHER FAMILY

Brenda and EC's child, Anna, moved to Tennessee after they divorced. There had been no contact from either side for many years. But one of Brenda's childhood friends called her about Clara's shocking murder in 1952. The same friend called her again two years later to tell her about EC's new wife, Katy, and their son, EC, Jr. Brenda was stunned to hear that EC had married for the third time and that he already had another child. More than anything, she was disgusted.

Other than her job, Brenda was devoted to her daughter, Anna. She spent lots of time with her and did everything she thought a good mother should do for a growing child. They had a great relationship and it really showed when they were around other people. Anna grew into a nice young lady.

Anna Cain got married in 1958. In honor of her mother, she kept her maiden name of Cain. She had a son, the second male child in the Cain family, whom she named Edward Earl Cain III. However, when he got older he decided to take his biological father's name out of respect for him.

For the first three years, things went well for this new family and child, and then tragedy struck. In 1961 Anna's husband was killed in a horrible accident at the Atomic Energy Commission Facility in Oak Ridge, Tennessee. Anna could not bear to stay in Oakridge and have to face her memories and reminders of the tragedy every day, so soon thereafter she and her son moved to Melbourne, Florida.

Anna was a kind and gentle woman, and even though she never knew her father growing up, and the fact that she lost her husband after three years of marriage, she became a great mom. She was not only attentive to her son, but also to her mother Brenda. She always had their best interests in mind and did everything in her power to make sure both were healthy, well fed, and loved unconditionally.

EC III turned sixteen during his senior year in high school. His early academic achievements allowed him to skip a grade earlier. Soon after he graduated, Anna sat him down to tell him Brenda's story.

Anna began, "Your grandmother was run out of the Fork in North Carolina by EC right after I was born. She picked up and moved us to Franklin, Tennessee, because she had kinfolk there. Her first cousin offered us a room until she could do better. It was really tough for Mama. She looked for months to find a job. Eventually, she got a job at a local textile mill as a seamstress. During the day, her cousin kept me until I was ready for kindergarten. That's the best Mama could do. Later, she was transferred to a better paying spinning job in Oak Ridge, Tennessee. Things got better for both of us."

"Mom, I don't understand why my grandfather treated my GranMa so awful. Was he just a very mean man?"

"Not really. He was too young, and he just wasn't ready to settle down. He wasn't ready for a baby at such an early age."

"Yeah, but he could've been nicer."

"I found out what a nice man was when I met your father," Anna said.

"Tell me all about my Dad."

"Well, several years passed, and I was growing up and looking good. One rainy night my Mama was on her way home from work and had a flat tire. She was having a hard time getting anyone to stop to help her. Suddenly a car slowed down, came to a stop, and a nice looking young man jumped out. He offered to fix the tire. After about twenty minutes in the rain, he said he couldn't fix the tire, so he offered to take Mama home. This man drove her home and walked her to our door. When I opened the door, I saw this handsome young man, and he saw me. His name was

Michael. It worked from the very first minute. We clicked liked two peas in a pod. Mama asked him to come in and dry off while she fixed him a cup of hot coffee and a piece of apple pie. Was I ever excited. Before he left that evening he asked for my number," Anna said, smiling to herself.

"Several days later that nice, handsome man called and asked if he could take me to a movie. Mama said okay, so we started dating. Your Daddy was a very special man. We got married on my eighteenth birthday in 1958, and we soon had a baby boy. You were that baby. What a godsend."

Your Daddy had a high ranking job at the Atomic Energy Commission Facility in Oak Ridge. Something to do with the labs. One day in 1961 there was a horrible accident – a deadly lab spill. Your father and seven other workers were killed. Naturally there was an extensive investigation, and the predictable conclusion was that there was no evidence of any wrongdoing by the Commission. Therefore the Commission was not liable and had no reason to compensate the families of the victims. It was obviously one of those government cover-ups."

"Did you sue where Daddy worked?" her son asked.

"No, I didn't have the time or money to get a lawyer."

"Was that a mistake?"

"In hindsight, probably."

"How long did you and Daddy date?"

"Long enough to make sure we were right for each," Anna said.

"Did I go to Daddy's funeral?"

"Yes you did, in a baby stroller. You were too heavy for me to carry."

"Was I aware of what was going on?"

"I'm not sure. You cried the whole time," Anna said.

"How long did it take you to get over Daddy's death?"

"I won't ever get over your father's death. Never. He was such a wonderful person. And, thankfully you've turned out to be just like him."

Anna continued, "Now, about your grandfather...your grandfather, EC, is a very selfish man. He never once contacted my Mama, your grandmother, from the day she had me and had to leave the Fork. Although she badly needed help, she never once tried to reach him. EC never acknowledged me as his daughter. Never. Not once. I have never seen him except in some photos. I have never tried to contact him either, and I never told him I got married or that he has a grandson. He did not deserve to know. If he knows, it came from someone else. It's doubtful he even knows we live in Melbourne."

"Mama," Anna continued, "knew very little, basically nothing in fact, about what had gone on in EC's life until a childhood friend called a few times in the mid-fifties. She told Mama about my half-sister Elaine, born out of wedlock, and that EC and Clara, his new wife, adopted her. Later, Mama heard that Clara had been murdered from all of those national news stories about the tragedy. Mama knows very little about EC's third wife, Katy, and their son, EC, Jr. That's all I really know, except you need to stay clear of your grandfather, EC."

"You think I want to spend any time with a man who treated you and GranMa so badly? Come on, Mom. You know me better than that."

"I just wanted to make sure that you know how he treated us in the beginning. How truly horrible he was to my mother, which indirectly affected me, as well."

"All I can say is he's not anybody I would ever respect or want to have anything to do with, now or later," EC, III said.

"That's really good to hear coming from you. You're a well-grounded young man, and I'm glad and so proud that you're my son. Don't ever forget what a wonderful man your Dad was and how much he adored every minute he spent with you."

"Don't worry, Mom. I promise I'll never forget this day and this conversation. Never. Count on that."

"Good," Anna said.

"I love you, Mom. I'll always love you."

Chapter 10
THE PEOPLE

EC's collection of friends included his partners and advisors. They became known as "The Insiders." Most of them lived in Groveland, New Ferry or the Fork. When EC began moving and shaking with his business expansion and with his illegal activities, he turned to his Insiders for help. He got it in spades. Again during all the trouble related to Clara's kidnapping and murder, EC turned to certain individuals in the group, including his immediate family.

There was a lot of talk around town about some unusual assistance from local county law enforcement agencies, but to what extent this actually happened was never fully revealed. The outcome of the investigation, however, suggests that many may have looked the other way – and more than once.

Ralph Thompson, an influential, well-heeled Groveland heavy equipment dealer, who had been closely associated with EC since the early days of their respective business dealings, had great connections of his own. He had amassed a great deal of farmland in the county, which was tended by tenant farmers. He was also landlord to many commercial businesses.

One situation Ralph chased until he finally got the deal he wanted was a large tract of oceanfront property on North Carolina's coast. It had been in the family of one of the state's largest Budweiser distributors for many years. The tract included five miles of oceanfront that went all the way back to the sound. The price Ralph negotiated with the owner was remarkable. To his credit, Ralph had the vision and the staying power to wait until the world discovered the benefits of Windsail Island. He was able to do this because of the favorable "interest only" loan he received from the seller.

About a month after Ralph closed on the beach property, he called Vinny Moser and asked him to meet for lunch. Vinny agreed and they met at the Riverside, their favorite seafood restaurant on the coast.

Ralph asked Vinny, "Have you ever had hush puppies anywhere in the world better than these?"

Vinny shook his head. "No damn way, no damn where."

They both ordered fried seafood platters that were a combination of the "fresh catch of the day," usually flounder, with local shrimp and oysters. Of course, the platters came with heaping servings of coleslaw, French fries, and hush puppies. Their glasses were constantly filled with sweet iced tea.

After they had devoured their seafood platters, Ralph began his pitch. "Vinny, I'm going to build a span bridge across the Intracoastal Waterway that will connect Windsail Island to the mainland. The beach side of the structure will actually have pilings that sit on my land."

Vinny raised his hand like a schoolboy asking a question in class and said, "How the hell are you going to do that?"

"Very simple," Ralph answered. "I will do it with help from people like Vinny Moser. We'll gather up a handful of state politicians we've both funded for years. We'll use them to set in motion a plan to connect the northern end of Windsail to the mainland with a span bridge over the Intracoastal Waterway."

Vinny replied, "Okay. And who's going to pay for it?"

Ralph had a short answer. "State and federal funding. This will be a major and very expensive endeavor. It'll be a monumental task. If successful, the value of my beach property will skyrocket."

Vinny asked, "What's in it for me?"

"Ocean front property or cash. Take your pick, and you get it once the deal is done. Let's go. I've got lunch."

Vinny said, "Count me in." The two men got up, shook hands, and left.

It took a number of years, lots of campaign money, and a great deal of arm twisting before the Department of Transportation approved the project and added it to the budget for immediate development. This bridge would bring the world to the doorstep of Ralph's property. The bridge pilings would actually sit on a portion of his land. The exposure for his property would be incredible. Once the project was completed and opened, Ralph was sitting on go.

What Ralph did next was incredible. It had not been done before in this market. He subdivided the tract into a combination of lot classifications. He had beachfront lots, second row lots, and sound front lots. He also had commercial lots with frontage access on the road he built that split his land. He saved some property for multi-family lots.

Additionally he saved some beachfront lots for Vinny, as his source of payment. Vinny's lots became very valuable over the years. Ralph had converted his property into an absolute gold mine, and he knew it. He priced the lots accordingly. Over time, not only did he make a huge fortune on this project, he earned the reputation of being a big time deal maker.

Another business that Ralph invested in later, but kept very quiet, was a loan shark type operation based in Richmond, Virginia. Supposedly, Ralph Thompson was a silent partner or passive investor, but most likely he was the main man in charge. The company, Freeloaner, opened branches all over the southeast in a matter of a few years. When the crunch came, the company collapsed overnight and millions were lost.

In good times or bad, Ralph Thompson had good cash flow. This was quite an advantage when opportunities arose. He also covered EC's back more than a few times, either at the bank or from his own pocket. It always involved money, lots of money.

There were a couple of feed and grain businesses in Groveland that were operated by friendly competitors. One, M&B Supply Co., which was an old converted general store and fertilizer warehouse with a feed mill built in the mid-1940s, was run by two very different partners that managed to gain success. One partner, Roy Browning, was the inside man, and the other, Cecil Miller, was the outside man.

This new business enterprise was very much needed and therefore was very well received in this farming community. Together they eventually grew and opened four different locations in several nearby communities. Later they became burdened with tax problems, which resulted in the dissolution of their partnership. After they split the assets of the operations, they continued on successfully, but separately.

The other feed and grain facility, Groveland Milling Co., was actually located at the Fork, just across the highway from EC's country store and next to EC's first drive-in movie. It was run by a very nice gentleman, Carl Barber, who had a silent partner, the local Ford dealer Vinny Moser.

Vinny was a nice looking, dark complexioned young man, tall and trim with jet black hair. He was quite attractive to the ladies when he got all dressed up, something he never failed to forget. To make matters even more enticing, Vinny lived in one of the two largest and most beautiful homes in Groveland. You could smell his money. He and his wife, Claudia, had two children. Claudia was a school teacher before she became a stay-at-home mom. She was an attractive, sophisticated, smart lady and they made a very handsome couple.

Whatever funding many businesses needed to grow and prosper, Vinny Moser provided. It was his modus operandi, and he was very successful at it for years. He was the money behind an oil jobber operation in the county. Vinny Moser was loyal to the community, the church, and the school. He showed his loyalty with his financial support, as well as hiring "just out of high school" young men to work in his various enterprises.

Most people knew little about Vinny's many other businesses. Besides his car dealership and some local farming operations, he operated other more cash intensive businesses around the state. He was known to be in his office at 5 o'clock every morning and on the phone talking with his business interests in distant towns until 9 PM or later.

The other car dealer, Henry Robards, was a Chevy man who inherited the business through his father-in-law, Doctor Battle. He married Alicia,

Dr. Battle's daughter, in the late thirties. They had three sons. After the war this dealership moved into a new facility on the bypass and grew into a very profitable entity. Later, Henry Robards (with a partner) became the Chevy/Cadillac dealer in the very lucrative military market of New Ferry. It provided Henry the funding to do other things like back other people in different types of businesses.

One was a very well-known drive-in only restaurant called The Spot Drive-In. It was operated by two brothers. One was a Trailways bus driver, and the other delivered papers. They were quite a pair of characters. For most young folks with access to cars, The Spot was the main social hangout, as well as the main place to eat out in Groveland. It became the meeting spot for thousands of kids over the years, even for people from nearby towns. A popular delicacy at The Spot was the fried bologna sandwich with mustard. Thousands upon thousands were sold over the years.

Henry Robards's major investment was the money and vision to back a very popular grocery store chain that wanted to expand in the eastern part of the state. He solicited a member from another well-known local family to become the operating partner. It was hugely successful for both families involved in the partnership. He coined a phrase early in his business career: "You can never go broke taking a profit." He was credited with that sage advice hundreds of times throughout his life.

The other large and beautiful house in Groveland was where Henry and Alicia Robards lived. It was Alicia's family home and they moved into it after her father, Doctor Battle died. Her mother was moved into a newer, but smaller house across the street.

The myth about these two car dealers was that they were bitter rivals and despised one another. Fact is, they were great friends and socialized quite often in each other's homes, at their clubs, and at many other social functions.

There was another oil distributor in town, Bobby Hanes, who was originally supported by Vinny Moser. He was also pretty good friends with EC. Bobby provided EC's country store at the Fork with a self-service gas operation and spearheaded the self-service gas operation in the county.

He became very successful in the oil business, along with his very attractive and loving wife, Anita.

Bobby was very active in the Jaycees and began dabbling in politics, the unpopular – at that time – Republican kind. Eventually he ran for the State House of Representatives as a Republican. He was soundly defeated. However, Bobby Hanes was probably the person most responsible for his county and the surrounding counties becoming two party counties in later years.

Then there was Preacher F. J. Moon. A character par excellence for sure. He was a farmer, a mercantile man, and a colorful businessman. Preacher Moon, Vinny Moser, EC, Ralph Thompson, and others were close buddies and were often seen together at the coast eating seafood and having a sip or two, while solving the world's problems.

Two important men who played a major role in this entire saga actually grew up in another county. Michael Banks and Horace Felton were both former bankers and both knew EC from their early childhood days. They were also close friends with Vinny Moser and Ralph Thompson.

Michael Banks grew up in the next county over. In his younger days he was a great student and a fabulous athlete. Once out of college, he started as a teller at a local bank. After a few years of learning how to be a banker, he decided he wanted to start a bank of his own. He solicited help from his childhood friend, Horace Felton, who was at that time working at a bank in Richmond, Virginia.

When the new bank concept arose, Michael Banks and Horace Felton were at every meeting. Then came investors like Vinny Moser and Ned Ellis from the coast, but Michael Banks was the man pushing the deal. He had lots of support from Vinny Moser, Ralph Thompson, EC, and Horace Felton. The fact that Michael Banks and Horace Felton had a combined twelve years of experience in the banking business served them well as they went about organizing their new bank. They knew how much capital they needed, and they knew where to go to legally raise that kind of money. They also realized the importance of a strong personnel structure. They were making big plans.

There were a number of local men, mostly young men, who worked for EC in his many business enterprises. They were Nelson Woodward, Enoch Woodward, Clem Houston and Earl Tardy. These four, along with some others, were involved in many of EC's enterprises. You'd see them at the country store, at the Fork, at EC's appliance store in New Ferry, on his delivery trucks, and riding around with EC in his fancy car. EC was not without access to bodies when something needed to be done. They would do just about anything EC asked them to do, anytime, anywhere; no questions asked. Sadly, sometimes that was not in their best interest.

Nelson and Enoch were brothers. They were nice, hard-working country boys who helped their tenant farmer father tend his crops. They did this until they grew older and were able to get paying jobs and leave home. They both worked for EC doing about anything he asked them to do. They could often be found at Woodrow's pool hall in Groveland. They would shoot some pool, drink some beer, and brag about what they were doing for and with EC. Sometimes when their tongues got really loose, they told more than they should.

Another unusual person in EC's collection of friends was Harvey Faison. He lived at the Fork and was a long distance truck driver. He was very proud of the big, shiny eighteen-wheeler rig that EC helped him buy and finance. He trucked freight of all sorts all over the country.

One day EC looked up from the cash register as a friend from Groveland walked in and started telling EC about his problem. It involved a commercial building he owned. His leased building was being operated as a furniture store by two other men and it was located at the Fork across the intersection from EC's store. The business was on the ropes after only a year or so of operation. The friend told EC, "These folks in my building are in trouble. They're going fuckin' broke and that is not going to help me at all. Can you find someone to torch the goddamn building?"

EC replied very calmly, "You know arson is a very serious crime, don't you? But, I can get it done for you."

The friend responded, "I know it's a serious crime, but I figured your boys won't get caught."

"I sure as hell hope not," EC said.

Later that night, EC called Harvey to his store and said, "Harvey, I need you to burn that goddamn furniture store down this week. You tell me which night you plan to set it on fire so I can be gone."

"Okay, if you say so," Harvey said. "If you need some Jewish lightning, I'll find you some." (Jewish lightening is when the mortgage rubs up against the insurance policy and causes a friction fire.)

"Give me three days," Harvey said.

Harvey went home that night and decided who he would get to help him torch the furniture store. He called a couple of boys he knew who had worked for EC over the years. He figured he could trust them to keep their mouths shut. They agreed.

A few days later, Harvey and his accomplices gathered up their needed supplies: some old dry burlap bags, newspapers, and several cans of fuel oil. Harvey sent one of the guys to the station to buy five gallons of gasoline. Once they were well fortified, they went to the building and spread the burlap bags and newspaper all around the store's perimeter. Then they drenched the materials with fuel oil. To make sure the fire made it inside the store, they broke the front door glass and splashed gasoline inside. Harvey set fire to the building. In no time flat the store was engulfed with flames shooting skyward thirty feet or more.

The store was destroyed, but Harvey Faison and his boys had done a sloppy job. They left too many clues. Much of the torch material did not burn completely. It was obvious to the arson investigators that the fire had been deliberately set. In a matter of weeks, Harvey and his two helpers were caught, tried, and sent to prison. It devastated his son, Mike Faison.

Mike Faison had often bragged to his classmates that he knew a lot about what EC was doing because his daddy told him. Mike talked openly about EC's criminal operations. Maybe he did know about them, maybe he didn't, but he talked a good game. He was shooting hoops in the high school gym one afternoon, when the school principal and a deputy sheriff came to tell him his daddy had been sent to prison for arson. EC, who got a suspended sentence, wasn't too excited that his name was associated with the crime. Mike Faison didn't like that one bit and was quick to let anyone know. He thought he should tell the law everything he knew, but he didn't because he was afraid of EC.

One of EC's insiders had connections to a major bootlegging operation in the next county. Supposedly, it was an underground operation designed and operated by a major poultry farmer. It rivaled an underground operation in Johnson County that was controlled by a gentleman farmer, Percy Flowers. In earlier years, his operation shipped thousands upon thousands of gallons of moonshine whiskey north. Flowers was indicted in 1958. A federal judge sentenced him to nineteen months. The sentence was eventually reduced to only twelve months. In one way or another, several folks from Groveland were involved in the operation in the next county over.

Sammy, one of several moonshine-seasoned drivers who hauled bootleg for the operation in the next county, was sitting in his car at The Spot Drive-In one night when a friend of his jumped into his car just to chat. The moonshine deal came up in conversation. The friend asked Sammy, "Do you know anything about that?"

Sammy said, "It's the largest moonshine deal in the state. It's so high tech that we simply drive into the underground site, and they do the rest. The first time I made a run, I asked the mechanic, 'Why are you putting overload shocks on my car?'"

"To keep the ass end of your car off the highway, you moron," the mechanic told me.

"Don't scratch my car,' I said to him. But he gave no answer. Then he loaded the cases of moonshine into my trunk. He handed me an envelope with instructions on where to deliver the moonshine. Not knowing any better I asked, 'Where is my money?'"

"He slapped me pretty hard on the back of my head and snorted, 'You don't get paid until you make the delivery, you damn stupid fool. Where the hell did they find you anyway?'"

"Once I arrived at a designated spot in a town on the way to DC, I drove into a garage. The overload shocks were removed from the car and the cases of moonshine were off-loaded. I was handed an envelope containing $250 in cash for the run to Weldon. It would have been $500 if I had driven all the way to DC. I never went past Weldon, so I always collected $250."

Sammy continued, "Many local boys, mostly teenagers, are involved. They can leave Groveland by six at night and be back right here at The Spot by 11 pm with $250 cash in their pockets. It was just too easy to pass up. Man, this has been going on for years."

At the time, Groveland only had one bank. That meant that everyone knew everyone's business just by asking. It was controlled by an old banking family from up state that provided much of the financing for all the growing businesses that sprang up after the war. The parent banking company continued to grow and expand and by the late 1950s had turned into the fourth largest bank in the state.

When the new bank was chartered in 1952, the established bank's management strongly suggested to a couple of their enterprising customers, Henry Robards and Vinny Moser, to forget about getting involved with the new bank. Robards was on their local board and acquiesced to their request. Smart move. Moser did not.

Vinny Moser had a family history in banking. Vinny's father, WB Moser, opened People's Bank in Groveland in 1913. He had a bank monopoly in Groveland until the bank closed in 1930 due to the Depression. It was named The Bank of Groveland when it closed. So for Vinny Moser, getting in on the new bank was a fairly natural thing to do.

There were other extraneous relationships that went unnoticed in the small village. Certain folks were attracted to the kind of criminal activity that EC and some of his partners were constantly involved in, in and around the counties. It was exciting, maybe even sexy, to some of their admirers. Nothing unusual about what types power and money attract.

A sexy blonde Swede, Patsy West, was one such person. Her parents operated a tulip farm in the northeastern part of the state. She was married to a high school teacher she met in Norfolk, Virginia, where he was stationed in the Navy. After getting out of the service, he landed a teaching job in Groveland, and they moved to town. The Wests had lots of friends. The couple loved playing canasta, and Patsy loved her vodka, which she was seldom without. Patsy worked at the Ford dealership for Vinny Moser for many years in several different positions.

There were a number of women around the counties that offered special favors to men like EC and his business associates. EC and many of his buddies took full advantage of most every situation they were afforded. They enjoyed what went along with their power and money.

Chapter 11

THE COUNTY SEAT

New Ferry was the county seat. It was surrounded by acres of flat farm-land, and as the crow flies, was fairly close to the coast. It was a military base town and very involved in the war. That's why the town grew faster and bigger than any other towns in the county. It was built on the banks of the New River, the only river in the state that begins and ends in the same county and is the widest river for its length in the state.

EC opened his third drive-in movie theater in New Ferry, on Vinny Moser's riverfront property. It is also the town where EC had opened an appliance store a couple of years earlier. The store was located on a busy retail street, just blocks from the center of town. EC was on a roll and other businesses followed suit.

As the county seat, New Ferry became the center for county business. Banks, law offices, the courthouse, the jail, the county sheriff's depart-ment, and the local newspaper were located there. It really was the busi-ness hub for the entire county. It was also where the new Bank started in 1952. The huge influx of a major military base payroll supported the growing local economic action.

New Ferry was located twelve miles east of Groveland, which was three miles east of the Fork. All three of these nearby communities had a great deal in common. They were all relatively small, close knit, and family oriented. Before the military base was built in New Ferry, all three towns were almost totally dependent on a rural sustainability.

In addition to crops raised in the fields, most families kept a garden. They also raised chickens for their eggs and hogs for meat. Most of the farm families were familiar with country ham, smokehouses, grits, red-eye gravy, collard greens, home-made biscuits, streak of lean, and banana pudding. They ate most of their meals at home. School kids rode the bus to school early in the mornings, home-packed lunches in hand, and returned late in the afternoons.

Many families in all three areas had family members who lived and-or worked in the other towns. This resulted in an overabundance of cross-over relations among the three communities, and everybody knew what everybody else was doing, at work and at home. There were not too many secrets among the residents. The one exception to this rule was EC's behind-the-scenes activities, though despite his secretiveness, many people believed that he was up to something illegal.

Before the military base was built in 1941 on the eastern side of New Ferry, the property was a huge tract of land, about 156,000 acres. It was owned by a few local families and was basically a forest brimming with wildlife including deer, bear, birds and great fishing holes, as well as an abundant coastline. The beachfront property was breathtaking, a sportsman's paradise. It had not gone unnoticed by the many wealthy northern outdoorsmen who came in droves during hunting season to the hunting camps they rented from the local landowners.

These wealthy northerners did not come alone. They brought their women and their liquor. They also brought their hobbies like gambling, gaming tables, slot machines, and yes, even money-making machines. The trouble had just begun. Talk of some of this illegal behavior had spread around the county. It became necessary for the sheriff to visit these "misbehavers" from time to time. The sheriff's department would raid these camps sporadically, but only with prior notice, so they would have time to hide the evidence. Notification came from the top at the sheriff's office.

Another factor in New Ferry's economic growth was US Highway 17 which cut through the city, bringing thousands of north and southbound travelers to the area every day. To accommodate these travelers, gas stations, motels, and restaurants opened along the route. These businesses had a steady, captive audience. Overnight travelers would also patronize the other shops in town during their stay.

The biggest financial boon to New Ferry's growth and expansion was the development of the Marine Corps base. Not only did it provide civilian jobs while it was being built, it also created the need for food and shelter for all of those workers who came to build the base. That meant homes, apartments, grocery stores, and restaurants.

Once the military base was completed, many thousands of military personnel passed through this base for training before they were deployed elsewhere. The base became home to about 35,000 troops on a regular basis, month in and month out. Any business in this part of the county prospered from the money Marines spent on their days off. The Marine base not only employed military folks, it provided jobs for thousands of civil service workers who lived in the county, another monetary boost for the local economies. This community was well on its way to becoming a mainstream southeastern city.

Not unlike Groveland, New Ferry had a couple of landmark drive-in restaurants of its own. One of these, the IT Drive-In, was on Highway 17, close to the river. It was a favorite of the military people when they came into town on their weekend leave passes. The sandwiches were great and the beer was very cold. It was always packed with customers.

The other drive-in was called The Whistle'n Pig, located on Lejeune Blvd. It was unique in that it had a small room on top of the building that housed a full blown DJ booth, occupied, most often, by Pat Patterson, the local music hero. He'd spin records that were requested by the dining patrons. It was quite an attraction that helped the 'Pig" succeed. Local residents were its mainstay.

The cross street, Court Street, was so named because it was where the courthouse stood. The main attraction there was a bevy of bars, pawnshops, tacky clothing stores, and eateries. The goal was to attract the attention of those Marines when they got leave and came downtown looking for wine, women, and song. There were beer parlors galore with live music and "go-go" girls dancing in cages well above the fray. They were the fore-runners to the pole dancers that appeared years later. Businesses along this street extracted a great deal of the soldiers' pay each month.

Kellam's, the corner drug store, was the place where EC, Ralph Thompson, Vinny Moser, Michael Banks, and their associates hung out almost every day. Most often in the early morning hours they would be deep in serious conversations over coffee and eggs.. It was like clockwork seeing them file into the drugstore several mornings each week.

Not too many years later, a major commercial developer from Raleigh realized the value of this military-based market. He bought several acres of land in the heart of New Ferry and built the very first shopping center in eastern Carolina. On the adjoining property to the shopping center, he built literally hundreds of apartments. The apartments filled up in a very short period of time. The shopping center was very successful and eventually became the location for the corporate offices of the new Eastern National Bank.

Chapter 12
THE MONEY

In the early fifties, the local Sheriff and several of his deputies made an unannounced raid on one of the fancy hunting lodges rented to wealthy northern sportsmen. The lodge was located on luscious hunting grounds on the river near New Ferry. They confiscated gaming tables, slot machines, and a money-making machine. It was a counterfeiting device with plates included. All of these items found their way back to the sheriff's office. Rumors abounded that some of these items fell into EC's hands.

Soon ideas began to materialize in EC's mind, as to how he could take advantage of this unintended opportunity. EC's knack for smelling a deal, legal or not, began to form. A short time later, EC called in a few of his powerful friends to introduce his plan. His plan was pure and simple. EC had decided counterfeiting was a way, if successful, for everyone in his group to get rich in a hurry, and he had the plates.

They began by finding a paper and ink man named Ed Spruce from Kingstown, thirty miles to the west. They bought a printing press up north and brought it back to the Fork. Now they were ready to crank up the operation and see where it took them.

They set up operations in the back of EC's furniture warehouse behind his store at the Fork. It was akin to setting up a newspaper press, but took less time. It only took a few of EC's boys to get it running and test the different parts. Then they had the job of getting the paper and ink synced. This was necessary so the bills printed were not only legible, but also the right size, and with the proper markings in place that made them look authentic. This took a lot of time, paper, ink, and plenty of trial and error, not to mention tons of patience.

Eventually, they ran some one dollar bills that looked pretty good, good enough to see if they could be spent without raising any suspicions. EC sent his boys to surrounding towns to purchase small items like gum, cigarettes, sodas, bread, gas and milk. To their surprise, they had absolutely no problem passing the counterfeit money.

The team was elated and began making plans to up the ante by buying more expensive items with this worthless paper. They wanted to be sure they could turn their bogus money operation into a giant money maker without getting caught.

Over the next several months the team continued carefully spending the counterfeit money in a growing geographic radius emanating from the Fork. However, some of their purchases were in fact questioned and became a problem. Since the crooks were mostly unknown men from out of town, authorities had a tough time tracking the origin of the bogus bills.

EC decided to chill out until they could better perfect their printing method. When the time came that the counterfeit money looked more realistic, they hoped the illegal bills would go unnoticed. They operated the business off and on over the next several months, as they continued trying to improve the quality of their new product.

One day, for a variety of reasons, mostly greed, they decided to try counterfeiting twenty dollar bills.

That plan was a major bump up in the overall scheme of things. Once printed, they needed a place to store the bogus bills, but more importantly, they needed a way to spend that much money.

In a short time, EC and friends reset the money press and began printing several thousand twenty dollar bills each day. They packed them in paper boxes and stacked them against the warehouse walls. Once the warehouse space was filled with boxes of counterfeit twenties, one of EC's trucks backed up to the loading dock, and EC's boys loaded the delivery truck with all of the boxes of worthless loot.

In the dark of night, the truck made its way to EC's appliance store located in New Ferry's busy retail part of town. It was only a few blocks down the street from the fast-growing Eastern National Bank.

EC's boys would then unload the boxes of counterfeit money and place them in the large deep freezer appliances on the store's showroom floor. They locked the freezers and placed red SOLD signs on the top. The freezers could hold about $800,000 of the fake money, a lot of real cool dough. Since the bills did not have seals or serial numbers, the question was how and where they could pass this huge unfinished batch of counterfeit twenty dollar bills.

The new counterfeit operation was going on during the conflict between the US and Cuba. During this time Castro was trying to start a revolution to overthrow Batista. The word got out that EC's group, through a connection with the Florida Mafia and Myer Lansky, was trying to switch funny money for Arms for Cuba There were stories of numerous visits to Florida and maybe trips to Cuba. Although this could have been one way to unload the counterfeit money, most of these stories were pretty far-fetched and didn't include any real specifics.

Another possible method for distributing the counterfeit money was pretty bizarre and included the new Eastern National Bank. This plan included using bogus money to advance the explosive growth of the new Eastern National Bank that started in 1952. The bank operations would take place at night. EC's minions would take all the counterfeit money stashed in the freezer lockers on his appliance store's showroom floor, and truck it down a few blocks to the Eastern National Bank. With outside help, they were able to get inside the bank. Bogus money would then be stashed in the "Old Money" bags that all banks used to send their old, worn, torn, cut, and damaged money back to their Federal Reserve Bank to be "Burned." The damaged and burned money would be replaced with a like amount of new and good money. When any bank sent their Federal Reserve $800,000 of "old money" to be burned, the sending bank received $800,000 back in good money. The money would then be deposited into an array of accounts, some real, some not. Under this plan most of the deposit amounts would be counted as new deposit accounts for the bank and would show a rapid rate of growth for the Eastern National Bank. It was good for the balance sheet, good for the rankings, and good for the investors owning the Bank stock. This version does have credible aspects.

In the Treasury Department building in Washington, DC, resides the Bureau of Engraving and Printing. In 1890, Congress established the Destruction Committee Members Program to make sure all worn out and damaged US currency bearing the green seal be collected and "Burned" by the government. The group was most often made up of vetted veterans of utmost integrity. Besides the Bureau, burning old money was also done at the other twelve Federal Reserve Banks around the country, including the one in Richmond, Virginia.

The money was brought in and holed, halved, and then put into the fiery incinerators and burned to ashes. Good currency, in like amounts, was returned to the participating bank. Every day millions of dollars of "money to burn " was received at Federal Reserve incinerators around the country.

Chapter 13
THE BANK

In October of 1952, only five months after Clara Mercer Cain had been strangled to death, an unusual group of men around the county decided to charter a new bank in New Ferry. There were about six original investors, according to the early application filed with the State. EC knew and was friends with most of these men. The investors included Michael Banks from the next county over, who spearhead the bank deal. Michael happened to be a childhood friend of EC's. Another one of EC's childhood friends, Horace Felton, was already working with a main bank in Richmond, Virginia, and he also became an investor. There were a couple of heavy hitters involved from Groveland. One was Vinny Moser, who happened to be the landlord of EC's drive-in movie theater on the river in New Ferry. The other was Ralph Thompson, the local heavy equipment dealer. Another investor was Ned Ellis from a nearby coastal village. All of them were buddies with EC. The Bank's corporate law firm, also located in New Ferry, was headed by Charles Moser, Vinny's brother.

Their bank application was accepted, but their request for the name was denied. It had already been requested on a previous application for another state bank. So they opted for another name, the Eastern National Bank, subsequently referred to as the "Bank." That name was accepted.

Horace Felton was also a childhood friend and classmate of Michael Banks. They had stayed in touch during their early years, as both men gravitated to the banking industry early in their business careers. When

Michael Banks started putting the new Bank together in 1952, he contacted Horace Felton, who was already working for a major bank in Richmond. Felton already had a reputation as a smart, savvy banker. They exchanged many communications during this time frame, and they also had numerous personal meetings. Many people considered them partners from the get-go.

Soon after the Bank was organized, EC and a couple of his close associates, along with the major Bank investors, held a secret meeting in Groveland at an old house across from the community building. There was little furniture in this old house and barely enough chairs around the big round table for everyone to have a seat. The only light on in the house was the ceiling light over the dining room table. The meeting started around 10:30 at night so as not to attract too much attention.

Because he was in charge, EC stood and began by saying, "We can print the money at the Fork, haul it to my store in New Ferry, and then move it over to the Bank during the night. It's a piece of cake." He outlined a plan about his counterfeit money operation. It was a very detailed explanation about how the bogus money would be burned and replaced with good money that would be utilized by the new Bank, both now and later. Later was definitely the operative word.

Michael Banks, the main banker chimed in, "I agree. EC has a workable idea. It only needs to be executed in a professional way. I have a few suggestions that will make things work quite smoothly." There were lots of raised eyebrows. Some of the men in the meeting could not believe that EC and his buddies were really going through with such an outrageous operation.

Outside that night, a couple of young guys, who were out later than usual, were cutting through that yard on their way to the downtown movie theater. In the old house they saw a room full of local men they recognized, all huddled around a table and talking in hushed tones. They never heard enough to get the reason for the meeting, but they did get the strong impression that whatever they were talking about in there most likely had to be illegal. They were right, and years later they connected the dots.

The new Eastern National Bank (the Bank), opened its first branch on the corner of downtown New Ferry's military section and its major retail avenue. Brad Hoffman was the first branch manager and loan officer. It was just five blocks from EC's appliance store on the same side of the street.

As the Bank grew at an amazing rate, so did EC's circle of business partners. They branched out into bootlegging and loan sharking operations, fraudulent land grabs, just to name a few. However, there was never any evidence of drug or prostitution activity. Some stories link the group to part of the southern Mafia, most likely from Florida. Maybe this connection was what pushed them to resume their counterfeiting operation. No one really knows for sure.

In late 1957, a national banking magazine named the Eastern National Bank, headquartered in New Ferry with only a handful of branches, as the fastest growing bank in America. That seemed impossible and very surprising in such a small rural community.

The Bank cut a major path in the banking industry for the next twelve years. The Bank changed its name to the State National Bank in 1970, still referred to as the Bank. It bought or merged with any and every bank available by doing some fancy footwork and issuing or trading millions of shares of stock. A new acquisition was announced from the Bank most every month, sometimes two per month. When banks wheel and deal as this Bank did, chances were they would pick up some undesirable or non-performing assets in their many transactions. The Bank got its share of these bad assets. It also inherited some unusual personnel. Some of the new shareholders that came along with the bank mergers were less than Wall Street types. Additionally, some of the newly acquired bank employ ees did not fit into the Bank's existing cultural profile.

When Michael Banks, the Bank's first CEO, died in 1972, Horace Felton, who had joined the Bank as its COO a few years earlier, was named the second president of the Bank. A lot of people, including many Bank shareholders, did not really understand how or why Horace Felton became the second Bank president. They did not realize how much and for how long Horace Felton had been involved with the Bank over the years. Actually, he was one of Michael Banks's closest advisors. He was instrumental in the Bank's early growth. Unfortunately, he inherited quite a mess and presided over the Bank during its many years of financial problems.

As often happens with so many rapidly growing businesses, many of the early employees of the Bank were local men and women, totally untrained in the various positions necessary to operate a bank. Thus, the Bank suffered some serious growing pains early on and even later when it began to aggressively expand across the state.

As years passed and the Bank opened more branches and made many financial acquisitions, the employee culture began to change drastically. The corporate offices in New Ferry began to change dramatically with the infusion of banking types moving in from other states and from other competitors' work forces.

As the Bank grew, its total asset value, deposits, and total outstanding loan balances also grew rapidly, and so did its Reserve requirements. The Bank began having trouble maintaining its Reserve limits to the extent that the Feds put a red flag on the status of the Bank's ongoing transactions. The Bank would ante up, get back in compliance with the Feds' Reserve requirements, and then would buy another bank and inherit more bad loans. There went the Reserve amount again. It appeared that the Bank, in an effort to continue its rapid growth rate and influx of new revenues and deposits, along with its insatiable appetite for unrealistic profits, chose a mantra of "grow at any cost." After many months of this kind of unsatisfactory behavior, the Feds put the Bank on the national watch list, not a distinction any bank aspired to. It was not too many years later that the Feds moved federal employees into the corporate offices of the State National Bank in New Ferry to try to salvage what was left of this struggling Bank.

The Bank was consistently a major source of gossip around the county. The stories never ceased. Some were true, many were made up, but they were all very interesting.

Horace Felton was there when the Feds came. He was there when Cliff Stevens from Charlotte became the Bank's largest shareholder. Cliff Stevens came as a white knight to the rescue. He was a wealthy financier from the southwestern part of the state. He put in gobs of money. He also had a great position with a regional bank in the western part of the state. When Stevens first met, at the request of the Federal Reserve, with Horace Felton, the CEO of the Bank, he told Felton right up front, "If I get involved with your Bank, I have to have more Bank shares than any other person. I also plan to bring in my own choice as CEO. Additionally, I plan to blend your Bank into a regional bank so your Bank can survive. Got it?"

Felton spoke very softly, "I will do whatever you ask me to do. I just want the Bank and its shareholders protected."

So Stevens became the Bank's largest shareholder. He brought in a new and seasoned CEO, John McCoy from Charlotte to give the Bank a new face and a new image. The Feds, even back then, were totally opposed to having any bank fail. They, along with Cliff Stevens, the white knight, hatched a plan to move the Bank into a larger regional bank. They merged the two financial companies in December 1982. Both parties were extremely happy. The remaining State National Bank operations changed its name once again to Crescent National Bank, and it was still referred to as the Bank.

Some of the early Bank shareholders, who bought their first shares in the Bank when the Bank filed a Reg. A stock offering in 1953, were able to exchange their shares for shares of Crescent National Bank, the regional bank. Although the exchange rate was quite low, they were happy to get something that represented some degree of value. For those who held their stock a few years, the value continued to grow. At least it gave many of the locals something new and exciting to talk about regarding their infamous Bank.

Chapter 14
THE SPECULATION

From the first time EC made headlines involving the murder of his second wife, Clara Mercer Cain, to the counterfeit money deals in 1958 and 1963, speculation about EC and all these crimes were at the top of everyone's conversations. Old folks, young folks, people who thought they knew something, and others who just made things up were talking everywhere. They were talking at work, at home, at church, at sports events, at social events, at the beach, at the courthouse.... just everywhere.

No one had any real answers about the murder. It was still unsolved, and no one had figured out the purpose and destination for the huge amounts of bogus twenty dollar bills. No one ever figured out where all the counterfeit money printed was hidden. Lots of people had an idea about where it was, and some were certain they knew where it was, but not one bogus twenty had ever been located.

Several times a month, many of EC's boys frequented Woodrow's Pool Hall in Groveland. It was like their social club. Woodrow's was a billiards hall from long ago. There were four great tables with slate and fine felt covers. Several cue stick holders were mounted on the walls. Sexy lamps hung over each table. There was a standup bar at the end of the room that sold beer and wine. In the corners were some older chairs and one old leather sofa.

Woodrow, the owner, ran his pool hall with a strong hand and kept the place fairly orderly. Sometimes, after too many beers and losing too much money at the tables, trouble broke out. The pool hall's location, just two doors down from City Hall, helped to maintain peace.

There were many pool sharks that passed through Groveland just to play some serious pool for some serious money at Woodrow's. The locals learned early on to be careful of players who came in carrying their own cue sticks in fancy cases. Best let the better players occupy the tables as long as the outsiders were there. It was not unusual for a really good player to walk out of Woodrow's Pool Hall with a couple of grand. The locals who were not damn good pool players knew it was best just to watch and keep their money in their pockets.

One night at the pool hall in Groveland, the Woodward brothers told the story about Clem Houston, who worked in the Bank's printing office in New Ferry. Clem made a statement about Horace Felton becoming the president of the Bank. Clem said, "I guess all you have to do to become the frigging president of the Bank is be in the goddamn counterfeit money business."

Enoch Woodward applied to the Bank for employment at the corporate office in New Ferry. He was uneducated and unskilled so his application was denied. Then Enoch said to the interviewer, "You better call Horace Felton and tell him Enoch Woodward is asking for a damn job." He was given a job on the spot. No questions asked.

In the late 1950s through the late 1960s a great deal of EC's manifested drama had invaded the small towns of the county. It had left most everyone shocked, perplexed, and concerned. Just who and what was this man all about? Many people were anxious to get some questions answered some way, somehow.

In the early seventies a small group of folks began meeting out of town to discuss the details of these strange ongoing events to see if they might find some answers on their own. They sincerely wanted to know what happened and why. They also wanted justice for Clara.

They would discuss what each of them knew personally, what they had heard from others, what they believed, what they did not believe, and who they might ask to gather more information. The number of meetings increased over the months as did the number of participants. Detailed notes were taken and logged at each meeting. The notes were kept in a safe deposit box in an out of town bank. These folks were serious about finding out what happened and why.

A great deal of their discussions involved EC's collection of friends and business partners. This was true whether they were talking about his wife Clara's murder or the counterfeit money scandal, or the Bank. Who was involved? Who knew what? Why did that person get involved? What was the Bank's role, if any?

The more information they gathered, the more the members of the group began to come to a consensus. As the years passed, there were lots of phone calls among these folks to discuss any new aspects of the crimes. Whenever these members happened to see one another, they invariably discussed the latest rumors and any new information they had, and it was all added to their file.

What is so surprising about this is that even after several decades, several of the members still conferred about the crimes and continued to collect new information about the murder and the counterfeit money. What encouraged them to persevere for so many years? It was because so many of their suppositions had been validated over the years. A great deal of the speculative comments that were entered into the file twenty or thirty years earlier were now being proven to be correct.

During this period, a couple of local deal-type guys went to meet a very wealthy oil man-investor about getting involved financially in a "cancer-free" cigarette deal they were trying to secure. He suggested they come to Winston Salem and meet with him and his attorney at the City Club on a specific date. They went and met Reginald Parker and his lawyer at the City Club. The lawyer was this little guy who was impeccably dressed and well-coiffed and certainly had a Napoleon complex. That is, his ass was built too close to the ground. (Later, the guys heard he lost his law license for drug abuse. Then he called to tell them he was in Nashville, Tennessee, becoming the greatest country and western singer of all time while waiting to become as a presidential candidate. He asked that all contributions be sent to his campaign chest in Nashville, Tennessee.)

Reginald Parker was a big guy. He was tall, broad and almost flamboyant with his Texas type cowboy hat, giant belt buckle, and boots. Don't forget the boots. He also talked loud and long. At first blush, one might think he was one of those "Big Hat, No Cattle" type of guys. But he told some great stories and he relished telling them. He was self-confident and self-assured. You could sense that he had been around and had most certainly made some money, and he probably owned lots of cattle as well.

After informal introductions, Reginald asked the boys, "So, where are you fellows from?"

When they responded in unison that they lived in Groveland, Reginald started firing off questions faster than they could be answered. "Do you know EC? What about Clara's murder? Do you know about the counterfeit money? How about Vinny Moser? Ralph Thompson? Do you know about the Bank?" He just went on and on to these boys whom he had just met for the first time. He asked about some interesting but serious events that these guys had lived with and knew all about.

Reginald Parker took little time in explaining to these young men how he knew and how he was connected to all of these folks and their bizarre activities. The boys tried to ask questions, but Reggie just kept talking over them.

Reggie said, "Before I got rich in the oil business and moved to Winston, I lived in Wilson. After fronting for and securing a radio broadcast license for a Mafia-related customer in Alabama, I became a heavy equipment dealer for Caterpillar in Wilson. It was usual practice to trade or borrow equipment from other dealers in order to fulfill a customer's order for some backhoe, or pan, or earth moving grader that I didn't have in stock at the time. So I'd go to Groveland and borrow or trade with Ralph Thompson, so I could make the sale." Reggie continued, "Ralph had a service and parts garage next to his dealership. On numerous occasions, I dropped in to visit with Ralph only to see the whole parts counter stacked high with counterfeit money. There was no security, no concern, no concern at all."

Reginald Parker lit a cigarette, took a sip of his sweet tea, and kept on talking. "Ralph Thompson called me one day to ask if I was going to the

Caterpillar convention in Nassau. I said I was and he asked me to meet him at the Nassau Airport on Monday when their plane arrived to give them a ride to the convention hotel. So on Monday I met Ralph's plane in Nassau as promised. Ralph and his wife Cindy Thompson, EC and his wife Katy Cain, Michael and Nora Banks, and Horace and Bette Felton each disembarked carrying black suitcases full of bogus twenty dollar bills. I believe they passed over a quarter million dollars of counterfeit money over that convention period. They would go out shopping during the day, all the time passing bogus money for items they were buying. At night they'd go out for drinks and dinner and pass thousands more fake dollars. Hell, Ralph's wife bought enough silver service set pieces to stock a castle!"

Then Reginald wanted to hear about the "cancer free/safer cigarette" deal. The young men were happy to tell him all about it.

They began by telling Reginald about two men from the Midwest, Jim Simpson and Jim Hinson, who were kind of like two circus barkers that flew their own planes. They had used USDA research conducted at the North Carolina Agricultural Station located in Oxford, to start a bug light company. The research determined that if three "blue lights" were placed in each square mile in a larger contiguous area that covered many acres of tobacco producing land, the lights would attract the moths (worms) that feed on the tobacco leaves. The tobacco could then be raised without the use of the pesticides that supposedly have cancer-causing carcinogens. This clean tobacco could be used in a new type of cigarette that could be marketed as a "safer cigarette."

"It was a fabulous idea!" they said.

The milling company in Groveland became the bug light distributor and helped convince the farmers in that county and the surrounding counties to participate in the program that could produce this cleaner, safer tobacco. A very large growing area of hundreds of contiguous acres was covered the first year. The costs of the bug light installations were paid for by the participating tobacco farmers based on their individual tobacco allotments relative to a percentage of the whole. So large tobacco farmers paid more than the smaller tobacco farmers did – very democratic.

Reggie was hanging on every word of this story. Then the visitors told Reggie the "kicker" in the deal. The two Jims had also started Continental Tobacco Company, headquartered in Columbia, SC. This was the second part of the deal. They had received only the fifth tobacco manufacturing sector permit ever issued in the US. They had also set up a non-traditional tobacco market in Vanceboro for buying this "clean tobacco" that would dictate premium prices per pound for the pesticide free leaf. The participating tobacco farmers could hardly believe they were getting such high prices for their tobacco, but they damn sure liked it a lot.

The company was looking for $100,000 investors. The deal had such sizzle that it attracted a good number of other high risk takers. Some real heavyweights got involved. There was even a White Paper type documentary on one of the Triangle TV stations right in the backyard of the other tobacco companies like Liggett Meyers and Lorillard.

The "clean tobacco" was grown, harvested, and sold to the company at premium prices. The company processed the tobacco. They hired a retired Reynolds blender to blend the product. Then it was sent to the manufacturing facility in Columbia that was furnished with cigarette making machinery from Germany and Italy. The end product was a safer cigarette called Venture. It was test marketed in Grand Rapids, Michigan. The market wanted filters. Smokers had already begun to like brands with filters, like Kent and Winston.

So a filter machine was secured, and before long, Venture Filters were on the market. The product sold like hot cakes early on, mainly because of its "safer" claim. But once the smoker inhaled the Venture cigarette they immediately got a serious headache. The tobacco was too strong, too green, too harsh, and had not been properly aged. Nor had it been properly blended with a milder tobacco. That was a major mistake the first time around.

Reggie interrupted their story and asked, "So what happened to the company? Get to the punch line, please."

One of the two business partners from Groveland answered, "Mr. Parker, the major investors bought the company and brought in some new money. The Chevy man from Groveland got in, as did the chairman of the ABC Broadcasting Company's executive committee from Southern Pines. Then this new group associated with US Tobacco Company in Richmond, Va. They re-designed the product and launched a new cigarette called Tryon Cigarettes, in a beautiful new blue package. This time they did it right and a real 'safer' cigarette was born. Reginald was sold. he became an investor.

Later one of these same guys needed a great attorney to represent him in a real estate deal gone sour with a very wealthy New York developer. He was introduced to Bryan Moses, also from Winston Salem. The lawyer was also a pilot, about sixty-five years old, but he was very active. He was well known for representing passengers in an American Airlines crash at O'Hare in Chicago. He also represented some of the families of victims of the Apollo crash. He was just the type of lawyer this guy needed.

The meeting took place at Bryan's home in Winston on a Saturday morning. It was obvious that Mr. Moses had done very well. His home, more like an estate, was on many acres of manicured grass and shrubbery and dogwood trees. The furnishings inside were very expensive.

They met in the kitchen – a glorious gallery of gadgets and art with an expansive view of the luscious manicured grounds outside. It was stunning. It would be quite a treat to prepare a meal in such a spectacular setting.

They exchanged pleasantries and introduced themselves. When Bryan discovered this young man was from Groveland, he was flabbergasted because Bryan had been raised just outside of New Ferry on Branch Road. You guessed it. The conversation immediately went to EC, Ralph Thompson, Vinny Moser, Michael Banks, counterfeit money, the Bank, the murder, and on and on.

Bryan told the young man that as a small boy he'd sat around the shop behind his house listening to his father and his father's friends tell stories about the hunting camps on the land before the military base was built. Those old men said the bogus plates were absconded by the sheriff's department. They told other stories too, about EC's 'friends', the money, the murder, and the Bank. He'd heard it all eavesdropping on his dad and his dad's friends.

Bryan told his new client that his very first legal case after he'd graduated from law school and completed a clerkship with a judge, was a land dispute case in this county. A large farmer, Harry Harrison, whose farm was around the Fork outside of Groveland, bought most of his farming equipment from Ralph Thompson. He bought on credit and agreed to a lien on his property to secure his financing. Harrison signed many of these land liens for Ralph Thompson. Over a period of time, Ralph claimed that the liens were in default, although they were not, and Ralph foreclosed on the land, which was the security for the liens. Ralph's 'bought' friends at the courthouse upheld the foreclosure and awarded the land to Ralph Thompson. These were thousands of acres of excellent crop producing land. It was worth millions of dollars.

The good thing that happened was that Harry Harrison was put in touch with Bryan. Bryan took the case based on its merits and his confidence in Harry Harrison's integrity. He also knew of Ralph Thompson's reputation. Bryan was warned over and again that he was about to lose his credibility as a lawyer. He was also repeatedly told that he would never prevail in the Devil's own backyard. Never.

Ralph Thompson even called Bryan one night late and threatened him with bodily harm by saying, "If you don't take your fucking briefcase and get the hell out of town, you'll find it very difficult to argue any more legal cases without a tongue! Do you get my drift, you low life bastard?"

Bryan told Thompson he'd assume he was drunk and would pretend he hadn't heard Thompson's threat. Bryan said, "Pop your goddamn whip, big boy, and I'll scc you in court."

Bryan Moses carried on and sued Ralph Thompson not only for the land in question but also for legal fees and damages. Things got very ugly, and many times it seemed like a lost cause. But he prevailed and won the lawsuit, returning the land to its rightful owner, Mr. Harrison. There were some very bad actors on the other side, mainly a group of friends of Ralph's and EC's. Most had strong ties to the Bank as well.

Bryan Moses agreed to and represented the young real estate guy with his shopping center suit, and he was able to secure the price and the funds that were due the young man.

The Bank had a very strange and mysterious relationship with the North State Bank in North Wilkesboro. The two banks were scheduled to merge, and at the very last minute the Feds stepped in and squelched the deal. Mr. Donovan, chairman and major shareholder of Northwestern, along with several bank executives went to prison for bank fraud. They used bank funds for their personal gain. Harry Kusak, Mr. Donovan's son-in-law, and his wife came to the Bank in New Ferry to work. He was later transferred to a bank in Melbourne.

Then there was one of those strange characters that came to the Bank by way of Melbourne, Florida, a mafia hotbed for sure. Eli James was his name and he was a nice man and very business-like. Not long after arriving in New Ferry, he started dating Veronica, a widow, who managed a lady's clothing store. Within a short time they married.

There was a tradition at Eli James's Bank. Every Christmas they held their company party at the Country Manor in the next county. It was always a great party, and only very close friends of the Bank were invited.

Eli and his new wife, Veronica, were in attendance and had an enjoyable time. But soon after they'd eaten, Eli started feeling ill and they had to leave the party prematurely. When they got home, Eli went straight to bed. He was most uncomfortable. During the night he became so ill that he went to the hospital. He died following emergency surgery. His wife Veronica couldn't believe what had happened or why and wanted to know why there was no autopsy.

Veronica James called her oldest son from the hospital, told him that Eli had just died, and asked him to go to her house immediately to make sure it was locked up. Her son agreed and when he arrived at his mother's house, to his surprise, he found five men, all Bank employees inside. He knew and recognized each one, who began to stream out of Eli and Veronica's house carrying briefcases, document files, and black bags.

The son demanded to know what the hell they were doing.

They told him they were "taking care of Bank business" and continued on their way. He was perplexed and angry and demanded answers, but no answers were provided.

The next day Veronica's son went to see an attorney friend, Mark Davis, who happened to be a partner in the law firm headed by Vinny Moser's brother, Charles. His firm was also the counsel of record for the Bank.

Mark Davis suggested that he forget what he'd seen happening at his mother's house the night before. "It will be in everyone's best interest to just drop the matter and go on about your own business," Davis told him. Terribly frustrated, the son left. How was he going to explain this to his mother?

Some months after Eli James was buried, friends asked Veronica James, "Just exactly what did Eli do for the Bank?"

Veronica told them that Eli would leave on Monday mornings carrying a couple of black bags and a personal suitcase and travel the country all week. He would then return home on Fridays with his suitcase and the black bags. The best way she could describe Eli James's role at the Bank was as their "bag man." She never actually said what was in those bags, but lots of people thought they knew.

A couple of years earlier, the same fate had befallen Michael Banks, the original Bank president. Michael died after having dinner at the annual Christmas party at the Country Manor. Again, there was no autopsy. The moral of this story, and the joke among the Bank's employees, was "Don't go to the Bank's Christmas party."

Another unusual character who worked for the Bank a long time was Barry Thomas, a childhood friend of the Bank's first president, Michael Banks. Barry Thomas was basically the Bank's main gofer. He did special tasks and ran errands for the corporate officers. He did a great job. He knew everyone and he had a great personality. But he was a serious alcoholic and many times he was drunk while working for the Bank.

One surviving story is that at one of the Bank's parties, Barry was well into the soup again and behaving quite badly. A lady at the party said to

Barry's wife, "If Barry Thomas does not shape up and sober up, the Bank is going to fire him."

Barry's wife's response was, "The Bank can't fire Barry because he knows too damn much about the counterfeit money operation." Did Barry's wife's statement simply mean Barry knew about EC and his counterfeit money operation. Or did it mean that Barry knew about the Bank's involvement with EC. Or did it mean that Barry knew that the counterfeit money was instrumental in the Bank's growth. What could Barry Thomas possibly say about the counterfeit deal that would damage the Bank? Whatever the case, Barry Thomas was never fired.

Then there was Brad Hoffman, the first Bank loan officer. He was the first close confidant of Michael Banks and Horace Felton. Brad Hoffman was very familiar with all the Bank's operations, including all its dark secrets.

Brad was born and raised in Groveland. He had one brother and one sister and his mom worked at the school cafeteria. Brad was a super athlete. He was a three letter sports guy. He was an end in football, the catcher behind the plate, and a fantastic basketball center. His height served him well in all three sports. Once out of high school, he spent a couple of years at a junior college before jumping at the chance to become the new Bank's first serious employee.

When Brad had his first heart attack, he was sitting at his desk in the Bank headquarters office in New Ferry talking on the telephone to... a customer? No, he was talking with EC. You have to wonder what that conversation was all about. It must have been very powerful or maybe, very scary would be a more appropriate description.

Chapter 15
THE FIRST ARREST

A series of events led to the initial "bust" of EC's counterfeit money operation at his appliance store in New Ferry. First, way too many people were involved in too many towns to keep this illegal business under wraps for any extended length of time. Second, there was neither accountability in place to keep track of the quality of the bills being printed, nor was there a record of the number of bogus bills printed on any given day. As a result some of these bills often ended up in the pockets of many of EC's boys, and they used them for personal purchases. For a smart guy like EC, not tracking these bills was very sloppy behavior.

In addition, the printing process itself had become sloppy. Some of the bills appeared faded in color. Other bills were printed without serial numbers. Still others were not cut to the official length of legal dollars. Alone or in combination, these failures in printing would certainly tip off anyone who had any suspicion at all about the validity of this currency.

There were other factors that occurred with the bogus money operation that helped bring about its demise. Clem Houston went to Atlanta to see his brother. During his visit, he and his brother went to several bars and a half dozen or so restaurants. They found it easy to pass the counterfeit money at these establishments. Once their bogus bills got to the business office and were being processed for deposit, many of the bills were identified as counterfeit and rejected. Those that slipped through and were deposited were discovered to be counterfeit by an Atlanta bank. Authorities were alerted about the bogus bills popping up all over town.

Likewise, Earl Tardy spent a long weekend in Washington, DC, with his girlfriend. He took her shopping, and they went to a Redskins football game followed by some bar hopping before they dined at the Tastee Diner. Two days later, authorities were notified about counterfeit bills circulating in the District.

There were all kinds of conversations among the locals in several communities about the bogus bills. A story about some counterfeit money being hidden in a sawdust pile not far from EC's store at the Fork made the rumor circuit many times over. Then there were stories galore about where the counterfeit money was printed, where it was being spent, where it was being hidden, and what it was being used to purchase.

When some of these facts found their way back to EC, there was hell to pay. He cursed at his boys in a way they had not experienced before. He even beat the hell out of Earl Tardy for his stupidity in going crazy and spending the counterfeit currency in DC. EC knew things were getting out of hand, and he tried desperately to get control of the situation. But it was too late; the horse had already left the barn.

In 1958, counterfeit twenties began to surface in and around New Ferry. Stories about this were coming out in the local media. Even a local young man serving in the Army and stationed in Germany read about it in an *Army Stars & Stripes* article that included a map showing spots in his hometown, Groveland, where the counterfeit money was turning up.

Then news stories began to show up in Richmond, Washington DC, Atlanta, and Charlotte. It was not long before the Feds were alerted, and the Treasury Department and the Secret Service got involved. Thanks to an observant citizen in New Ferry, the Feds caught a huge break.

To no real surprise, one day a local civil service person dropped into EC's furniture and appliance store looking for a freezer. After looking at several freezers, the customer asked the salesperson, "Can you open that deep freezer over there that has the 'Sold' sign on top?"

The employee told him the freezer was sold and was being delivered later that day.

The customer pressed the salesperson and said, "I just want to see how the inside is laid out. What will that hurt?"

Afraid he would lose a sale, the employee said, "Okay, let's take a look."

He opened the freezer and the customer saw what looked like a box full of twenty dollar bills. He exclaimed, "What the hell is this?"

Thinking quickly, the salesperson said, "That's just 'play money' we use in store promos!" Then he quickly closed the lid. The customer, somewhat puzzled, left. But he did not let it go.

When the civil service guy got home he called a Secret Service friend who was in town looking into the counterfeit money that had been circulating around the area. He told his friend what he'd seen at EC's appliance store and that he thought it might be related to the articles about counterfeit money he'd been reading in the local paper.

The two men collaborated and the Secret Service agent was able to get a search warrant from a local commissioner. EC had openly opposed this particular commissioner's appointment the previous year. When they returned to the store the following day to check out their suspicions, they would be able to use the warrant to search the premises, if necessary.

Both men, along with several other Secret Service agents, arrived at EC's store the following day. They found the same freezer with the Sold sign on top. The Secret Service agent, posing as if he wanted to buy it, asked the same salesperson from the day before whether he could look in the freezer with the Sold sign on it.

He got the same push back from the salesman, who once again told him the freezer was sold and would be delivered that day.

The agent showed his badge and demanded that he "Open the damn freezer so I can see the inside!" The sales clerk opened the lid, and there it was... a freezer stashed full of counterfeit twenty dollar bills. It was definitely not "play money." The Secret Service agents produced the warrant and confiscated all the money – all $789,000. The Secret Service agents went berserk. They acted as if they'd just won the National Championship of something.

EC and five of his boys were arrested shortly thereafter. EC posted bond.

There was a news frenzy. The newspapers and TV stations had the county on its ear about all this bogus money. They posed questions like... Where was it going? Why? What was it going to buy? Who was involved? Was there more? The questions kept coming.

The Secret Service released very little information relative to this development and their investigation. They had just started making their case, so they kept most things close to their vests. The local sheriff's department had not actually been a party to the raid, the issuance of the warrant, or the confiscation of all of that "funny money," so there was very little they could add to the narrative, even if they had wanted to be involved. Not all the local authorities were excited about the situation. There was some obvious discord between the local, state, and federal agencies.

Chapter 16
THE FIRST TRIAL

In 1959, EC's first trial was held at the courthouse in Wilmington, North Carolina, with circuit Judge Sauter presiding. It was a relatively small courtroom, and it was packed to the max that morning.

EC's lawyers were scurrying around the defense table making sure they had all their files. Then they got busy making sure all their character witnesses had shown up, as promised. They were not disappointed because EC had an incredible number of people show up as character witnesses. Almost anybody that was anybody in the county stood tall for EC. It was like old home week at the Fork. It was easy to understand why most of them showed up for EC.

The trial itself attracted all kinds of folks: customers, curious Fork residents, some of EC's family, his wife, and his twelve year old daughter, Elaine. Lots of EC's friends showed up, too, so did the press, both TV and print. Also present were EC's business associates. There were lots of people there who wanted to know the whole story. It was not just about the counterfeit money. This man's wife had been murdered only six years earlier, and the murder was never solved. There were many questions. Who else was involved? Were these crimes connected? What happened to the money? Why was all that money found in a deep freezer in EC's appliance store in New Ferry? Everyone wanted answers.

The Feds showed up en masse. The group included FBI agents, Secret Service agents, and federal prosecutors with lots and lots of files, documents, and exhibits. They hustled around their prosecutor's table anxiously waiting to begin their assault on EC. They figured they had the goods on him, and they were confident they were going to send EC away for a long, long time. Their ace in the hole was the $789,000 of counterfeit money. What else could they possibly need to get the conviction and sentence they wanted. It certainly seemed like a done deal.

The word on the street was that EC thought he was in a pretty good position to walk away unscathed from this legal bump in the road. Actually, he was pretty smug about the whole deal. He figured with all the character witnesses, the best law firm, and even the judge he wanted, he had everything he needed to get off. He also felt he had added insurance against a conviction because of the other "important" people involved. EC showed up in a grey, pinstripe, three-piece suit with a light blue tie. He was very dapper looking indeed, and he had an air of total confidence and calm about him. It took him about ten minutes to greet all his well-wishers before the judge rapped his gavel and declared court in session. EC was feeling good about the outcome.

After the judge's opening remarks and the official reading of the charges filed against EC, the prosecutor stood to deliver his opening comments. He minced few words as he laid out the nature of the crimes EC had committed. Then he started describing how he and his team were going to prove beyond a shadow of any doubt that EC and his co-conspirators had, for a number of years, participated in the manufacture, possession, and distribution of counterfeit money.

The prosecutor called witness after witness to the stand to relay their knowledge of the crime, how they knew what they knew, and when they knew what they knew. He called the civil service worker who had first seen the funny money in the freezer at EC's appliance store. Then he called the Secret Service agent who had also gone to EC's appliance store and seen the counterfeit money. Next he called the salesperson who had reluctantly shown the "Sold" freezer to the two previous witnesses. At last, he called the Secret Service agent who had arrested EC. Their testimony was tedious, textbook, repetitive, and boring, but very damaging just the same. Several times during the morning session, EC's lawyers objected to testimony being delivered by witnesses. Some objections were denied, but many were sustained. This went on for hours before the judge called a recess for lunch. Thank God for small favors.

When court resumed after lunch, the prosecutor began placing one exhibit after another on several easels set up near the bench. He took his precious time in identifying each exhibit and explaining in detail its relevance in the case. This seemed to go on forever. The gallery was getting antsy and folks were squirming in their seats.

Just when it appeared that the prosecutor was about to conclude with this part of his presentation, he turned and pointed to the double doors at the back of the courtroom.

The doors flew open and two federal agents entered the courtroom pushing two wheelbarrows piled high with hundreds of bundles of counterfeit twenty dollar bills.

The crowd gasped and stood up in awe of such an incredible site. Almost $800,000 of counterfeit money was right there in the courtroom in full view. The judge pounded his gavel and called for order. Not many people had ever seen such a dramatic introduction of evidence in a court case before.

The prosecution had made its point, if not its case.

Now it was EC's defense team's turn. They paraded streams of folks to the witness stand to declare their love and support for EC. You have never heard such an outpouring of accolades for an individual who, by most anyone's standards, had been caught red handed with a very big hand in a very big cookie jar. So what was the deal with all of that bullshit.

When EC took the witness stand to give his side of the story and respond to cross-examination by the prosecutor, his testimony, in summary, amounted to a great deal of "yes" and "no" answers. Also heard was of "I'm sorry" or "I apologize," or "I just want to go home," or "I'll never do anything like this again." Some of his testimony and answers were almost childlike.

In spite of the circumstances, the overwhelming amount of damaging testimony, and the material evidence presented in the exhibits, EC kept his cool. He remained calm and collected and never once lost his temper or raised his voice. In fact, he spoke so softly that the judge had to ask him to speak louder on several occasions.

The theme of EC's defense seemed to be shaping up as an objection to many of the legal technicalities involved in the discovery of the bogus money in EC's appliance store. The basic legal issue was the subsequent issuance of the search warrant and actual arrest of EC. It was not so much about whether he was guilty or not guilty.

EC's attorneys had bet on the technicality aspect, but they lost that bet big time. They were not just surprised by the judge's ruling of "guilty as charged," they were dumbfounded.

EC was numb. He looked around the courtroom at his attorneys, the judge, and all his friends as if to say "What the hell went wrong here? Where is Vinny? Where the hell is Ralph? Where's Horace? Why doesn't someone fix this? Now!" He even rejected an offer from the judge to say something to the court before he was sentenced.

EC and several of his boys were escorted out of the courtroom on their way to prison. To many observers, it was surprising that EC received a sentence of twelve and a half years and was fined $10,000. His attorneys immediately filed an appeal.

EC was despondent. He never thought this would happen. Before he realized what was going on, he was loaded into a prison van with wire separating the driver section from the passenger area. Boy, did that get his attention. He wondered where they were they taking him, and why now.

What EC had not been told was that the state and federal authorities had agreed to place EC in Central Prison in Raleigh while his appeal was heard. No need to go to all the trouble, time, and money to put EC in a federal facility until his fate had been determined.

Once EC arrived and was processed into Central Prison, he was in total shock. To begin with, his cell was much smaller than he'd anticipated, and it smelled like old urine. There were no partitions, so privacy was non-existent. The bed was horrendous and the toilet facilities looked older than EC, who was beginning to get a severe case of indigestion. He had never been around so many hard core criminals. They were all staring at him, mocking him, and calling him names. EC was truly frightened. He was not prepared for this sudden change of environment. However, he had no recourse, and he knew it. This was what was so scary for EC, and this was the really sad part for him.

EC remained in Central Prison for over a year. Some days he felt as if he'd never get out of that hell hole. A federal prison had to be better than this, he hoped. If his appeal was denied, he'd find out soon enough.

Chapter 17
THE FIRST APPEAL

EC's appeal was argued in August of 1959. Once again the courthouse was a zoo with hundreds of people clamoring to get inside. EC's followers were there to show support and the media frenzy was in full gear.

The appeal was based on the issuance of an illegal search warrant, and EC's attorneys had presented case law after case law to show why the search warrant and arrest had violated their client's rights.

In October 1959, EC won his appeal, and his sentence was overturned. EC and his boys were immediately released on probation.

EC's sentence was overturned due to a legal technicality in the way the search warrant was secured and issued. The warrant had been obtained based on information provided by the civil service worker who had visited EC's appliance store looking for a freezer. The Secret Service agent, along with two other agents, asked a commissioner of the court to issue the warrant on the premise they would have the warrant in hand should they discover counterfeit money in the freezer when they visited the store. The commissioner granted their request, and the search warrant was issued.

The appellate court judge determined that the information about the location of the counterfeit money was not personally known to the agents who asked for the warrant. Furthermore, they had not told the commissioner that their information had come from an unidentified source.

The law is adamant about "unreasonable" searches and seizures and prohibits the use of evidence that is uncovered by a search that violates the Fourth Amendment rights of an individual.

So, EC and his band of renegades caught another break. Their sentences were overturned and everyone was released on probation. It did not take long for these men to get back to their respective homes and begin restarting their lives.

The federal prosecutors were seething. How could they have screwed up so badly? They were mad as hell at the judge, but hell, it was their own stupid mistakes that set EC free. How ironic. All that money rolled into court in wheel barrows, and EC still skated. That had to be awfully hard to swallow.

Despite EC's release, the gossip and rumors were still running wild. Everyone wondered who got paid off and who had the power and influence to get their sentences not just reversed, but overturned. EC and his boys had been caught with their hands in a cookie jar filled with $789,000 in counterfeit money. Everyone knew it, it was a *fact*, and yet they were free.

Things did not stop there. No indeed. You'd think a rat would learn how to run through a maze at some point in its life, but some don't, neither did EC. He simply wanted to crank up the money machine again as soon as possible, get those bogus bills as close to perfect as he could, and start churning out thousands of them every day. EC was ready to implement his plan to get thousands of bills printed each day and stash them where EC had originally intended them to be hidden.

One major problem EC faced in resuming his counterfeit operation was the Feds had seized his original plates. EC's crowd started looking for a new source of plates and they succeeded. Within just a few months, the machine was humming again. It was rumored that the new plates came out of Chicago, but that was never confirmed.

EC and his band of renegades shifted their focus to a new location in Richmond, Virginia. EC sent one of his main men, Earl Tardy, to run the deal. Once EC was satisfied with the quality of his new bills, he set the operation into full action mode. He told his boys their quota was a $100,000 worth of "good" bogus bills *a day*. That meant five thousand individual bills had to be printed every day, a big order for a few country boys in the back of a rented warehouse in Midlothian, Virginia.

One would think that after seeing EC and his cohorts walk away from their prison time on a technicality, the Feds would have at least put a tail on EC or one of his boys, just to make sure that the counterfeit operation did not start up again. They didn't nor did they even consider it. EC was free to get things going, and very soon bogus bills were flowing by the thousands.

Chapter 18
THE SECOND ARREST

Over the next four years, EC and his partners were a bit more careful as they moved a lot of fake money around. But in time, too much of their counterfeit money started showing up in both states. This time, however, it took extra special effort by the Feds to catch EC.

What the Feds did not know was that EC had moved his entire operation to a warehouse in Midlothian, Virginia, across the James River from Richmond. It was in a desolate, secluded area and not on anybody's radar at the time. EC sent Earl Tardy to Virginia to head up the operation.

Another reason it took so long before the counterfeit currency was detected this time around was because EC demanded that the bills be almost perfect before they were circulated. That rule applied to all bogus bills, whether they were headed to the Bank, the storage facilities, or destined to be spent on the street.

In mid-1961, some of EC's bogus bills began showing up in small towns in Virginia. It didn't take long before these fake dollars got the attention of the Treasury Department. Once the Secret Service was brought in on the case, they surmised that EC might be up to his old tricks again. The Secret Service set up surveillance groups in the guise of road crews around EC's retail store at the Fork so they could monitor EC's daily routines. They wanted to know who stopped by, who visited, and by all means, who called. They followed his car when he traveled to other towns assuming he had the plates in the trunk of the car. The joke was on the authorities because the local police had tipped EC off about what the Feds were up to with their surveillance.

When the Secret Service caught on there was a leak or a mole in their organization, who was tipping off EC, they abandoned the surveillance teams. They replaced that operation with individual Secret Service men shadowing EC along with about a dozen of his associates, both in North Carolina and Virginia. It took about another year, but they were able to obtain enough hard evidence to file for another arrest warrant for EC and many of his boys.

On Easter morning in April 1962, while EC and Katy were fixing breakfast for Elaine and Will, who were tearing into their Easter baskets, federal agents stormed onto EC's property. They surrounded his residence. The agents were armed with both a warrant for EC's arrest and a search warrant to enter and search EC's home. They knocked on his door.

EC answered the door holding a cup of coffee, recognized the agents, and as cool as he could possibly be said, "Good morning and Happy Easter. Please come in. We're having breakfast and celebrating Easter. Won't you join us? Coffee anyone?" There were no takers.

The smell of fried bacon wafted through the house. Katy was making biscuits from scratch. There was a pan of grits on the stove alongside a cast iron skillet full of scrambled eggs. The table was set, and orange juice filled four glasses. They were all set for a Happy Easter breakfast.

The agents fumbled around and pulled out their warrants and handed them to EC saying, "EC, this is a warrant for your arrest for the manufacture and distribution of counterfeit money." The agent handed EC the second warrant and said, "EC, this is a search warrant that authorizes us to search your house. Any questions?"

EC said amiably, "Looks like you've got it all covered boys, legally. Help yourself. I have nothing to hide."

The agent in charge spoke very officially when he said, "EC, you are under arrest." Katy, Elaine and Will were shocked beyond words. You could see the fear on the faces of Elaine and Will even though they did not totally understand what was happening. Katy started crying.

EC responded abruptly, "You guys are a bunch of low-life bastards arresting me in front of my wife and children. You could have done this at my store any day of the week. But no, you had to show your asses by coming into my home to terrorize my family on Easter morning. There's a place in hell for folks like you. Do whatever you have to do and get it over with so you can leave my family alone. I hope all of you rot in hell!"

The Feds confiscated about $100,000 in bogus twenties from EC's house. They were very good looking twenties as they had consecutive serial numbers and the official seal. These counterfeit bills looked like, felt like, and spent like the real McCoys.

The arresting agent was the same Secret Service agent that had seized the $789,000 in counterfeit money at EC's furniture and appliance store back in 1958. According to Elaine, EC's associates, Sheriff Tim Madsen and Deputy Henry Merit from the New Ferry sheriff's department, were there at the time of his arrest. This was the same deal, just a different time.

When they hauled EC away in handcuffs, Katy and the kids were in total shock. They were all crying and hugging one another. What started out as a very nice Easter morning had turned into a total nightmare. There'd be no Easter bunny at the Cain house today.

EC was taken to the sheriff's department in New Ferry where he was officially charged, fingerprinted, and photographed. He was relieved of all of his possessions, including his clothing, and issued a jailhouse uniform. He was led to an interrogation room where he was questioned for hours on end. He was given food, water, and allowed to use the restroom facilities as needed.

Finally, around dinner time, EC was introduced to his new living quarters, a five by ten jail cell. It was standard issue with a cot, mattress, blanket, pillow, towel, wash cloth, soap bar, a toilet and a sink. It was all EC would need for a very long time. His meals would be brought to him in his cell.

EC asked for permission to make his "one phone call." He called Ed Pascal, the lawyer he'd used so many times. His conversation with Ed was short and direct, "Ed, you got to get me out of this fucking jail. I cannot stay here long or I'll go bat shit crazy. Please post my bond and come and fucking get me as soon as possible."

"EC, I'll see what I can do," Ed replied. "But today is Easter and tomorrow is Easter Monday, a holiday, you know. So it'll probably be Tuesday before I can do anything to help you get out of this mess."

"Ed, make it as soon as possible. I've got to get the hell out of here. Please."

"Give me a couple of days, EC. That's the best I can do. I'll be in touch."

EC did not sleep a wink that night. Neither did he eat one bite of food. Anxiety had set in big time.

The game was over. It was his turn to pay the piper, and he knew it. The jig was up, and he was most likely going away this time, and probably for a long, long time.

In the morning, EC was surprised at how early things got started in the jail. The noise level was over the top. Everybody talked at once – and loud. It really annoyed EC, but there was nothing he could do now to change things. It was too late. Things were not looking good for him.

About mid-morning, federal agents showed up again. They took EC back to the same interrogation room. The agent in charge said, "On Tuesday morning we are going to take you to the courthouse for your arraignment. You need to be ready for us to pick you up around seventhirty. Your appearance in court is set for ten o'clock. You will be told by the judge exactly what you are charged with and what applicable laws you have violated. The judge will also tell you when your trial date will be. You can ask the judge any questions, if you don't understand. I'd recommend you get an attorney."

EC responded, "I know all about that bullshit. I already have an attorney."

EC was led back to his cell. He knew it was going to be a long and tedious journey before he got back to the Fork.

Chapter 19
THE SECOND TRIAL

EC's second counterfeit trial began in May of 1963 in New Bern with Judge Joe Larder presiding. It was different from his first trial in many ways. There were no large crowds and this time there was no media frenzy. For almost five years, EC's counterfeit fiasco had been written and talked about so much that it was now old news. People had finally tired of hearing about it. What *was* unusual was that Judge Larder, who was from nearby Trenton and who knew all of the movers and shakers in New Ferry, Groveland, and the Fork, was presiding. Many people thought he should have recused himself from the case. This was the reverse of the "fox in the hen house" scenario.

This time around things were much more serious, and one look at the inside of the courtroom made that very clear. The Feds were loaded for bear. The prosecutor had two full tables stacked with files and boxes of evidence. They had brought every single piece of evidence from the first trial, including trial transcripts, testimony, legal documents with notarized depositions, charts and photos, and actual counterfeit bills. In addition to that mound of evidence, they had several new deposition files, new photos of EC's home, and specifically a photo of the hundred thousand dollars of counterfeit money they found in EC's bedroom the day he was arrested. They also had scores of exhibits they could rotate on several easels positioned at the front of the courtroom during the trial. They were making absolutely certain that EC did not slip though their noose this time, as he had so easily done back in 1959.

The prosecution had honed down the charges and chosen just three counts with which to charge EC: possessing, manufacturing, and distributing counterfeit money. They had the goods to back up those charges, and to the best of their knowledge, they had crossed all the t's and dotted the i's.

The Feds had another weapon on their side. They had "turned" one of EC's boys, Fat Jake, who believed that EC had given him up as the fall guy. The prosecution's case was in part based on testimony that Fat Jake gave on the stand. He sang loud and clear with facts, dates, and names. He was very damaging to EC's hopes of getting off again.

The Feds brought in many other men who had been arrested and turned to give testimony against EC. They brought in the counterfeit paper man, Ed Spruce; the front man in Virginia, Earl Tardy; and a few of EC's local flunkies, Nelson and Enoch Woodward, and Clem Houston. Most of the men who turned on EC and testified for the prosecution did so in an attempt to get leniency in their own trials. However, none of these rats were rewarded for their pleadings. They were all convicted and were sentenced to many years in prison.

EC was toast. He pled guilty to all three counts, and he along with several others were convicted as charged. EC was sentenced to 15 years in federal prison and was fined $10,000.

Chapter 20
THE SECOND APPEAL

EC did not give in so easily, however. His attorney immediately filed an appeal based on ridiculous and non-existent facts. EC had been had by his own greed. This is one fact he neither wanted to accept nor believed. It was actually happening. EC was definitely in trouble this time, and there was very little, if anything, his attorneys could do to change the course of events.

His appeal was based on five points including having incompetent counsel, a guilty plea he claimed had been illegally coerced, and his sentencing terms. This would have been the right strategy had there been any substance at all to any of his claims, but every one of them was as bogus as his twenty dollar bills.

Because most people knew by now that the jig was up for EC, there were no crowds in the courthouse, and there was no media frenzy. EC was basically alone in his predicament. Some of his partners had even turned against him. He did not look so calm and confident now, in fact he looked despondent and weary. He was beginning to show his age. EC's world had been turned upside down, and so had Katy's, Elaine's, and Will's.

The judge denied each of EC's claims and explained his reasoning in each instance. This appeal was argued in September 1963, filed and finalized in early 1964. The court reprimanded the appellant for filing such a useless case, thereby wasting so much of the court's time and money.

For once EC worried about what would happen to his family: his wife, Katy; his sixteen year old daughter, Elaine; and his young son, Will. EC was going to prison for a long time. Things were about to change in a very big way for a great many people. Some would adjust. Some would survive. Others would not.

When EC left the Fork in 1963 to spend a few years in the Federal penitentiary in Atlanta, he left his family in one hell of a mess. He had always made all the decisions at home and for all of his business ventures. Katy and Elaine had no idea about what was coming, much less what to do about any of it. They were totally blindsided.

Katy really had her hands full and didn't know which way to turn. She struggled to keep the store at the Fork operating. That in itself was quite a job for her. She also had Will, who was just ten years old, to look after. There was the appliance store in New Ferry to manage. This was all too much for Katy to handle alone. So she just let things slide, and slide they did.

The store at the Fork lacked the proper attention to maintain a profitable business. The shelves became sparsely stocked with inventory. About every three days, the gas pumps were empty. Eventually, even their most loyal customers went elsewhere to shop.

Katy spent most of her time, when she was not tending to Will, in the appliance store in New Ferry. This was no surprise because going to the store in New Ferry got her out of the house and away from the Fork. She felt more comfortable there for a number of reasons. Because she lacked the basic business sense she needed to buy and sell appliances, her job was very difficult.

Reports around the county said that Katy was trying to sell the three drive-in movie theaters. No one was offering anything close to what they were worth, much less what Katy was asking for them. It became obvious that some folks were trying to take advantage of Katy because she was a woman, and because her husband was in prison.

Elaine was a huge support to Katy and Will, helping in every way she could. She even babysat Will for days on end while Katy tried to save the "empire." She worked at a part-time job as often as possible. Both Katy and Elaine did whatever it took to survive from one day to the next, from one week to another. It was tough going, and it took a toll on both women. Even Will suffered from confusion and neglect. It was not until 1965 that they both got a bit of relief when one of EC's newest "friends" showed up.

Chapter 21
THE PRISON TIME

In 1963, Atlanta was a growing metropolis. It was booming with new people, new businesses, new homes, and new manufacturers. Red clay was being moved everywhere. The web of interstate highways that connected in the city was impressive and scary. Where did all those cars come from. Where in the world were they all going. The city even had a new minimum security federal prison for low risk felons. This is where EC was sent. It was not exactly a country club, but it was certainly nothing like a normal state penitentiary.

EC felt this was about as good as he could expect considering his crimes. He decided to make the best of it. In the early days after his arrival and being a man accustomed to being in charge, he decided he was going to let the existing prisoners know that he was pretty tough and would have something to say about how things were going to be in prison.

That was a major mistake. The pecking order in this prison had been established long before EC arrived. His arrogant approach did not sit too well with the guys in charge inside the prison. It did not take long for EC to find out that he'd made a huge miscalculation. One day in the exercise yard, a group of hard looking guys approached EC and asked, "Who the hell you think you are? You come in here and in three days you think you're going to take over? You think you're going to tell us how things will be run when we've been in here for years? What kind of goddamn fools do you take us for? You got any answers for that, white boy? Speak up you son of a bitch."

EC was sweating profusely. He had no idea how to talk himself out of this jam. He knew he was too outnumbered to fight them. Finally he said, "Look, I got no beef with you guys. I just wanted to be a part of the system. Understand?"

Out of nowhere one of the men hit EC right between his eyes. He doubled over in pain. Then one guy grabbed EC's arms and pulled them behind his back. Two other guys started hitting him all over his body. Each blow brought a loud groan from EC. He was badly beaten. He had never had that kind of beating. Even worse than that, he was thrown into solitary confinement for a full thirty days. EC was charged with inciting a riot. That gave him some time to figure out what he had done so wrong.

EC's rude awakening had begun. He had to totally rearrange his attitude and his way of thinking in order to get along in this new environment. That was not an easy task for a man who in his previous life had always called the shots.

Several days after EC was released from solitary confinement and was adjusting to his new lifestyle, he was called to the warden's office. The warden gave EC some valuable advice about what he should and should not do to get along in prison. EC listened intently. The warden also suggested that EC file a petition asking to be placed with the printing work division.

EC asked the warden, "What does that mean?"

"Several years ago, in an effort to be more community inclusive, the *Atlanta Constitution* newspaper decided to outsource all of its printing needs relative to publishing a daily newspaper. They agreed to train enough inmates to get the newspaper on the street each morning. They came to us to see if our prison would like to be involved. We jumped at the opportunity to do something constructive, not only for our inmates, but also for the Community Inclusive Development Program. So early every morning, the inmates involved in the printing division are bussed to the paper's printing facility at the business park off of I-85. They operate the presses, print the newspaper, eat lunch, print the ad inserts for the next day, and then are returned to the prison by dinner time. So far it has been most beneficial for all parties involved. Would you like to give it a try?"

EC wasted little time with his response, "Count me in. I'd love to be involved with the printing work force. At least I'd get out of here each day for a few hours and be exposed to the outside world at the same time. It sounds like something I would enjoy."

The warden stood up, reached across his desk, and shook hands with EC. He said, "That's great. Then it's all settled. Now you'll be involved in printing again, but this time you'll be legal. Just submit your request by tomorrow so you can start your new job on Wednesday."

EC felt better already.

As days and months passed by, EC began a friendship with his cell mate, Pete Hamilton, an inmate imprisoned for fraud and bank scams. Pete was a bit younger than EC. He looked like an all American boy, tall and slim with red hair and freckles. He had a formal education, but he was not as shrewd as EC nor did he have EC's street smarts. But he was charming and had the gift of gab, a great trait when you're swindling your investors. Together they made a very interesting pair of jailbirds.

Pete was from Alabama and had graduated from Auburn. After graduation he started working for an investment banker. It did not take Pete long to figure out how to con, swindle, and defraud investors out of their money. He had a good two year period during which he raked in lots of money from his scams before he was caught by the Feds. His first offense did not bring too much of a prison sentence. Once he was paroled, he went right back to doing the same old things again. The only difference was he had moved to Georgia where no one knew him. He was a likable, believable, fast-taking guy who could easily convince investors to buy whatever he was selling. Again, he was in the chips in no time flat. It took about three years before Pete was once again arrested and convicted of bank fraud. This time he went to the "big house" in Atlanta for a spell.

Once EC and Pete bonded, they talked endlessly about who they were, where they were from, what they had done, and what they wanted to do when they were released. They became very good friends. Pete Hamilton became EC's confidant. One day, after EC had become quite comfortable with Pete, he said, "Sit down. I need to tell you some very important stuff. If you don't think you can remember it all, you might want to take notes."

"EC, I went to Auburn," Pete replied. "I can remember anything I choose to remember."

EC said, "Sit down, smart ass! I'm going to tell you all the details of my counterfeit money operation." It was almost as if EC was asking Pete to resurrect the money deal once he was paroled. EC told Pete all the secrets that everyone had been trying to figure out for years. He told him how he made the money, how much money he had printed, where all the bogus money was hidden, and how to access that hidden money and convert it into spendable funds. EC spilled it all. Pete made mental notes of everything EC told him about the counterfeit money and about the Bank. Secretly, Pete knew he needed to write some of these facts in his journal. He fully intended to cash in on this opportunity once he got out. That is exactly what he did.

What Pete *did* put down on paper was what EC told him about how he tracked where the millions in counterfeit money were hidden. EC told Pete, "I had a ledger notebook where I recorded each batch of bogus bills, where they went, the name and address of the bank, the safe deposit box number and access information, and how much money was in each box."

Pete's first question was, "Where is that ledger now?"

EC laughed and replied, "Pete, your greed is too obvious. Before I left the Fork for my second trial, I took the ledger and hid it in plain sight in my store. There is a Pepsi Cola standup display box against the back wall. It has shelves where bottles of Pepsi products are stacked. The bottom shelf inside the case is flat and square. The black ledger book fits perfectly into that space and it appears to be part of the fixture. That's where it is now, right there for the world to see through the glass door of the display case."

"EC, that is brilliant, you clever devil."

Pete Hamilton would be getting out of prison long before EC, and in response to EC's obvious trust in him, told EC, "I'm willing to help you. I'll go to the Fork and help look after your business interests until you get paroled and return home. I also promise to make sure that Katy, Elaine, and Will are doing okay in your absence."

EC was overwhelmed by Pete's offer of assistance, and Pete would certainly made good on that promise. Once EC was allowed visiting privileges, Katy and Elaine made several trips to Atlanta to see him. They made a point to try and convey to EC how much he was missed and how much they loved him. With every visit they always promised to wait for him as long as it took.

Elaine, who was sixteen when her Dad was sentenced in 1963, was growing up and had found a lot of interests. She had no problem attracting suitors because she had become a very attractive young lady. On one of Elaine's trips to visit her Dad, EC did not fail to notice Elaine's changing looks, and he seemed to be very proud of her. EC said to Elaine, "Baby, you are a real knockout. Men folks are going to have a time with you. When are you going to get married?" She didn't answer him because she didn't know if that was a compliment, or if EC was just being vulgar.

EC was glad to get visits from his family as well as the other friends who came to see him over time. Most visitors saw a very different looking and acting EC. He'd lost some weight, maybe too much for such a small man, and he'd also lost his confidence, his most precious trait. He was a changed man. His physical appearance, as well as his disposition, really surprised a lot of folks.

Elaine thought it was so sad what was happening to her Dad. It hurt her very much, because she still really loved him. She was excited that EC had found a friend like Pete Hamilton while in prison, and she was grateful that Pete had decided to help EC. Maybe this meant things would get easier for her, her stepmother, and her brother.

Pete Hamilton was released from the Atlanta prison in the fall of 1965, and as promised, he set out for the Fork. He had told EC he'd go back and take care of all of EC's business interests until EC was himself freed or paroled from prison.

Pete Hamilton jumped in with both feet. The first thing he did was locate EC's ledger book. It was exactly where EC said it would be, cooling in the Pepsi display box. Pete decided to leave it there for safe keeping. Then he set about making good on the promise he'd made to EC.

He assessed EC's different businesses and saw that both the store at the Fork and the appliance store in New Ferry needed lots of inventory to fill too many empty shelves. Next Pete took a look at the employees at each business. He decided the stores needed younger blood so he replaced a few of the older employees with newer, younger ones. Then he called in all the drive-in movie workers to see what needed to be done to get better control over these revenue producers.

Pete went to the Eastern National Bank and secured a commission letter written on the Bank's stationery and signed by the Bank's president. The letter agreed to pay him a percentage fee for any and all large deposits he caused to be placed in the Bank's depository. It was a commission letter to a felon. This letter surfaced only once in the major morning state newspaper. Pete Hamilton was able to do this because he knew EC and because the Bank owed EC big time.

During his first few months at the Fork, Pete spent very little time with Katy, as he was too busy changing things around. He did submit a written monthly report both to Katy and to EC in order to keep them abreast of what he was doing in each part of EC's empire.

It did not take too many months before Pete and Katy began meeting for business lunches. Then they started meeting for business dinners. Then the monkey business began as they became quite chummy. Not only were they spending lots of time together keeping EC's businesses afloat, they were spending lots of private time together. Where you saw one, you'd see the other. Elaine was the first to notice this new relationship between these two "strangers," and she did not like this development one bit. She let everyone know in no uncertain terms.

Elaine caught Katy alone in the kitchen one morning making a pot of coffee and asked her, "What the hell's going on between you and Pete? Just because Daddy is in prison doesn't give you the right to be fooling around with Pete. You are still married, you know."

Katy dropped the coffee pot on the floor, spun around from the kitchen sink and yelled, "Stay the hell out of my goddamn business, you nosy little bitch. I'm a grown woman, and I'll do whatever the hell I choose to do. I'm trying to cook us some breakfast this morning and you come in here with that shit. What the hell is wrong with you?"

Elaine shouted back, "I don't want any of your frigging breakfast. I'm not hungry for anything you're going to fix. You can't cook worth a damn anyway. Mama could run circles around you in the kitchen. She knew how to cook real good country meals. You don't hold a candle to her. Let's get back to the point about what you and Pete are up to. You know damn well Daddy will find out about you and Pete. He always does."

Katy threw the frying pan full of scrambled eggs into the kitchen sink and stormed out of the house. Things were beginning to crumble in EC's world.

Chapter 22
THE HOMECOMING

EC was paroled in 1967 from the Atlanta prison. In light of his good behavior, his sentence was commuted to his five plus years of time already served. He was picked up by family members and whisked back to the Fork. What EC had in store for him when he arrived home was nothing short of phenomenal. People were everywhere. There were family members, including Elaine and his sisters. There were also customers, neighbors, curiosity seekers, and law enforcement members. Even Vinny Moser, Ralph Thompson, Horace Felton, and F.J. Moon showed up. There were balloons, music, food galore, and a carnival-like atmosphere second only to the State Fair. It was as if a war hero had come home from the war.

It seemed that everyone in town had shown up to welcome EC home. Everyone except Katy and Pete Hamilton. Those two had run off into the sunset long before EC got out of prison. Both Pete and Katy knew it would not be prudent for them to be around when EC was released from prison and returned to the Fork. They were living off money from EC's business enterprises and were not putting any of the earnings away for EC. Pete and Katy were enjoying all the pleasures of a married couple, although Katy was still married to EC. Under normal conditions, this could have been a death sentence for both of them. They picked up all their belongings, including all the money available in the stores, and moved to Virginia Beach, where they rented a house. Katy took Will, EC Jr., now thirteen years old with her. They felt safer being across a state line from

EC. It may have had something to do with EC's probation that limited his travel. Pete was still hustling deposits for the Bank as a means of generating income. Katy got a job at the Lighthouse Restaurant. Pete took the ledger book with him just in case he might need it one day. In 1968 Katy divorced EC and married Pete.

EC's Welcome Home party just got bigger, better, and more incredible. EC looked around and there was a brand new Oldsmobile, a gift from Dan Toler. Then he saw the brand new double-wide mobile home delivered by Jim Pearce, another gift. EC was getting repaid in spades. It certainly seemed as if he was being paid back for taking the fall for a lot of important folks.

When EC stepped into his old country store, he expected to find it had gone to hell since Katy and Pete had run off together. He was certain it had fallen on hard times, again. He did not expect there to be any inventory remaining on the shelves. To his utter surprise, the store had been completely restocked by his friends, his customers, and his vendors. EC was back and so was his business.

About two hours into his homecoming celebration, EC climbed into the back of a pickup truck and addressed the crowd. "Ladies and gentlemen, I want to thank all of you from the bottom of my heart for all your support. I want to thank my family, my friends, my customers, and my neighbors for everything you've done to help me return to a normal life. I made a very bad mistake, and I have served my time. I have learned my lesson, and I can promise all of you that anything I do in the future will be honest and honorable. Your future friendship and support will be greatly appreciated by me and my family. I want all of you to know what your presence here today means to me. Thank y'all so much."

The applause was deafening.

That night at supper, EC sat down with his sisters and Elaine and told them, "I have written Katy off. She is out of my life and I plan to go on without her." With a scowl on his face, EC said, "As for Pete, his days are numbered. What goes around comes around. He'll get his in spades one day when he least expects it."

EC wasted little time getting back in the swing of things. He decided he wanted to develop some land by building houses along Branch Road. People wondered how he could do this having been in prison the past six years and supposedly lost everything. Simple. EC called in his green stamps at the Bank by putting the heat on Horace Felton. EC had taken the fall for many others, and now it was payback time. EC easily secured the necessary construction loans and began building single family homes. The Bank even financed the buyers' loans.

It was also Horace Felton who made sure EC was taken care of once he got out of prison. Even before EC was paroled, Felton had signed the Bank commission letter to EC's cell mate, Pete Hamilton, when he was released from prison. It was a Bank commission letter on the Bank's stationery and addressed and signed by none other than Horace Felton, himself. This was the letter that had appeared in the main state newspaper.

If EC needed any financial assistance, he knew he could count on Horace Felton. EC's daughter, Elaine, thought very highly of Felton and his wife, Bette, and admitted being treated kindly by both of them over the years.

EC took advantage of the fact that he'd taken the fall for some pretty big boys. They were obligated, and they performed. He called in his chits often. EC's business pursuits required financing, but that was no problem. The Bank had now become his silent partner.

It surprised many people who knew EC that after Katy divorced him and ran off with Pete Hamilton to Virginia, he never sought revenge against either of them. That was a complete turnaround from earlier years, when he would have literally unloaded on both of them for what they had done. They could count their blessings that EC had mellowed out and was a totally different person now. Prison time had done a number on EC's head, and he knew it. He wanted no more of that kind of life.

EC jumped in with both feet and began working non-stop trying to recapture what he had lost. His friend, Judge Hank Barnes, allowed him to file for a personal bankruptcy of $18,000 and then allowed EC to buy his assets back for $18,000. What a gift this was for EC. He operated his stores, and he built homes. He was a man on a mission.

EC still found time for women. He became friends with a younger man, Tom Packard, who operated a grocery store in New Ferry. Tom was also a political operative and had been elected to the state Senate. Although there was quite an age difference between them, EC and Tom Packard spent many days and nights chasing women up and down the coast. Their favorite party place was on a friend's yacht in Myrtle Beach, South Carolina. They often took their "party" to a well-known establishment just down the road from Myrtle Beach in Georgetown called the Sunset Lodge. It was quite an attraction for out of town men from several surrounding states. The Sunset Lodge was an exquisite oceanfront resort facility. The furnishings were first class, the food and beverage services were top notch, and room service was more than any man could ask for – as in hot and cold running young women, mostly hot. Their responsibilities were simple and straightforward. Their job was to please any and all male inhabitants' requests. No exceptions. The place prospered beyond imagination. Tom was always having some type of party, and he entertained quite often. EC was most always invited, and he did not miss many of Tom Packard's events, especially if women were involved.

At fifty years old, it was as if EC was starting another career, about his fifth one it seemed. This time around he had sworn to himself and others that whatever he got involved in had to be and would be legal. EC had come to this new way of thinking while he was doing his prison time. He began to reflect on the things that he had done over the years that were legal and how those had turned out. Then he compared those to the things he had done that were illegal and how they had turned out. It didn't take a rocket scientist to distinguish the two outcomes. EC decided right then and there that he'd be buying into the legal aspects of business from that time forward.

In addition to his home building project, EC and a friend built and opened a super market food store in Groveland. It was larger than a convenience store, but smaller than a regular grocery store. It was a marginal success for a few years before he sold it. Then it changed hands several times.

EC also built a retail food store on Branch Road in New Ferry that was sort of an on again off again operation. Neither of these stores ever came close to being as successful as his store at the Fork. Over the years they were marginally successful as bingo parlors.

The store at the Fork had been spruced up by EC and had been completely restocked with all kinds of inventory. EC continued to operate this store for many more years, as it provided him a base of operations as well as a living income. He had an amazing following of loyal and faithful customers who kept his store running profitably for many years.

His appliance store in New Ferry did not fare as well. While EC was in prison, Katy and Pete Hamilton tried very hard to salvage the store, but they did not have the expertise or money to keep it afloat. It closed for good about three years after EC left for Atlanta, and he never got over the disappointment.

Surprisingly, EC showed very little outward emotion about Katy running off with Pete. It was almost as if his attitude about them was "good riddance." Once he adjusted to his regained freedom, and had reorganized his business affairs, he got busy working on the rest of his life. There were so many things he wanted to do, and he felt that he had to make up for all those lost years. He didn't have the time or inclination to worry about some woman, who had run off with his cell mate. He knew where he could find plenty of other women and lots more friends.

Chapter 23
THE AFTERMATH

In 1965, while her Dad was still in prison, Elaine turned eighteen, fell in love, and wanted to move on with her life, as her home life was no picnic. Katy had taken up with Pete Hamilton in her Dad's absence and Elaine just wanted out. She ran away with her young boyfriend and got married. This marriage lasted less than two years before Elaine moved back to the Fork. Once her Dad was out of prison and back living at the Fork, Elaine felt more secure. She liked spending time with EC again. She had really missed him all those years he was in prison. He helped her get a job in New Ferry, and she began to prosper. Then he helped her buy a house in New Ferry closer to her job. Soon Elaine started dating a local military guy pretty regularly. In less than a year she married again. Soon after her second husband got out of service, they picked up and moved to California. They had a challenged child, who eventually had to be institutionalized. After six years, they divorced and Elaine moved back to the east coast. She transferred her child to a facility in Atlanta.

In late 1969, Katy and Pete separated. Their money ran out. Pete was getting little or no money from his banking commission scheme, and Katy's job was seasonal. Poverty came in the front door and love flew out the window. Katy and Will, who was now fifteen, moved back to New Ferry. Will and his father got back together and resumed their relationship. This was something Will needed, a little fatherly love and advice. They saw each other most every weekend, and they re-bonded. Their relationship grew every year. After Will graduated from high school, he did two years at the local community college. Then he got married and had a child, a girl. He landed a job as a county deputy law enforcement person, thanks to his father.

A few years after Will had been sworn in as a deputy, he was cleaning his firearm, when the weapon accidentally discharged and shot him in the chest. He was rushed to the local hospital where everything known to medical science was used to try and save his life, but to no avail. Will, EC Jr., died later that night. Many wondered if it was an accident or suicide. There was a lot of speculation about Will's death, and depending on whom you asked, opinions varied. Not too many months after this tragedy, Will's wife and daughter moved away.

When Will died from the gunshot accident, EC went absolutely berserk. He couldn't believe it. He simply could not accept that his only son was dead. He wanted to blame somebody for Will's death. He just wasn't sure who he should blame. Will's death affected both EC's and Katy's lives dramatically. It hurt both of them as much as anything ever did in their entire lives. The child EC had with Katy, his namesake, was dead and gone forever. Neither one ever recovered from that tragic event.

A lot of EC's problem with Will's death was that Will was only thirty years old, and EC had not been around to help raise and guide him for ten or more of those years. EC's guilt was overwhelming. It was another consequence of his prison time.

Katy had a very difficult time with Will's death as well. She could never quite reconcile how he had died, and that piece followed her forever. Will's tragic death, mixed in with her failed marriage to EC, plus her subsequent marital and financial problems, turned Katy into a reclusive and despondent old woman. Today she lives on the North Carolina coast, where she languishes in despair.

During Elaine's middle aged years, she made a good living working as a mortgage broker and real estate salesperson. She moved several times and lived everywhere from California to Florida and other southern states. She had a rollercoaster life style, much to EC's disappointment. Later in life with her health breaking, she fell into a desperate situation. She moved back to the Fork into a rented mobile home, where she still resides.

One unbelievable story Elaine tells is about what happened to her one night after she moved into her rented double-wide. It was not too far from EC's home and his store, and where she lived as a child. Her mobile home sat off the country road about fifty feet, and it was at least two lots removed from her closest neighbor. The fields around her modular unit were head high in corn and tobacco.

After Elaine had gone to bed, she heard a knock on the front door, which was very strange at that hour of the night. Her gut told her not to open the door, but she did anyway. When she opened the door, she knew immediately she was in big time trouble. A drifter pushed her aside and came into her trailer. He was waving around a long switch blade knife and soon held her at knifepoint.

The man said he'd seen Elaine at the Piggly Wiggly earlier and realized she was EC's daughter. He followed her home and waited until it got dark. He told her that he knew her father had lots of counterfeit money from all those illegal deals he'd made. It was never found, so it must be hidden somewhere, and she must know where. He waved the knife threateningly and told her he wanted the money *right now*.

Elaine explained she had been away from the Fork for many, many years and had no idea where her Dad's money had gone. He had it all wrong, as far as she knew there wasn't any money.

The guy swung at her with the knife, sliced her leg, and demanded that she tell him where the goddamn money was right then or he would cut her fucking throat.

Elaine knew she'd better keep talking or start screaming immediately. She barely survived his attacks by dodging his swipes and screaming her lungs out. She screamed so loudly that she actually scared off her attacker and attracted the attention of some of her neighbors.

Neighbors heard the commotion and came running to help. They found Elaine bleeding from several knife slashes and lying in a pool of her own blood in her shredded pajamas. Elaine had caught a break, she was still breathing.

Another time, a man EC had known in prison walked into EC's store at the Fork. He was not exactly someone EC was happy to see. The man pointed a gun at EC and told him to hand over ten thousand dollars. He said he had to have it that day, and if EC didn't give him the money, he would kill him.

EC casually took the cigar stub out of his mouth and told the robber in a serious tone that he didn't have that kind of money lying around. EC convinced the robber that he could go to his daughter Elaine's home in New Ferry and probably get the money from her. The robber agreed. So they went to Elaine's home. When Elaine answered the door and saw her Dad and this other man standing there, she immediately sensed that something was wrong. When her Dad told her that he needed ten thousand for his friend, she figured out the situation and knew what she needed to say.

Elaine looked the robber squarely in the eyes and told him in no uncertain terms that there wasn't any goddamn ten thousand dollars in her house. She told the robber that he must be crazy because she could hardly pay her own damn bills, much less have that kind of money lying around. She told him that he had picked the wrong house and to get the hell out.

The robber decided that he and EC should go back to the Fork and figure out how to get the money there. As they started for the door, EC asked Elaine if he could use her bathroom before he left.

In the bathroom, EC wrote a note to Elaine telling her he was being kidnapped by the robber who planned to kill him, if he did not get the ten thousand dollars he was demanding. He said he would get the robber to stop at the Spot Drive-In in Groveland on their way back to the Fork. The note directed Elaine to call the sheriff's office and tell them what was going down. As EC was leaving, he hugged Elaine good-bye and pressed the crumpled up note into her hand.

On the way back to the Fork, EC coaxed the robber into stopping at the Spot Drive-In for a sandwich. The police and sheriff's deputies were there waiting. The kidnapping and EC's possible murder were thwarted, and the felon was taken into custody without a shot being fired.

There were years EC did not talk with Elaine, and that hurt Elaine badly. She kept on going. She kept on working, striving, and surviving. There was a great deal of sadness in Elaine's life, and on top of that, her three marriages did not work out.

In the last ten years of EC's life, Elaine and her father had a somewhat better relationship. They spoke. They visited. They shared time with grandchildren. Elaine never tried to take advantage of the relationships EC had with the folks he took the fall for when he went to prison. Why she didn't, no one knows. She suffered for it. She never regained her confidence or enough stability to get back on her feet. The last several years have been difficult for Elaine, even though she is now back home at the Fork among folks she's known forever.

Nothing much seemed to change at the Fork during the last years EC operated his country store. The store building began to show signs of wear and tear, but EC did nothing to improve the facility. He just let things go. Maybe he knew there would be little return on any investment he made in the bricks and mortar. There were not too many people left in the Fork, and very few new people arrived. As a result, few new homes or businesses were built.

As the years passed, people seemed to forget EC's earlier transgressions. They treated him as they would any other neighbor and businessman. EC blended back into the community and lived what most people would consider a normal, non-eventful life. It appeared that EC had calmed down and was satisfied with the status quo. He had probably learned his lesson in prison. He certainly did not want any part of that again.

When EC was 71 years old, a local lady from the Fork came into his store with her sixteen year old daughter, Faye. The woman said, "EC, for twenty five thousand dollars, you can have my sweet little daughter as your wife."

Initially, EC thought the lady was kidding, but after a little more conversation, EC knew that Mama was dead serious.

EC asked Faye, "Do you agree with what your Mama said?

"Yeah," Faye answered.

Will you agree to marry me if I pay your Mama the money she is asking for?

'Yeah," she responded.

Are you sure?

"Yeah," she said.

Do you understand what it means for you to marry me?"

"Yeah," she said again.

Amazingly, after some more conversation, Faye nodded her head while looking at her mother and said, "Mr. EC, I'd be honored to be your bride."

EC, smiling from ear to ear, said, "I'll take your offer."

He paid Faye's mother the money in cash. A week later, EC and sixteen year old Faye went before the Justice of the Peace at the courthouse in New Ferry, said their vows, and were declared legally married. EC took Faye to Myrtle Beach for a weekend honeymoon.

As you might guess, the relationship did not last long. While it lasted, EC got lots of kudos from his male friends and lots of looks of total disgust from his female acquaintances. That was about EC's last fling.

EC remained in fairly good health, even in the last dozen or so years of his life. That was pretty amazing considering all he had been through. He did slow his business activities somewhat, but he never gave up his favorite hobby. EC still loved to go down to the coast and do a little fishing with his buddies. Most often they spent their time sitting around the store talking about old times, usually EC's old times.

Although EC never outgrew his need for attention, he loved to relive the old days and the incredible events he'd experienced. He boasted about being an important part of the new Bank that went on to become such a famous Bank. He could recount every detail of his two trials for counterfeiting and seemed to relish in retelling those stories – although he would never talk about his days in prison. His audience, no matter who it happened to be, was always attentive to EC's wild, even bizarre tales.

In his last years, EC and Elaine reconnected once again and were able to spend some real quality time together. They often met at her house for supper or just took long drives together. They'd talk for hours about their lives, making up for missed time. No topic was off limits. EC talked openly about his meager beginnings, losing his parents when he was still a teenager, and being a bouncer in his Aunt Emily's whorehouse. Even though it embarrassed him, he told Elaine about being arrested for armed robbery and spending nine months on a prison farm.

It seemed to Elaine that EC almost bragged when he told her about getting his first real girlfriend pregnant. However, he at least showed some remorse about annulling his first marriage immediately after Anna was born. Somehow he justified running Brenda and their daughter, Anna, out of town. EC never talked about his second wife Clara's abduction and murder.

Elaine opened up to EC, too. She still carried anger about her Dad marrying Katy so soon after Clara's murder. She still missed Clara, the woman who adopted her as her own, and the only mother she'd ever really known. Although Clara's murder was still painful for Elaine, she also loved Katy and her half-brother Will. She was grateful for their love and support while EC was in prison. Some of Elaine's best memories were how much her Dad had helped her when her first marriage ended in divorce and she moved back. That had been a very low point in her life, and for once EC was there for her.

EC still lit up when he talked about Will, EC Jr. His untimely death had been painful and devastating for both Elaine and EC, as well as for Katy. They shared lots of stories, some were good, others, not so much. EC still had a hard time understanding his own feelings about Katy. The hook up between Katy and Pete Hamilton, his former cell mate, had been quite a surprise.

Both EC and Elaine were grateful for the chance their time together gave them to lay their ghosts to rest. It also gave them time to reconnect as father and daughter, and move forward.

Elaine, along with help from some of EC's living siblings and friends, gave EC a very exciting 80th birthday party at the Fork. It was attended by all sorts of family, friends, and well-wishers, and it was a big surprise for EC.

EC stayed pretty close to home until he was moved to a nursing home in New Ferry, where he lived until his death in 2001. His funeral was held in New Ferry and was well attended.

PART TWO

Chapter 24
THE MYSTERY MAN

In 1977 a young man, who called himself Mr. Jones or just Jones and who was attending the university on a soccer scholarship, returned to Chapel Hill to begin the fall semester of his junior year. Jones, who had adopted his deceased father's last name as his nickname, was a handsome lad about six feet tall. He had an athletic build and his body was well toned from years of competitive soccer. He had lots of sandy colored hair and a nice summer tan. The consensus among the coeds was that he was "very easy on the eyes." He had spent the summer out west with three of his fraternity brothers.

The four lads, all DKE fraternity brothers, started out in North Carolina and headed west, where they had secured jobs with the Green Giant company at their packaging facility. Along the way they stopped in Colorado at the Coors brewery to sample the product. Their appreciation for the popular beverage may have been a bit too enthusiastic as they were politely asked to leave. So they moved on, taking turns driving so each could relax and enjoy the scenery. They hit Salt Lake City by storm, but the girls they met were more interested in converting them to Mormonism than engaging in what the boys had in mind. On they went, stopping in Sun Valley and then Lake Tahoe before reaching Waitsburg, Washington, where they would spend the next six weeks working twelve hour days, living in a bunkhouse with the other workers, and spending their time off in the nearby city of Walla Walla, so loved by its founders it was named twice. The boys loved it too. Walla Walla was wide open with lots of bars and nightclubs. There were plenty of men's clubs and houses of ill repute. The city offered most any vice that anyone might desire, and they indulged in all of them. Most nights they would go into town after getting cleaned up and return to the bunkhouse, just in time to change clothes and be back at work by seven.

Two weeks into their stint at Green Giant, the boys met some Chi Omega sorority sisters from the University of Washington. They were nice, attractive young women who loved to have fun – the kind of fun that hadn't appealed to the Salt Lake City girls, and the boys spent many nights exploring the city with them.

On July 4th, near the end of the canning season, the Waitsburg facility's staff and summer workers set the world pea canning record for canning the most peas in twenty-four hours. It was a major event and there was lots of celebrating. Jones was surprised at how pleased he was that he had been part of setting that record.

When the pea season ended, the boys moved on to a wheat farm where they had new jobs waiting for them. For three weeks from sunup to sundown, they drove trucks loaded with harvested wheat to the grain elevators where the wheat was offloaded. That done, they returned to the fields to pick up another load and do the whole thing again – and again, and again. Those were long days, but they got three squares of delicious farm cooking every day.

They still had time before they had to be back at school when that job ended, so they headed to San Francisco. Then it was on to Acapulco where they had even more fun than they'd had in Walla Walla. Fortunately, they managed to avoid anytime in a Mexican jail. They made it back to Chapel Hill safe, sound, and healthy.

Jones reflected on his summer as he walked across campus toward his fraternity house, a big, beautiful colonial brick house on the corner across from the Carolina Inn. He was looking forward to seeing his roommate, Donnie Barden, and recounting some of his adventures. Donnie wasn't in the room, so Jones dropped his stuff and headed downstairs to have a beer and listen to the house's free juke box.

Donnie was there, singing along to the music and already into his second beer. They greeted each other with handshakes and few back slaps and Donnie said, "Jones, I gotta hear about your trip, how was it?"

Jones grabbed himself a beer and started to tell Donnie about the long days at Green Giant and driving the trucks loaded with wheat.

"No, no, I want to know about Mexico. I heard you guys spent some time down there. Did you get laid? Did all of you get lucky? How often did this happen?"

Jones laughed, "God, Donnie, you never change. I can't answer for the other guys, you'll have to ask them."

"It seems like I heard something about you and the daughter of the plant manager of the Green Giant operation. Any truth to that?"

Jones looked at Donnie and smiled. "You dirty old man. You should try to get laid yourself once in a while – or once even – and quit worrying about who everybody else is screwing. I admit that Mr. Warren, the plant manager, had a daughter named Jane. I will say that she was interested in seeing that some of her dad's better workers had a good time. She was always inviting them home for a nice warm meal. You'll have to use your imagination from there."

"Then tell me about Acapulco," Donnie pressed. "What happened there? Lots of wine, women, and song?"

Jones fetched another beer, took a swig and continued, "We'd sleep late every day then head for Hungry Herman's, a diner with modified American food. We would eat enough to last until we returned later that day. It was about the only place we trusted. None of us wanted to get the dreaded Tourista. In the afternoons we'd head to the cliffs where professional divers dove off the 80' to 100' cliffs for money. We'd spend the whole afternoon there drinking Cuba Libres and watching those crazy guys jump off the cliffs. It was a blast."

Donnie interrupted, "Isn't tequila the thing to drink down there? Rum and coke, what a bunch of wussies."

"We drank what we wanted to drink and had a hell of a great time. At night we'd get cleaned up and go bar hopping. First order of business every night was to hire a mariachi band to follow us around from bar to bar. It was a riot, not to mention an excellent way to get attention. You know, like rich Americans or crazy gringos. We had a ball. After we had a few drinks, we'd head out to some famous place like the Casa de Rebecca. The women were absolutely beautiful. Some were gorgeous enough to take home to Mama. Really."

"How much did they charge?" Donnie asked.
"Not enough."
"What did they do?"
"Anything you can imagine."
"Did you try to get the price down?"
"Hell no."
"Did everybody get laid? Come on, Jones, tell me the truth."
"Anyone that had enough pesos."

Jones ignored most of Donnie's questions and said, "One last tale, Donnie. One night when we were leaving the Casa de Rebecca, a group of locals followed us out to the parking lot. Sensing that trouble was getting ready to happen, we jumped into our car and locked the doors. One of the guys opened the pocket under the dashboard and pulled out his German Lugar. He rolled down his window, stuck his arm outside, and fired five rounds. That cleared the parking lot. Those locals ran like scalded dogs."

To Jones's satisfaction, Donnie's eyes got huge.

"To finish my story, we had so much fun that we had to sell one of the two cars at the free trade zone in Laredo, Texas, just to have enough money to get home. Even then we couldn't stay in motels, so it was non-stop driving, eating Krystal Burgers along the way, and drinking Red & White beer until we reached North Carolina. It was one helluva summer."

"Sounds like it," Donnie said, yawning. "You guys had so much fun that *I'm* worn out. I need to go to bed and get some rest. Night."

"Night. I'll be up after I listen to one more Elvis song," Jones said.

Three weeks later, Jones was walking through Y Court when Donnie ran up and grabbed his arm. "There is a state trooper at the house who wants to talk with you right now. He says it's urgent. Come on, I'll go with you."

Jones removed Donnie's hand from his arm, stepped back abruptly and said, "What the hell? Why would a state trooper want to talk to me?"

"It's probably just something like some unpaid parking tickets. Everybody on campus gets them at one time or another. It's no big deal."

"Bullshit. That doesn't sound right to me," Jones said. "Old parking tickets aren't urgent. Hell, let's go see what he wants."

When Jones reached the fraternity house he saw the patrolman standing on the front porch. He introduced himself and asked, "You have something urgent to tell me?"

The policeman shook Mr. Jones' hand and said, "I'm Captain Larry Richards of the North Carolina Highway State Patrol. Can we go inside and sit down and talk?"

Jones said, "Sure. Follow me." They went inside into the small TV room just off the foyer and sat at the table next to the fireplace.

The officer began, "Mr. Jones, we got a call this morning from the Melbourne, Florida, police department. They told us some very bad news. They asked that we come here and deliver this message to you in person and offer any assistance to you that you may want or need."

"Is it about my mom? Tell me now! What's wrong with my mom?"

The officer reached across the table and placed his hand on Jones's hand and said, "Mr. Jones, your mother was killed this morning during a bank robbery where she worked. I have very few details other than there were three robbers who stormed the bank, got nervous about some movements behind the teller windows, and they opened fire, killing your mother and several others. I am so sorry to have to tell you this. I'm here to help you in any way."

Jones started screaming, "No! No! No! This can't be true! She can't be dead. She's all I've got. Tell me it isn't true! How can I get there now? I've got to go home now!"

Several of Jones's fraternity brothers came running into the TV room when they heard Jones's cries. The officer explained the tragic news he'd just delivered. The fraternity brothers surrounded Jones and put their arms around him trying to comfort him.

The officer spoke again, "Mr. Jones, we can take you to the Raleigh airport and fly you and several of your friends to Melbourne today on our State Highway Patrol jet. We can get you there before dark, if you want us to."

Jones sobbed, "Thank you so much. Let me get my stuff. I'll be ready in ten minutes. Let me see if a couple of my brothers will go with me."

Jones and a few of his friends flew on the state highway patrol jet to Melbourne that afternoon. They found out when they arrived that there was an ongoing hostage situation. This was about more than Jones could stand.

The tragedy ended when the SWAT team stormed the bank two nights later and killed all three robbers, but not before two more bank employees and bank customer were killed. It was more than tragic. Jones was overcome with grief.

Jones's mother, Anna, had a funeral service that had never been seen before in Melbourne. It seemed as if the whole city turned out to pay their respects and say goodbye to this wonderful woman. One very touching moment during the service was when each one of Jones's seventy-five DKE fraternity brothers came marching into the church and placed a white rose on her casket. There were no dry eyes in that church that day.

Several weeks later Jones returned to Chapel Hill for the remaining fall semester to resume his education and complete his degree. Sometime before the Thanksgiving holiday, he decided he'd about had enough of the college scene. Although he knew it would have been upsetting to his mom if she knew he quit before graduating, he was ready to make some money.

He decided that he wanted to break into the banking industry and he began to lay out his plan. Jones spent some quality time in the university library doing research on the top in-state banks. By chance, and through sheer luck, he came across an old archived article in the Raleigh newspaper. It was about a man, Pete Hamilton, who had convinced a bank, then called the Eastern National Bank, to pay him a fee for causing large sums of money to be deposited into their coffers. Printed in the paper was a copy of the commission letter on Eastern National Bank stationery signed by the Bank president, Horace Felton. What the article did not say was that Pete Hamilton was an ex-felon whose knack for financial trickery with other people's money had landed him in the "big house" in Atlanta in the mid-1950s. The article also omitted the fact that Pete had been the cellmate of Edward Cain, the counterfeit money king from the eastern part of the state.

Jones wasted little time in mounting an effort to locate Pete Hamilton so he could meet with him as quickly as possible. It took him a few days before he got in touch with Pete, who was then living alone and barely existing in Virginia Beach. After a brief conversation, Jones asked Pete to meet him about half way between their two cities, and Pete agreed. A few days later Jones met Pete at Parker's BBQ in Wilson.

Parker's BBQ started years ago as a way to feed all of those tobacco farmers when they brought their tobacco to one of eastern North Carolina's foremost tobacco markets. It was a family business located on US Highway 301, the main north south route from New York to Florida through North Carolina. Car traffic was heavy, as was the diner traffic seeking that delicious barbecue that was soaked in the vinegar-based sauce, only found in eastern North Carolina. Along with fresh slaw and deep fried hush puppies, the eating at Parker's was some of the very best "cue" in the state.

Pete was amazed at how busy the place was and how reasonable the prices were considering the size of the portions they served. He loved all the farm tools hanging on the walls along with all the old photographs. The wagon wheel light fixtures hanging over the tables were his favorite furnishings. He couldn't believe the hustle and bustle going on in each section of the restaurant.

After they had talked generally about the bank industry and stuffed their bellies, Pete Hamilton got to the point. "Look, let's cut out the bullshit and level with one another." That broke the ice and the two men got down to business. Actually, they seemed very comfortable with one another. Mr. Jones confessed his motives and how they related to his mother's death. Pete admitted his past. They had a heart to heart talk about who they really were. In this very short time, they managed to bond in a significant way. What Jones learned from Pete Hamilton would change his life forever. He was given information that no one else knew.

Pete told Jones, "What I'm telling you are little known facts about what some, but not all, banking industry officials will do in order to further increase their bank's assets and deposits. Some banks will and do reward certain individuals if their actions or connections benefit the bank. It is not a very well-known fact, and in most instances, allegations to this effect will be denied over and over again. It is possible to get paid by increasing a bank's deposits in more ways than one. Believe me, that's the operative phrase, in more ways than one. No one has to know."

"One other thing," Pete Hamilton said, "Jones, you can get lots of Bank stock or lots of money without risking a dime of your own money."

"Man, you're talking my kind of language now," Jones said. "I'll take that deal." Jones had already set his sights on getting in bed with this Bank, the sooner the better. As it turned out, it would be real soon. Jones' college days were definitely over.

Within two weeks of meeting Pete Hamilton, Jones made an appointment with Horace Felton at the State National Bank's headquarters in New Ferry. It was a private meeting just between the two men. Not all the details are known as to what actually went down at that meeting, but one thing is certain, Jones had a new job. The one he wanted, with the Bank, in the Strategic Development Division, and he wasted no time in getting started.

Seven years after the State National Bank had changed its name in 1970, nineteen year old Jones was in the capitol at the back of a crowded news conference, when another acquisition was being announced. He was there because it was his first time participating in such a big deal. It was big to him anyway. It was only the beginning of his incredible whirlwind career in the banking business. When the Bank began its major expansion, Jones was always one step ahead of the game. It seemed that he knew in advance which new bank had been targeted for the next acquisition. Many wondered how he knew, what he knew, and when.

In 1982 the Bank, operating under duress by the Feds, was folded into Crescent National Bank, a major regional bank based in Charlotte, Jones was at a gubernatorial campaign rally in Charlotte when the deal was announced. He never said a word. He never shared any public limelight. He was never seen at any shareholder meetings. He was only seen in the Bank headquarters sporadically. However, according to the Bank's cleaning service, he had a very private office deep down in the bowels of the corporate office headquarters.

What was so strange and intriguing was that Jones never interacted with other Bank employees, at least not in public. Clearly whatever he did or did not do for the Bank was highly secretive and very private. No one seemed to know what Jones knew, and that was scary. It was almost as if Jones was calling the shots.

This is a mysterious aspect of the Bank's history not commonly known by most people, in or outside the Bank. It involved the activities of this very quiet, unknown, individual, Mr. Jones, who always dressed in a dark Baroni pinstripe suit with a red tie – always a red tie. Most often he had an expensive attaché case chained to his left wrist. There was unending concern and speculation about what was in that case. He was the kind of a person you couldn't quite put your finger on. Nobody really knew where he came from or exactly what he did for the Bank, much less his position there. He'd go in advance of the Bank people and be in the city where each new acquisition took place. The advance Bank people, the numbers guys in town to conduct the audit of new purchases, would invariably see him when they went out for meals or drinks. He was always around. Nobody knew why.

Over the years, this quiet, almost reclusive man was known simply as Mr. Jones. No first name. No middle initial. He was just plain Mr. Jones, and an unbelievable Mr. Jones at that.

The stories about this man have no end. One year a Bank employee saw Jones on TV at the Macy's Thanksgiving Day parade in New York with a lady celebrity friend. The very next week the Bank bought a small Manhattan bank. An avid college football booster said he often saw Jones in the box seats at the university stadium with a lady friend by his side. A bank vendor claimed he'd seen Jones in the bar at the White Elephant Hotel during Christmas Stroll Week in Nantucket. Again, he was with a lady friend.

A month later the Bank closed a merger in Boston, but not before Jones had a chance to dine at Legal Seafood down on the waterfront. Then he left Bean Town.

No one knew where Jones lived and slept. Did he own a home or a condo or did he live in an apartment? No one knew where he lived. No one knew, but there was plenty of gossip about his constant traveling and how he got from place to place. Some said he was always seen getting in or out of a chauffeured limousine. Others wondered if maybe he owned a private customized train car that also served as his home. It was an ongoing source of speculation and mystery. One unidentified loan officer with the Bank told a story about being called one day about approving a sizable loan for Mr. Jones. The banker checked out Jones' credit and found him most creditworthy. He asked about the collateral that would be required to secure a loan of this amount and was handed a stock portfolio of incredible value. He immediately approved the loan. Now the question became why Jones needed to make such a large loan. No one knew that answer either.

Jones was not just a borrower. Years earlier he proved himself to be a pretty damn good investor. On one of his trips to Atlanta he ran into three Carolina guys in the Atlanta hot spot, The Underground. They drank some whiskey – actually they drank a lot of whiskey – told some tales, and after an early morning breakfast at the Waffle House, started talking business. Jones asked the guys what had brought them to Atlanta.

One of the guys, Roy, answered, "We're in Atlanta because we have just signed a deal with Texaco allowing us to place and open thirteen modular restaurants on and adjacent to, operating Texaco gas facilities located on many southeastern interstate highway sites.

"Where'd you get the restaurants?" Jones wanted to know.

"We just purchased these modular cafes at a bankruptcy sale from Satellite 3 in 1 Corporation for $20,000."

$20,000 is all you paid for thirteen stores?"

"Yep, Texaco is interested in proving that selling food in conjunction with their gas operations on interstate highways would increase gas sales by as much as 50%."

"Do you think that selling food at gas stations will mean selling more gas?"

"Don't know for sure, but you can damn well believe we're ready to prove them right."

Joe, another one of the three guys, continued, "We've already cut a deal with Screen Gems, a division of Hanna-Barbera Productions. We met with Hone$t Ed Ju$tin at his New York office on 5th Avenue. Ed was the head guy at Screen Gems and he was quite a character. We cut a deal with him that granted us the license to use the Flintstones name and image for our restaurants."

Jones about jumped over the table into their laps with excitement. He said, "Cut me in for a 25% equity piece, and I'll provide all of the financing you need."

Tom, the quiet one of the trio, jumped to his feet and shouted, "Welcome aboard, partner!" It was settled, Jones became an investor and provided all of their funding.

The boys went on to open all thirteen stores, and they even had the gas operations at some locations. Texaco had already begun building three new brick and mortar restaurant-gas units for them on Interstate 75 in Auburn, Alabama, on Interstate 24 in Monteagle, Tennessee, and on Interstate 40 in Greensboro, North Carolina. Texaco identified three hundred other sites for possible conversion to Flintstones Foods-Gas operations. These guys and Jones were on their way to making a real fortune. Everyone involved was excited about the progress they were making.

About five months later the boys got a call from Texaco's vice president for operations. He suggested they all come to Atlanta for a strategy meeting. They went down, including Jones. They were picked up at the airport and driven to a Holiday Inn close by. The VP suggested they have a drink. The boys knew that a drink at that time of the morning meant something was wrong.

Then the vice president spoke: "Boys, I have just received an executive order from the New York office that orders me to shut down any and all development projects in my region immediately. That includes the three new Flintstones stores we're building for you."

The boys were in shock. "Why?" they wanted to know.

"Energy Crisis," he said.

"What the hell is an energy crisis?"

"In short, it means that the gas supply has about run out, which means there will be little or no interstate traffic. This is very bad news indeed for all gas and food service units on the interstates, including your Flintstones."

This was not the way this deal was supposed to turn out. Everyone knew that. They also knew that the circumstances were beyond their control, but that did not take away the pain and the hurt. Jones assured the guys he understood and that he would simply write off his losses. Too bad the others could not do the same. It was a very long and sad plane trip home.

Not all of Jones's investments went south. He loved his Dell Computer stock. He was also thankful he had been lucky enough to get in on Apple's IPO. He had also bought into a Chicago-based fund called the National Equity Group. It dealt mainly in distressed commercial real estate and was managed by Stewart Chan. Chan was known as the "grave dancer" because he was always buying depressed or foreclosed properties for pennies on the dollar.

Jones told a business associate, "I heard that Stewart Chan had won the purchase bid for the Purple Pickle Building in Durham, North Carolina. Then I heard he got it for an absolute steal. Then I found out that after doing some minor cosmetic repairs, he was putting it back on the market at twice the price he paid. That's when I decided to buy into Mr. Chan's fund."

Over the years, Jones accumulated quite an impressive stock portfolio. He never concentrated too heavily in any one stock sector, but seemed more comfortable owning a variety of stocks. He did not buy bonds, nor did he buy "penny stocks." He also left the commodities alone after dropping several hundred thousand dollars in just his second foray into that complex market. Above all, he never believed in mutual funds, and he limited his financial institutional buys to shares in his employer company, the Bank.

He never believed that some broker, sitting in a cubicle somewhere, would really have his interest at heart. As far as he was concerned, he believed for most of them it was about churning accounts, so they could generate more fees.

For that reason, Jones stuck with investments that he personally bought. He restricted his investments to deals that he understood and didn't have to be concerned with the operations or the management. That turned out to be a great decision that served Jones quite well in the years that followed.

Chapter 25
THE CONVERGENCE

In 1982, the Crescent National Bank sent Jones to northern Florida to head up the purchase of the top bank in that area, The Sunshine State Bank of Lake City (SSB). It was a test run, and a challenge to see if Jones really had what it took. It was a big prize the Bank wanted badly, and Jones was ready to prove his merit to his boss.

The first thing Jones did before he left for Florida was call the chairman of SSB and set up a private meeting. Mr. Jones thought it was about time, indeed, the right time, to burn some of that counterfeit money. He believed it was the perfect opportunity to re-introduce the "Old Money" program from the Federal Reserve Burn Center. He decided that he may as well resurrect the money-to- burn program now and see if what Pete Hamilton had told him to do with all that counterfeit money in the safe deposit boxes at SSB would, in fact, fly. Jones was anxious to get some of the thousands of counterfeit bills out of those safe deposit boxes and on their way to the Federal Reserve Burn Center. He was also looking forward to getting his $50,000 share and Pete's $5,000 share from each one of over two hundred safe deposit boxes that were stashed full of thousands of EC's counterfeit dollars in this bank. He had gotten that information from EC's ledger which Pete had given him earlier.

Upon arriving in Lake City, Mr. Jones checked into the Cabot Lodge, a nice place, but not too showy. He called and made dinner reservations at Jessica's Bistro for eight o'clock. It was rated as one of the top two restaurants in town. Next, Mr. Jones phoned SSB to confirm his eleven o'clock meeting the next morning. Everything was in place; the chairman was scheduled to see him at eleven.

When Mr. Jones walked into SSB at exactly 10:50 the next morning, he asked the secretary for a cup of coffee and a local newspaper. She brought him both. Five minutes later, he was ushered into the chairman's office. The two men shook hands, made comments about the weather, and sat down. Mr. Jones asked the chairman what he thought about selling his bank. What came next was a bit surprising. The chairman said he did not think his bank needed to be sold. Mr. Jones stood up, lit a cigarette, and said, "Joe O'Brien, your goddamn bank is going fucking broke. You're crazy if you don't take my deal."

"What are you offering?" Joe asked.

"Joe, you and I both know about the counterfeit money stashed in dozens of safe deposit boxes in many of your branch banks."

"What the hell are you talking about?" Joe said.

"Give me a break. Look up these safe deposit box accounts." He handed Joe the paper with the typed box numbers. "There is $100,000 of bogus money in each one of those two hundred and twenty-five safe deposit boxes.. Don't try to deny what we both know is real."

"Okay. What can we do about this money so no one gets caught?"

Mr. Jones laid out the deal. He told Joe, "Send the counterfeit money as 'Old Money' to the Federal Reserve Burn Center. Don't ask questions and your bank will get $45,000 each time one of the safe deposit boxes is emptied. The bogus money will be burned and good money will be sent back to your bank. I can also guarantee you our bank will buy your bank. We got a deal or not?"

Joe said, "Count me in." It was just that easy. Jones knew he was onto something really big for both himself and for his Bank.

Jones had chartered a large fishing boat and arranged to take the top seven executives from the bank to the Gulf Stream the following day for some great fishing, drinking, eating, and casual conservation. During that outing, he never once mentioned the Bank deal that was on the table. When they returned to the mainland he told the guys, "Next week we're going to the Dolphins game." The following Sunday he took the same group to a Miami Dolphins football game against the Tampa Bay Buccaneers. The Bucs won. After the game Jones told the guys, "Grab your wives. It's their turn. Next week I'm flying you and your wives to Bermuda for three days of wine, food, and shopping. It's all on the house!" The bankers' wives had a great time. That was the clincher. Their husband executives, along with the chairman, approved Jones' bank acquisition terms.

The next week the Bank closed the deal for the bank in northern Florida, the largest bank in the state with over six hundred branches. Jones had stood tall. He was implementing the Bank's new defensive strategy of growing bigger and richer to avoid being swallowed up by other larger banks.

During the late 1980s when the savings and loans got into major financial trouble and began to fold and shut down all over the country, the Feds stepped in with a recovery program called Resolution Trust Corporation, or RTC. It was complicated, expensive, and cost many shareholders their life savings and retirement funds. It was massive and very pervasive nationwide. That industry was truly in trouble, and the Feds had to get involved and get involved fast.

As the Bank continued its search for acquisition candidates, they looked to Texas where the opportunities seemed limitless. In the spring of 1988, Mr. Jones was sent to Dallas. Some very big deals had to be put together with some healthy financial companies that could absorb the damaged properties. Mr. Jones got right in the middle of the major problems that had arisen with a large number of S&Ls in Texas, specifically the Lone Star State Bank Corporation of Dallas.

Before Mr. Jones did anything else, he met with the CEO of the Lone Star State Bank. He got absolutely no push back relative to the bogus money burn program. Once he had laid out the details to the CEO, and they had agreed as to where the "good money" would go, the two shook hands and Jones left. According to EC's ledger, this bank's branches had some sixty of these safe deposit boxes filled with counterfeit money. Jones had it figured out; the older, larger banks, with hundreds of branches, obviously had the highest number of safe deposit boxes stashed with EC's bogus bills. EC had done a masterful job of getting so many $100,000 batches of his fake bills stashed in safe deposit boxes all over the southeast and southwest.

Jones recognized that this project would take lots of his time and effort, so he rented the penthouse suite at the top of the Fairmont Hotel in Dallas. He was certain he'd need to wine and dine some key folks in the deal in order to get what his bank wanted. There was no better place than the Fairmont to make the right impression.

Jones was really good at his job. He had great people skills, and good looks. He knew how to make people feel comfortable around him. His best attribute may have been his ability to do good things for the people he was dealing with and not have them think there was some type of quid pro quo, or that he was kissing their asses.

In January, Jones told all of the RTC executives working on the S&L deal, "You are all invited to attend the Cotton Bowl football game between Notre Dame and Texas A&M. Box seats for everyone." Jones continued, jokingly, "I'm doing this because I like Lou Holtz, the Notre Dame coach."

What he did next was incredible and ingenious. In April, Mr. Jones took all former Lone Star State Bank Corporation executives, along with their age appropriate kids, to the Michael Jackson Bad World Tour concert at the Reunion Arena in Dallas. They all had front row seats and Jones got right in the middle of all of those kids as if he were one of them. They all loved it, and he made a lot of points that night.

In order to make sure no one felt left out, Jones took over the convention ballroom at the Fairmont Hotel. Jones called the top executives to the conference room. After he gave a short update on the proposed deal, he said, "I'm inviting all bank executives and their wives on both sides of the deal, about four hundred of you altogether, as my guests, to a dinner concert with entertainment by none other than the Eagles. I hope you can find time to attend."

Within a couple of months, everybody in Dallas had heard of Jones, and in a very good way.

In 1988, after months and months of wheeling and dealing with the RTC, the Bank was offered an absolutely huge financial windfall. It would receive a large portion of these assets, and the FDIC would assume the old loan portfolios. The RTC did everything possible to keep the banks from outright bankruptcy and dissolution. Jones knew where the buttons were on both sides of the deal, and he did not hesitate to push them. He knew that the deal was too good to turn down. He also knew it could propel the Bank into the national arena faster and better than anything else the Bank could possibly do on its own. Both the Bank and the RTC agreed to the deal Mr. Jones had worked out over several months. The transfer of assets finally closed on New Year's Day. It was a huge gift for the Bank.

The next few years were a blur of sorts in the banking industry. It took some time passing before the Bank could fully digest the deal they made with the RTC. It took a while before they realized the promised return. Some sketchy loans, overstated assets, and a weak economy made times a bit harder for the Bank than they had anticipated.

Over the past several years the Bank had gone ballistic in bank mergers and acquisitions. They bought little banks. They bought medium sized banks. Now and then they even bought large banks. The Bank was growing like crazy. In a span of about four years, the Bank bought several hundred thrifts and community banks with the help of the FDIC. The Bank's numbers continued to rise. It gained more assets, more deposits, more cash reserves, more cash flow, more profits, and higher stock prices. Everyone involved with the Bank was doing extremely well, including Jones. Rumors surfaced that he had purchased a multi-million dollar penthouse apartment on the Upper East Side in New York, and he probably had.

Now the Bank was buying or merging with banks all over the country. Jones was seen everywhere. Everyone wanted to know what the hell Jones was doing. They wanted to know who or what he controlled, if anyone or anything. Lots of folks were asking lots of questions about Mr. Jones, but they were getting absolutely no answers, at least not the kinds of answers that satisfied anybody's curiosity.

At least one thing had changed drastically for Jones. His exclusive method of travel had become a very fancy Lear Jet. Even though the plane had the Bank's name on its fuselage, Jones was its sole user. That was big time. That was power. Jones was flying high in grand style. The fact was that he had to have his own means of transportation. It had to be fast enough and effective enough in getting him to the far reaching destinations he travelled to every week. His schedule was demanding, and it only increased with the Bank's growth.

The Bank was on a fast track to grow as it never had before. In 1989 Jones was dispatched to Atlanta to head up the Bank's efforts to buy the First Georgia Bank, a major regional banking operation in that city. He tried some time-tested efforts, but to no avail. He was getting stonewalled from every direction.

For some reason Mr. Jones was reticent about talking to the First Georgia Bank's chairman about the safe deposit boxes full of bogus money in his bank. Something just didn't feel right, so he changed his tactics. He rented the Sun Dial revolving restaurant on top of the Westin Peach Tree Plaza in downtown Atlanta on New Year's Eve. He even brought in Sir Tom Jones (no relation), the Welsh crooner. He invited the bank's top 100 shareholders and their wives to dinner. There were guest bags filled with very expensive items for all who attended. Hidden inside each bag was a personal letter to each shareholder asking them to pressure the bank management to accept Jones's offer. Even that ploy failed, so Jones went home.

As a defensive move, First Georgia Bank merged with Virginia State Bank. This time Mr. Jones' deal was over, and he was damn glad he listened to his gut feelings, his intuition, or both. These inner voices had told him that the First Georgia Bank was maybe too big to buy.

However, when the deal came up again a couple of years later in 1991, most folks had no idea what the Bank's CEO did to make sure he got the deal this time. He had a focus group set up to train him in what to say when the First Georgia Bank guy spoke. The Bank guy knew he had to be more respectful of the concerns of the seller. He knew what the First Georgia Bank guy disliked about him and his business style. He was considered too rude and too abrupt. The seller wanted to know what would happen to his employees, and how many would be retired, and would the CEO have a job.

When the merged bank, First Georgia Bank-Virginia State Bank, got into serious financial trouble because of its bad merger, they were ready to talk again. Mr. Jones and the Bank CEO returned to Atlanta. This time they had the leverage and they used it magnificently. The Bank CEO was on his best behavior. Fortunately, Mr. Jones was able to meet privately with the chairman of the First Georgia Bank/Virginia State Bank and he got the safe deposit bogus money matter straight before the deal closed. It was short and sweet. The chairman had to agree to the bogus money deal or he'd lose the bank merger deal. In other words, the chairman had to send the counterfeit bills in his bank's safe deposit boxes to the Federal Reserve Bank to be burned. Mr. Jones and his CEO wasted little time and next to no money. They sealed the purchase in record time. Jones got a little bonus for himself as well, but he got an even better promotion. He was named the Senior Vice President for Mergers and Acquisitions for the Bank. SVP for M&A had a good ring to it. He was now a senior management team member. What really made Mr. Jones smile was reading in EC's ledger that there were almost two hundred "bogus bill boxes" at this bank.

About the time of this acquisition by the Bank, a new CEO, Harold McNair, took over its management. He had been groomed for this job ever since he joined the Bank after his Marine Corps service ended. He was strong, pro-growth, ambitious, and hard-nosed. He suffered few fools. Over the next few years the Bank consumed a couple of hundred thrifts and community banks. The Bank was on a tear, and so was its value. The Crescent National Bank, in an effort to more appropriately reflect its new position in the country, changed its name to National Bank, but was still referred to as the Bank.

In 1992 Jones rented an apartment in Annapolis, Maryland. He would be there several months while he did his research and due diligence on the Bank's latest target, Eastern Shore Trust Corp. There was also another reason. Jones loved sailing, and for him there was no better place to sail than Annapolis.

Like many other of the Bank's acquisitions, this one was in financial trouble as a result of a shaky merger. Jones took a hard line position on the terms of the proposed deal, and then he dug in. All he would say to any of the seller's counter offers was a resounding "No!" Then he explained the safe deposit counterfeit money deal to the bank's president: "Sir, the two deals go hand in glove. You don't get one without the other. You must understand that your bank is in serious trouble, and I'm not going to pay you a fortune for it. However, I'm willing for you to participate in the "good money" we get back from the Federal Reserve Burn Center. Now, do we have a deal or do I have to go to your board?"

The president of Eastern Shore Trust, waving his arms wildly above his head, answered, "Mr. Jones, just show me where to sign. Let's do it now." He agreed to the deal and that changed the whole attitude of the selling bank.

It would take several more weeks of shareholder meetings by all parties concerned to secure shareholder approval of the deal, so Jones decided to wait on his sailboat. He went sailing most every day and spent most nights in fancy eateries in the area. Then he'd go to the nightly "hot" spots where the locals hung out. He was having a grand time with all those single women.

Once he consummated this deal, it was on to the next deal.

After a couple of years digesting what it had purchased in early 1995, the Bank got back on the acquisition path by sending Jones to Atlanta to buy the Peach State Bank Corp financial institution. *First things first,* Jones thought. He took the PSB chairman to the Ichiban Restaurant for dinner. Atlanta is where this chain started. He requested a private table. After a couple of drinks to loosen up his guest, Jones explained to the PSB chairman, "As we both know about the safe deposit boxes filled with bogus money, here is the deal." Then Jones elaborated about the finer parts of the plan, and how the "good money" would be shared.

The PSB chairman responded, "I'm not too sure I understand what you are saying. Is this legal?"

Jones slammed his palm to his forehead and said, "Legal? Are you some kind of fucking idiot? Where did you ever get the idea that counterfeit money is legal? You gotta be a goddamn fool!" Jones, who was not exactly sure he believed the chairman could not understand what he had just been told, added this caveat, "If you want to sell your bank, you have to agree to the bogus money deal. It's your choice, but I've got to have your answer in the next five minutes."

The chairman ordered another martini and said, "I'm sorry to act so contrary. But yes, you can count me in."

Jones muttered, "Thanks a lot. Jesus Christ!"

This was a fairly straightforward deal that could be wrapped up quickly. This deal was going to be easy. Jones loved deals like this because it gave him a chance to take some personal time for things he wanted to do and see. He had already decided he would attend the upcoming Super Bowl in Miami. He always had such a great time on those Super Bowl weekends. He enjoyed lots of wine, women, and song, not to mention some great football. The 49ers almost doubled the score on the Chargers. The Super Bowl weekend was what he really needed to offset his too hectic work schedule. Jones was on a roll.

Next Jones went to South Carolina and bought Investors Trust over a weekend. He had dinner with the Investors Trust executives in Charleston on a Friday night at the Charleston Grille, he played golf with them on Saturday at the Kiawah Island Golf Resort, and he closed the deal on Sunday over lunch at the Hilton Head Inn. Because he had worked out the safe deposit counterfeit money situation over the phone in advance, this was about the easiest deal he ever made for the Bank.

In 1996 it was now time to move west, so the Bank went after the Marine Bank Trust group in St. Louis, Missouri, at the time the 30th largest bank holding company in America. Mr. Jones was very excited about buying this bank. According to EC's ledger, this bank had hundreds of branches, and about one hundred and fifty of them had safe deposit boxes filled with EC's counterfeit money. The bogus money deal would increase Mr. Jones's bank balance by millions.

So Mr. Jones went straight to the CEO's office and delivered his spiel about the bogus bills. Upon hearing the tale, the CEO jumped up out of his chair, crossed the room, grabbed Jones's hand and starting shaking it violently. He told Jones, "This is like manna from heaven. Man, you are going to make me a rich man. Count me in."

Jones, smiling, said, "I can see your wheels turning as you add up your share. Just be glad I'm willing to share. Not everyone would."

Mr. Jones was smart. He had figured it all out ahead of time. He was pretty much convinced that if he shared the spoils of the counterfeit money that came back from the Federal Reserve with the captains of the banks, most all of his deals would fall into place. He was fairly certain the bank executives getting the money weren't in the least bit concerned that the money was illegal. They just wanted their share. Mr. Jones was right on the money, as they say.

The Marine Bank Trust deal would add some serious value to the Bank's balance sheet. Jones liked being back in St. Louis again. He could now do some of the things he hadn't gotten to do before, like go up in the Arch and a ride down the Mississippi on the Delta Queen. He was certainly taking advantage of a few of the gambling boats at night. EC did not miss dining at all of those famous and delicious eating places.

Then it was off to Chicago to make a deal for Burlington Securities. The Bank wanted to get into securities, derivatives, and foreign exchanges. This challenge was a bit different for Jones as it was not just buying a bank. Mr. Jones did his homework, and he was prepared when the meeting started. He laid out his parameters for the deal and told the seller, "If you can fill in the blanks to my satisfaction, we've got a deal. Each time the parameters change, your sales price will be substantially decreased." After a couple of days and several meetings, Jones was able to close the deal much to his liking.

Before he knew it, Mr. Jones found himself back in Florida in 1997. This time the challenge was a bit harder. Buying South Florida Bank, the largest commercial bank in Florida, would take some shrewd negotiations and some hard core bluffing. The first one to blink would lose the deal. This deal was probably the toughest deal so far for Jones, and it was very important to the Bank. The South Florida Bank chairman, listening to Mr. Jones explain the safe deposit counterfeit money deal, asked by far the most probing questions. He really pressed Jones for more details than Jones wanted to give up. He kept pressing Jones to tell him what would happen if the Feds discovered what they were doing. "What are you going to do if I call in the Feds? What then?" the chairman demanded.

Jones, really pissed by now, said, "Are you really that goddamn stupid? How are you going to explain to the Feds why your bank has these millions of dollars of counterfeit money stored in your bank? You got an answer for that, dumbass?"

The chairman turned red and responded meekly, "I guess you got me there."

Jones stressed the urgency of getting the merger completed. Finally, the chairman relented.

On the weekends, Jones would fly down to Nassau for some fun in the sun, not to mention the late nights of gambling in the casinos on Paradise Island. He knew how to win, he was a great poker player and he won a lot. One weekend he was there when they were filming a James Bond movie. That was very exciting. Mr. Jones and the movie cast and crew did some heavy drinking and played some high stakes poker. They Bonded, you might say. Mr. Jones was always back to work on Monday, ready to do battle. Those folks at South Florida Bank were tough and very smart, and they had a great bank with balance sheets to back up their tough talk. This deal was going to take some patience because it was very complicated.

There were so many different entities it was very confusing and difficult to determine a real value.

The South Florida Bank deal took over a year to close, but when it did close, it elevated the Bank's reputation and status.

Mr. Jones had used the counterfeit money EC had stashed in multiple safe deposit boxes in so many US banks. It was leverage to persuade each of those banks to take his acquisition offers. In short, Mr. Jones black-mailed target banks with the threat of exposing their counterfeit money deposits in order to close the deals. His ace in the hole was that he always had the power to cancel any deal.

All of a sudden the National Bank was not just another bank. It was making a name for itself in more ways than one. It was becoming a major, top tier bank. The Bank's stock value continued to rise.

Chapter 26
THE SOCIAL LIFE

One thing Mr. Jones knew from experience was that all work and no play made him a dull man. So whenever he could, he made sure to mix in all types of ball games. He loved pro football, college football, World Series baseball, and his absolute favorite was college basketball, ACC style. More specifically, he breathed Carolina basketball.

He kept his social life alive with Mary. Her name had finally surfaced as the lady friend who was so often seen with him while he traveled around the country. Because of Mary, Jones scheduled his demanding agenda around special social events whenever possible. There were highbrow cocktail parties here, a youthful wedding event there, and fine dining experiences in most of the Five Star restaurants around the US. He was never lacking in invitations to a multitude of very exciting events, and he and Mary missed very few.

Where did Jones find this lovely blonde lady? No one knew for sure, but rumor had it that while jogging one day in Central Park in early 1999, he ran across this stunning young woman. She was trying to scoop up scads of files and documents that had tumbled out of her open briefcase onto the sidewalk. He stopped to assist her before the papers all blew away. When she looked up and he saw that gorgeous face, he was hooked from the very first moment. Mary thanked him profusely and began to scurry away. "Wait," Jones called out to her. She stopped and he introduced himself. Lucky for him, he had picked up one of her business cards that had fallen out of her briefcase. Mary smiled thankfully and walked away.

Two weeks later while visiting New York on banking business, he called Mary Whitmore. She was an attorney and already a partner in a very prestigious firm on Wall Street. Her specialty was securities. Jones cheerfully asked, "Can you meet me for lunch tomorrow at Babbo's?" This was a tony little cafe at Waverly Place in the Village.

Mary said, "I can't wait." The stars and the planets must have been in alignment that day, because Jones and Mary had such a great lunch that they bonded from the very start. They talked non-stop for hours. That was the beginning of an exciting relationship.

Later that same year they were seen together on Nantucket. Yes, it was for the Christmas Stroll. Mary's sister and her husband were also there staying at his parents' house in Siasconset. What a beach house it was, right on the ocean. His father had written the Big Fish book that became that famous movie with the four letter title.

Christmas Stroll week is the week when thousands of people from all different places came to the island to Christmas shop in Nantucket. Other than it being a beautiful and exciting place to visit, there are some very meaningful discounts given by most of the local retailers during Stroll Week. Paying customers receive half of a numbered stub for each purchase. The corresponding half of each stub goes into a giant revolving wire basket. On Saturday of Christmas Stroll week, after Santa arrives, winning stub numbers are drawn from the basket for all types of prizes ranging from coffee makers to $15,000 in cash. You have never seen so many affluent people with all of the members of their families hanging out in the town square near the courthouse in freezing weather waiting to see if they had the winning ticket. It is an unbelievable sight. Almost everyone on the island shows up for this event and has a fabulous time.

Mary's sister called and argued, "Sis, you and Jones have got to stay through New Year's Day. It's First Light and it's going to be an amazing and exciting time to be on the beach in 'Sconset. We're going to be able to see the very first sunrise of the 21st Century right here on Nantucket. Besides, several of your friends from college and from New York here. You have to stay so you can introduce them to Jones."

Mary was convinced and screamed, "Happy New Year!" You could not have pulled Mr. Jones away with a team of mules. He was loving this, and Mary too.

Coincidentally, Melissa Brown, one of Mary's Dartmouth College roommates, had been on Nantucket since leaving Boston's Beth Israel Hospital in late October. She was recovering from a stem cell transplant she had undergone for her lingering illness. Her parents had rented a home in 'Sconset while she regained her strength. This allowed them to go back to Boston each week for Melissa's follow up treatments. So far things were going well.

Mary and Melissa met the next day for lunch at the Sea Grille, a great spot where all the locals hung out. Melissa's first question for Mary was, "Where in the world did you find Jones?"

"He was jogging in Central Park. I dropped my briefcase and papers were flying everywhere when he stopped to help me gather them up. It was quite accidental, and he did call me two weeks later."

Melissa smiled and said, "It appears that you two may be an item. What's your answer?"

"Let's not get the cart before the horse just yet. Now, tell me about yourself. How are you feeling?"

"I feel wonderful, Melissa replied"

"Have your doctors got things under control yet?"

"Yes, I hope so."

"Are you improving?"

"Absolutely."

"You must be getting better because you look absolutely gorgeous!"

Melissa smiled and spoke quietly, "Mary, you always know the exact right thing to say. You are amazing. Are you and Mr. Jones really serious?"

"I hope so."

"Where does he live?

"Everywhere, but mostly New York."

"What does he do?"

I'm not really sure. Something in banking."

"Are you living together yet?"

Mary laughed and said, "Melissa, you'll never change, thank God for that. I've missed you so much. I'm so glad you're here. Tell me about your art. Tell me about you and Jake."

The two young women continued talking for hours catching up on Mary's job, how much she liked being a lawyer, and discussing where Melissa was with her painting and her illness. It was outstanding therapy for both of them. Their close friendship was stronger than ever.

All of these friends got together several times that week. First it was one restaurant, and then some other bar. It was a delightful time leading up to New Year's Eve. It was such fun having such good friends. Everyone was impressed with Jones. They loved his style but, most of all, they were attracted to him because of his mystique.

There was a great New Year's Eve party at the home of the Mayor of 'Sconset. Everyone showed up with some type of covered dish and plenty of booze. It lasted into the wee hours.

All those who could remember it said they had a great time. It was like destiny had brought all of these people together on Nantucket.

By about 5:30 am January 1, 2000, bodies began to show up on the beach at 'Sconset. Just a few to begin with, then the crowd grew fairly quickly. Some were bright eyed and bushy tailed, others were pretty hungover. No one wanted to miss this historical event. Most everyone was wearing Nantucket shirts that read FIRST LIGHT 2000! Mary and Jones were there with Mary's sister and her husband. Then Melissa and her boyfriend and parents arrived. Then scads of young folks whom they all knew showed up. Then, as if by magic, a glow began to rise in the east, far off in the distance, even beyond the water horizon. 6:30 am became 6:45 am. The crowd became anxious and boisterous. The minutes were now flying by and the crowd grew larger and louder. At precisely 7:06 am eastern time, the First Light of the new century peered over the horizon onto 'Sconset. This group of close friends had witnessed First Light in the US in 2000. They were all thrilled.

After the excitement of the sunrise was over, the entire crowd went to Melissa's cottage for an early morning breakfast that her Dad and boyfriend prepared. But before anyone could eat, they had to consume a few drinks. It was an amazing New Year's Day. It was the culmination of an extraordinary time for everyone, but probably, most especially, for Melissa and her parents.

The next day Jones and Mary jumped on his jet and scooted back to New York. The week had been an incredible time for both of them; seeing all those people, some friends, some relatives, but all of them connected by some stroke of fate. Being at First Light with all of these folks, they'd never forget that experience.

Jones had places to go, people to meet, and banks to buy. He was anxious to get back into the swing of wheeling and dealing. It was time to get back to business, the Bank's business.

It had been his first love, but maybe now it was his second. His interest in Mary was heating up.

Mr. Jones really felt as if things at the Bank were getting close to a major breakthrough in its quest to become one of the major financial institutions in America. He didn't know exactly how things would go, but his instincts told him that the next few years were going to be very exciting. He knew he had to keep a close eye on any signs in the industry that might give him and his Bank a clue as to what was changing, and how the Bank could take advantage of any new direction.

Jones planned to increase his networking activities by calling most everyone of any importance in his business several times each quarter. That way he felt if anything was changing, good or bad, he would have an inside track on becoming aware of those changes. He'd be able to inform his CEO and help him steer the Bank in the most favorable direction.

Jones was both excited and worried about what new challenges both he and the Bank faced in the coming years.

Chapter 27
THE TOP TIER

Jones kept pressing the National Bank to move upward, not laterally. He insisted they continue to acquire any financial institution worth its salt, if available. They had competition in many of the deals they were now pursuing. So in order to get the deal, now they had to pay more. Mr. Jones really pushed this strategy, and the acquisitions continued.

By early 2000, the National Bank was a major player on the national banking scene. It had reached the upper tier of its industry. As a result of the Bank's growth and notoriety, the Bank became a rumored takeover target itself. It went from being the hunter to being hunted by several other larger banks. This was making Mr. Jones very nervous.

Several upper tier banks made subtle overtures to the Bank, but the Bank did not respond. The Bank charged Jones with the task of finding out which of these upper tier banks would be most vulnerable to a takeover. This was a monumental undertaking that would require lots of time, lots of secrecy, and lots of negotiating skill. Jones accepted the challenge in stride and set out to get the answers.

The next six months were quite demanding not only for the Bank, but also for Jones. The Bank was becoming the subject of many merger rumors. What was so frustrating to so many bank analysts was the Bank's total lack of response. The Bank neither denied nor confirmed the reports, which confused industry experts. The situation was putting a great deal of pressure on Jones to expedite his search for the most vulnerable bank that could possibly be acquired.

Jones crisscrossed the country again and again. He spent an inordinate amount of time in New York, but at least he got the chance to enjoy his penthouse apartment during his off time. Then he was off to Minnesota for several days. He flew back to Baltimore, and then back to the west coast. He was repeatedly seen in some of the obvious hot spots in California. The French Laundry in Napa Valley was his favorite. Mary liked it too. What they both liked about this part of California was being able to drop into an In-N-Out Burger. Their fabulous burgers and fries were to die for.

Jones was getting a great deal of use out of his jet. He was running up some serious air miles. The jet was his right hand man, so to speak. Other than the arduous bank work he was involved with, he was having the time of his life. He was doing what he had always dreamed of doing, and he was making a bundle of money at the same time.

Jones knew that the next major bank deal could very well propel one of the top tier participating banks to the position of being the biggest, largest, bank in the United States. He also knew his bosses at the Bank were counting on being that bank. He knew the monkey was on his back to make this deal for his Bank, not to mention his reputation.

Some of the other banks had different ideas.

It wasn't so much the merger that mattered as it was which bank would be the surviving bank, retaining its name, its headquarters location, and its president and chairman positions. Having all those assets on one balance sheet would be very impressive for the surviving bank. That turned out to be a tall order, even for Jones.

What really surprised Jones was waking up one morning in March of 2000. He was in Indianapolis to see Bill Guthridge's UNC Tar Heels play in the Final Four for the NCAA National Basketball Championship, The next morning he read in the WSJ about the possible merger between two of the top banks in the US, Urban Bank & Trust in New York and Golden

State Bank in California. The front page story did not list the name of the National Bank. That was a shocker. So was Carolina's loss. Jones' phone was ringing off the hook. It was Harold McNair calling with questions and more questions that he could not answer. This was a real game changer. He had to find out what they were thinking and fast. Harold McNair did not like excuses.

That afternoon Jones hopped on his Citation X jet and flew to New York. This was a very logical move because one of the two banks named in the merger article was headquartered there. He did not wait until he got to New York to start making calls. By the time his jet touched down in the city that never sleeps, he had a good idea of what was going on with this deal. He assessed all the information gathered from his many phone calls and determined that one of the banks was not at all serious about the deal. It was merely trying to establish a price for its stock. Jones relaxed just a bit, but he still needed to get a reading on the other bank. What was their game and how should he play it.

Chapter 28
THE DUE DILIGENCE

About this time, things began to get a little testy for the Bank and for Mr. Jones. It wasn't as if he were a secret or an unknown factor to the competitor banks. They had long known of some of his amazing feats in securing deals for the Bank. He was infamous, if not famous. The other banks had begun trying to check him out years ago, but had never been able to really get any personal information on him. All they knew was he worked for the Bank, and that he had done a great job moving their growth strategy along. As far as they were concerned, he had done *too* great of a job. He seemed to get every deal he went after and they had no clue about how he did it.

Jones was back in New York to meet with a very reliable source regarding the other bank in the merger rumor story. They met at Gallaghers Steakhouse on West 52nd Street at 6:30 sharp. What a great place to meet, if only to see all the photos of famous people on the walls who had eaten there over the years. Jones had graciously turned down several offers to put his own photo on the wall. This place always had lots of folks and lots of noise. It would be very difficult for anyone at the next table or booth to overhear other conversation. The place smelled delicious with the aroma of cooking steaks filling the air.

Patrons were everywhere, standing at the bar, seated at tables, and some just milling around. After a couple of drinks, perfectly cooked ribeye steaks and Caesar salads, the two men got serious. The informant opened the conversation with, "I got lots of interesting bank news for you, Mr. Jones, some good, some bad. Some of it may seem troubling. Golden State Bank wants a deal. They want to be the buyer, the acquirer, and the survivor." He continued, "Furthermore, they want to keep their headquarters in California. Most troubling of all, they want both the CEO and chairman positions filled by their top two executives."

Mr. Jones was squirming in his seat; he knew his work was cut out for him now. Jones said, "For God's sake, please tell me the good news. I certainly can't find anything good in what you just told me."

The informant smiled faintly and added, "The west coast bank's top gun is in failing health. I think he could probably be pushed to make a deal now, before he gets any sicker."

Jones thought that was the good news and said, "Thanks a million for your help. Here's your check for your time and trouble, and don't buy any bank stock." He gave the guy a pat on the back as he left the restaurant.

After that meeting Jones returned to his penthouse apartment only to find the door ajar and the entire place ransacked. He knew now that the real fight had begun. He felt confident that the intruders had not found anything of any importance that could be used against him or the Bank. He was confident because all documents of any significance were either in his attaché case attached to his left wrist or in the safe aboard his jet. No one knew about the safe as it had been installed in the plane as a wet bar, inside a metal case with a non-pick combination lock. He made a mental note to himself to check out who was working the building security that evening. More importantly, he wanted to check that person's bank balance over the next several days to see if any sizable deposits had been made. He wanted to find out which bank was behind the break-in of his penthouse.

Jones made a trip back to National Bank's headquarters in North Carolina to confer with their top executives about his latest information. They would need his input in order to formulate a new and exact strategy to go after the top prize. It was going to take some hard line negotiating, serious bluffing, outrageous lying, and lots of balls to pull this one off. However, in Jones' opinion, the Bank had just the man at the top they needed to carry out the Bank's role in its "reaching for the top" endeavor. The current CEO McNair had a military background, and he was smart, strong-willed, unwavering and very much a bulldog. Let the games begin.

Chapter 29
THE MERGER

After Mr. Jones's debriefing of his New York meeting, the National Bank decided to do an incredible thing. First they contacted Urban Bank & Trust, which was only looking to establish a price for their assets, and informed them they were submitting an official offer to buy their bank. They did not tell Urban Bank & Trust that they were going to submit a very low ball offer that would obviously be rejected, and most likely depress that bank's worth in the banking marketplace. It worked. Second, on the same day, they contacted Golden State Bank and told them they wanted to deal. They suggested they meet to structure a merger. Their offer to meet and talk was accepted.

Jones represented the Bank in the early meetings. He was tough, tenacious, indifferent, and he opposed most everything the other bank proposed. These types of meetings were off and on for several weeks. A couple of times Jones completely broke off the talks, and he made sure that he could not be reached at all by the other bank for weeks on end. After five months of this behavior, Golden State Bank walked away.

Once that happened, the National Bank's CEO immediately called for a full senior management meeting. All hands on deck. It was time to re-strategize to make sure this "plum" did not get away. The CEO had the number crunchers update the combined financials of the proposed merging banks. The numbers were absolutely stunning. In fact, they were spectacular. It was more than obvious what this deal could do for the Bank.

The consensus of the meeting was that the Bank had to do whatever it took to close the deal. They must see the merger through to its end, no matter what. That meant it was time to enact the attack dog mode.

Privately, the Bank's CEO and Mr. Jones met to discuss their new strategy. Very casually Jones said, "I think we need to divide and conquer on their demands. We should very slowly agree to their keeping the executive positions, while demanding the corporate headquarters be moved to North Carolina."

Harold McNair jumped up out of his chair and yelled, "The hell you say. We ain't buying that goddamn bank for some other goddamn fool to run. You got that, Mr. Jones? Jesus Christ! Whose goddamn side are you on anyway? For Pete's sake!"

Mr. Jones had never seen McNair so upset. This type of behavior was more becoming a Marine drill sergeant than a bank CEO. He knew he'd better respond with the right answer. Very calmly Jones suggested, "I would still recommend that we at least split the top two executive positions and bet real heavy on their chairman's declining health. If what we have been told about his personal condition, and what we have ascertained about his deep desire to make a deal now is anywhere close to being true, we can push him really, really hard to make the deal. Then we can make it right thirty days later, if you get my drift."

Harold McNair, who had regained his composure, sat down on the edge of his desk and spoke very softly, "Jones, you are a very bright kid. You have done a great job for our Bank over the years. My gut tells me that I should listen to you and let you call the shots on this bank merger deal." McNair continued, "So here's my decision. Go get the goddamn deal closed. Whatever it takes. Get it done."

McNair started to walk away, but stopped and turned to Jones and said, "Once we get this damn deal put to bed, I would like for you and Mary to come spend a weekend with Sara and me at Figure Eight Island. We all need a little R & R, and there's no better place to relax than Figure Eight. There are lots of real nice folks there, most are North Carolinians. It'll do both of us a lot of good. You'll have a great time, I guarantee it."

Jones gleefully responded, "My RSVP reads Invitation Accepted."

They shook hands and bade farewell.

Once the talks collapsed between these two banks, other banks tried to enter the fray. This just made everything more confusing, something Jones did not like at all. So he went into full attack dog mode. He attacked every other bank brave enough to raise its head. The harder the other banks pressed, the tougher Jones reacted. He attacked their management. He ridiculed their balance sheets. He exposed their reserve short falls. Jones took no prisoners. He was viscous. During the ensuing months he received several calls of encouragement from Harold McNair, which really lifted his spirits and gave him cause to continue. It got really nasty with a certain New York City based bank. Harry Peters at Treasury issued a warning to both banks to cut out the bullshit if they ever wanted Treasury to approve any subsequent deal. So Jones cooled down a bit, but he did not back off his position. He finally disposed of the feud with the New York bank, and dialed in again to the west coast bank. It took months of real down and dirty haggling before serious talks resumed between the two banks.

In early June 2000, the talks between these two banks were in high gear. A deal was getting closer by the day. Mr. Jones was making some very good moves for his bosses. Many of the stumbling block issues had been resolved and the attitude among the two banks was improving. Jones had convinced his side to agree to let Golden State Bank keep the name. He convinced his National Bank folks to let the other bank keep the chairman position as long as the CEO and bank headquarters moved east. Jones was still betting big time on the poor health of Golden State Bank's chairman.

Golden State Bank fought like hell to change the deal, but each time, as he had done so many times in the past, Jones threatened to break off the talks. The chairman of the other bank knew it was now or never for him. He was obsessed that the deal go through. So he acquiesced and agreed to meet with all the top executives of both banks in California in mid-July of 2000 to approve the documents for the merger.

Chapter 30
THE WEDDING WEEKEND

Jones checked his calendar for the date of a social event he and Mary had accepted some months ago. There it was, July 15, 2000. He had promised to attend if at all possible, depending on his work schedule. It was the wedding weekend for Melissa, Mary's friend and roommate from Dartmouth, a young woman from eastern North Carolina. She was drop-dead gorgeous as he recalled and an aspiring artist. He thought he remembered she had some type of medical problem. Maybe she was better now. The rehearsal dinner on Friday night would be held at the incredible Hess Collection Winery in Napa, California. It was to be followed the next evening by a 6:30 wedding ceremony in Sonoma at the Atkins Ranch, a working vineyard, outside and under the stars. No one in their right mind would want to miss all of that.

Jones decided he would be able to schedule his time in California so he could take care of his very important National Bank duties and attend the wedding parties as well. He knew that would make Mary very happy, and he was certain that he wanted to keep Mary happy. In fact, Jones was making a concentrated effort to go the extra mile. He went out of his way to be more considerate of Mary. They had only been dating for a little over a year, but Jones was developing strong feelings for this lovely young lady. *Well, it's about time I started loving somebody since I'm already forty-two years old*, he thought.

They were both very excited about the upcoming weekend. Mary was ecstatic that they were going to Melissa's wedding. She realized that Jones had done some magic tricks with his schedule to fit this wedding in just for her. She also thought she may know why. It was so important that she attend this wedding of her closest friend. Mary knew the situation and had prayed that she could spend this weekend with Melissa.

Jones made plans for them to arrive in San Francisco on Thursday morning. That way he had up to three o'clock on Friday to spend time with the Bank consultations to conclude the biggest deal of his life. This was shaping up to be one hell of a weekend, both business-wise and socially.

By 3:30 Friday afternoon, most all of the Bank merger documents had been reviewed and approved for the proper signatures when the official closing date arrived. There. He had taken care of all of the business de-tails. Now it was time to start the weekend. Jones rushed back to the very elegant Fairmont Hotel. He called out to Mary, "Are you ready to party down, Babe?"

Mary laughed aloud and said, "Change your clothes and call for the car while I re-pack our bags." By 4:15 they were on their way to Napa, ready for a great evening at the Hess Collection Winery rehearsal dinner.

The Hess Collection Winery was nothing short of spectacular. As the wedding party came strolling in, their mouths fell open and their eyes got big at the sheer awesomeness of this place. There were beautiful works of art expertly hung on every available wall. There were wide open and split level spaces everywhere with lots of glass. The shellacked hardwood floors glistened in the evening light. Everything was pristine and beautiful. The facility itself was a museum piece.

Then in walked Melissa Brown, the bride to be. She was stunning and elegant. She was bubbling with joy and anticipation. Her weekend had finally arrived. (This event had been planned for the same time and place last year, but it had to be rescheduled due to her illness.) This time she was going to see it through. You could see it in her face. Jones could not see one single indication that this lovely young woman was ill. Then a whole host of young and very handsome older folks began to trickle inside. What a lovely group of friends and relatives on both sides of the aisle. This was going to be very fine evening, and fine it was, indeed.

Jones distinctly remembered two things about that night. When he met Melissa's mother again, he knew immediately where Melissa's beauty came from. No doubt about that at all. Jones also thought Melissa's Dad's toast to his daughter was probably one of the best he had ever heard. He must have been right because when it was over, Melissa's father got a standing ovation. Wow!

It was this part of the toast that made Jones just about fall out of his seat:

Melissa was definitely high maintenance, and she had that reputation,
Hillary said it takes a village, but I'd say it's more like a nation!
As in a Nation Bank!"

Hell, his Bank's name was part of the toast! That was just too damn good.

Jones got up early the next day, smelled the warm summer air, grabbed some hot coffee, and decided to make a few phone calls. He checked with his bosses back east to make sure all was well with the merger process. All he got was great news, plus loads of accolades on what a fine job he had done. He made several other calls tying up loose ends here and there. He also received a tip on his answering machine that he had waited weeks to get. This information would definitely help him with the Bank deal.

Then he went in to wake up Mary. "Get up, you blonde goddess," he said as he handed her a cup of hot coffee. "It's time to collect our belongings and move over to Sonoma for tonight's festivities. If tonight is any better than last night, it will be overwhelming."

Mary yawned and stretched and moaned, "I'm not sure we can handle anything better than last night." With that she rolled out of bed and headed for the bathroom. While taking her shower, Mary began to think about if and when she might get married. She wondered if Jones would be her husband. She questioned if her wedding would be in an exciting place like Melissa's. She wanted to know if she was really in love, and if she was already getting serious feelings about Jones. How would she know, and how could she be sure.

"Hurry up, Babe," yelled Jones. "We gotta get going."

In Sonoma they went straight to the MacArthur Place and checked in. It was a exquisite, relatively new facility nestled in this small wine country town. Many other wedding party members were already there. They ran into some of Mary's and Melissa's old college buddies and joined them in the bar for drinks. The celebration had begun.

After a couple of cocktails, Jones and Mary went to their room to catch a quick nap before dressing for the evening festivities.

As Jones drove through the Atkins Ranch gate he could see all the white-clothed tables arranged on the grassy area in front of the stone house. There were grapevines for miles in every direction. It really was a working vineyard. There were lamps and outdoor heaters, if needed. Rows of chairs were lined up under a big oak tree for the actual wedding ceremony. Lots of formally dressed people, drinks in hand, milled about on the grounds. Jones mumbled aloud, "I think we're in the right place."

"You think?" Mary said, smiling.

By six o'clock everybody was in place. The wedding party, the guests, the pastor, the bartenders, the caterers, and the band were all there. Everyone was ready. It was an incredible gathering of so many special people. Someone or lots of someones had done a masterful job of pulling it all together. The flowers were exquisite. What a job. What organization. What a day.

At precisely 6:30 Melissa's father escorted her through the vineyard to stand beneath the old oak tree. Melissa's mother was seated just three feet away in the first row of chairs. The time had come. The guests took their seats and waited for the ceremony to begin. The pastor began to speak. It was a somber service, short but joyful, simple but beautiful. When

Amazing Grace was sung, there was not a dry eye anywhere. To top it all off, a double rainbow blessed the event.

Next came lots of drinks, and then more drinks. There was a photo booth, a cigar bar, and a port wine bar. An outrageous wild woman named Sugar Pie and her band cranked up the music, and everybody started dancing.

The caterers brought out the most delicious sea bass anyone could ask for, along with expertly prepared sides: salads, soups, breads, coffee, tea, milk, wine and champagne, and anything else one might ask for. It was all absolutely, undeniably delicious.

Soon the sun began to sink below the horizon. The air got still. The lamps were lit. The full moon rose in the night sky. There was a festive mood everywhere. It was nothing short of a truly magical evening. There was a Cinderella there who whispered to her mom and dad, "I don't want this to ever end!" One of her dreams had finally come true as she danced until midnight.

When Mary and Jones finally made it back to their room at MacArthur Place, they changed into some casual clothes, grabbed a bottle of wine, a couple of wine glasses, and went and sat by the pool. The full moon was still hanging high in the Sonoma Valley sky. After a few minutes of reliving the weekend, Mary said very quietly, "You think we'll ever have a weekend like this one, Jones?"

Jones sat up straight up in his chair and cracked a wide smile and asked, "Is that a proposal?"

"No, you crazy man. I was just thinking out loud."

"Pretty provocative thinking, I'd say."

"You didn't answer my question. Or do you need more time to think about it?"

"No. Wait. Yes. No. I mean I think so. Yes, I've thought about it."

"Talk about confusing. And you're in charge of Mergers and Acquisitions?"

They both laughed at that and the ice on a delicate topic had been broken. They knew their relationship had moved to another level that very night.

Jones and Mary were so glad they were there to witness and participate in such a warm and wonderful evening shared by such nice and friendly people. It was probably one of the best times they had ever shared together, and they both hoped not the last great time they would share. Jones was betting on that big time.

Melissa's wedding was a great omen for Mary and Jones. It helped unlock their feelings for each other, and that was a good thing.

Chapter 31
THE TRANSITION

In late 2000 the merger between the National Bank and the Golden State Bank was completed. It was one hell of a major deal that changed the dynamics of the entire banking industry. However, what was even more incredible than the deal that had been consummated, was Mr. Jones's ability to keep the safe deposit counterfeit money operation with his bank completely under wraps while the merger was being negotiated. He could do this because he knew which of the merging bank's branches were involved. He simply looked in EC's ledger book and made a list of each branch involved. Then with all of the nerve and gusto of Superman, Jones took it upon himself to contact the bank heads of all of these branches and convince them, under the threat of job loss or exposure to the Feds, to start sending the counterfeit bills to the Federal Reserve Burn Center. All one hundred and eighty branch managers did exactly what Jones instructed them to do. Every one of them, and never once was any of this discussed with anyone.

Several weeks later, the Golden State Bank chairman was retired (fired), and all the important executive positions were moved east. At Mr. Jones' suggestion, the board agreed to change the bank's name again to a more representative name, American Bank Corporation. Mr. Jones and his very hard-nosed CEO, Harold McNair, had taken the Bank to the pinnacle of the banking industry. They were now the American Bank Corporation, the biggest and largest bank in the USA. They had completed a major accomplishment, but why should they stop now. They kept on keeping on with one more purchase after another. "Greed goeth before the fall."

In 2001 two other leading banks in the state started talking. Soon the word was out and the date was set for a First State Bank and Winston Bank merger. Winston Corporation was the name of the merged company. However, many of the top executives who survived the acquisition were from the First State Bank. They brought with them a more lax and free-wheeling attitude toward banking. Later that proved to be a major problem for the bank.

The Bank did not get every deal it went after. Many other bank deals were done right under the Bank's nose.

The Bank sent Mr. Jones to Nashville, Tennessee, to check out an up and coming bank called the Fifth Third Bank. What Jones and his Bank did not know at the time was that the Fifth Third Bank was already in serious talks about merging with Suntrust Bank in Atlanta. Also, the Fifth Third Bank was well on its way to doing a deal with CCB in Durham, North Carolina. While Jones was snooping around town and asking a lot of questions, the Fifth Third Bank cut a deal with Suntrust Bank, who in turn slipped into North Carolina under the radar and plucked a major old line family bank called CCB headquartered in Durham, right out from under the Bank's nose. To summarize, before the Bank could make an offer for the Fifth Third Bank, the Fifth Third Bank had closed on a deal with Suntrust, who then sealed the deal with CCB. Two big fish had slipped away. It was quite a coup.

Then Sentry Bank merged with North American Bank from Canada, only to be swallowed up by Penn State Bank later. More fish that got away. Disappointed but not depressed, Jones decided to make the best of being in Tennessee.

Jones had already been thinking about the fact that he and Mary had not been anywhere special or had any private time since the wedding weekend. Maybe they could continue the conversation they had started at Melissa's wedding. He knew damn well that he'd had a tough nine months. He also knew that Mary had been working overtime with some very demanding clients. One of her clients was in the middle of an IPO. That took a lot of her time and energy. She just refused to pass her high dollar clients off to any other partners – and for good reason. First, she wanted to make sure her clients were treated properly. Second, she wanted to make sure they got the very best legal representation possible. Third, she wanted to make sure that she received payment for the legal services she provided. It had a lot to do with her desire to be self-sustaining and independent. Not a bad way to do business. Jones thought she deserved a break. He called Mary in New York and asked if she could catch a flight on Thursday to Knoxville to meet him for the weekend.

"Hell yes," was her answer. She was having a terrible week and wanted out.

Jones picked her up at the airport Thursday morning and they headed east.

When Mary got in the car, Jones said, "Do I ever have a surprise for you. I've heard about this deal for years. Now we're going to see what everybody has been raving about."

"What deal? Where are we going? Tell me?"

Jones had made arrangements for them to attend the International Storytelling Festival being held in Jonesborough, Tennessee, over the next three days. He had heard about this event for years and decided it was time for them to check it out. He thought Mary would really get a kick out of hearing all of those stories.

This annual event had been going on since 1973, and it just got better every year. The whole town got involved, opening their hearts to the 10,000 plus folks who attended every year. It was a phenomenal event that attracted thirty to forty of the very best storytellers from all parts of the world. Ten stages were set up under giant tents for the storytellers to tell their stories for audiences of up to 2,500 listeners. The tents were scattered all around town. The event was run like a finely tuned clock. Everything was scheduled right down to the minute.

186

Jones wanted to kill two birds with one stone on this trip. First, he wanted both of them to experience the Storytelling Festival to see if it lived up to its fabulous reputation. Secondly, he was anxious for them to slip away to this unique little hideaway in eastern Tennessee where he and Mary could have their much needed quiet time.

Maybe the best part was yet to happen. It was just about an hour's drive from the Storytelling event to Butler, Tennessee. This is where Mr. Jones had made their reservations for the weekend. He'd seen this unique place advertised in a banking magazine. He wanted to stay there because it had character and offered some serious interaction with other folks. He had also heard it belonged to a former, much older fraternity brother. It was at a convention-corporate retreat kind of a place called Sugar Hollow. A doctor from the Raleigh-Durham area had bought the 300 plus acre farm a few years back. He had spent a small fortune converting it into a rustic and charming facility. It included a horse barn that had been renovated into an incredibly handsome lodge with several suites. Individual cabins and full-size homes also accommodated guests. There was a commercial kitchen in the lodge that provided the food service for different events. The lodge had a bar, a great deck, and an unbelievable back porch for viewing the numerous deer and wild turkeys that showed up most mornings and evenings. There was also a corporate center for meetings, and an outdoor amphitheater for plays. The place had just about anything you might need for a weekend conference. It soon became a very busy place for weddings.

Marty, one of the caretakers for Sugar Hollow, was an amazing person. She did it all, from checking in visitors, to cleaning rooms, doing the cooking, feeding the deer, tending bar, and running errands. Hell, she'd even built her own house with her own two hands.

This particular weekend had for years been very special at Sugar Hollow. The doctor always invited an array of his friends and colleagues up for the Storytelling Festival. The mixture of folks was always interesting. They all had strong personalities and unique interests, but they still seemed to have a great deal in common, like eating lots of great food and drinking lots of wine and whiskey. There was a thread that ran through the group, whether it was their UNC pedigree, a DKE brother, a business affiliation, or an old army buddy connection. It was amazing how well they complemented each other. They never seemed to tire of hearing the same old stories, the ones they had been hearing for what seemed like centuries. It was a hell of a group, and one that spent a lot of time laughing, mostly at each other.

Jones and Mary checked in and were awarded the Appalachian Room in the Lodge. This suite had an outside entrance that opened onto the incredible back porch patio. The rooms all had names that reflected their decor. They were glad they booked a lodge room so they would be close to where they guessed the action would be each night. They could not believe how nice everyone was and how well accepted they were into this group of folks that obviously had known each other for many, many years. Jones and Mary felt right at home.

Soon after they arrived, a man came into the lobby and asked for everyone's attention. He was slightly older than Mr. Jones and Mary and appeared to have some type of vision impairment. He was upbeat and had a note of excitement in his voice when he said, "Welcome to Sugar Hollow. My friends call me Surry. I'm so glad all of you are here. Allow me to tell you what we have planned for you regarding tonight and early tomorrow morning. Tonight at 6:30 we are leaving for town to eat at this fabulous restaurant that serves real southern food, family style. It has a set menu, and you can eat all you want. But be forewarned to save room for some dessert."

Mary and Jones surmised he must be the doctor/owner. The doctor went on, "Tomorrow, if you want to go to the Storytelling Festival, you must be ready to board the van or bus by 8:30 or you will be left behind. So I suggest everyone catch a quick bite for breakfast, and be ready for a very exciting, but a very long day. We will stop in Johnson City on the way home and have dinner."

So far Jones and Mary had no objections.

On the ride into town and during dinner, Jones and Mary met several of the other guests. They were amazed at the many different places the guests lived. They came from as far away California, Oregon, and South Carolina. Then there were all of those folks from Raleigh; the Cobbs, the

Whedbees, and the Woods. It was a charming and varied group. Jones and Mary were delighted to be part of it.

For dinner, they went to a place called Shirley's Restaurant and was it ever country rustic. The staff was as friendly as anyone could ask for and the food – oh my goodness; fried chicken, mashed potatoes, string beans, corn on the cob, biscuits, fried fish, slaw, hush puppies, butter beans, ribs, and barbecue. Don't forget the sweet tea and the desserts like lemon meringue pie, chocolate custard pie, and apple pie with ice cream. Everything was so delicious, so tasty, and there was way too much of it.

When they got back to the Lodge, lots of the guests said their "good nights" and went off to bed. They wanted to be rested up for tomorrow. A few old timers had a night cap and then retired.

Next morning everybody made roll call on time, jumped on the bus, and off they went to the Storytelling Festival. What a day that turned out to be with stories and more stories. Some were funny, some sad, and some quite informative. Some were better than others, but they were all outstanding. Jones and Mary were overwhelmed from the very start. They had never seen anything like this before, and they were so glad they came. They had a blast.

What a day. It felt good just to get back on the bus and head back. As promised, they stopped at a steak house in Johnson City where most everyone had a cocktail or beer before feasting on some great steaks and fresh salads. Then they were back on the road to Sugar Hollow.

Back at the lodge there was some conversation about the storytellers, who had liked whom best, and about how much fun everyone had. But before long, everyone was heading to bed. It had been a long day.

The next day, Saturday, was more of the same. Most guests returned to hear more stories at the Festival. One or two avid football fans decided to remain at the lodge and watch the football game on the wide screen in the TV lounge. That night dinner was being catered at the lodge. When they all loaded the bus and started back to the lodge, the folks were still talking about their favorite storyteller and why. Most of the guys were thinking about a nice cold beer or a bourbon and water, maybe two, and soon they hoped.

When the bus arrived at the lodge, everyone went to get refreshed and ready for cocktails before dinner. Jones and Mary walked into the lobby and ran smack dab into Melissa's parents. This was too much for them to understand. Mary exclaimed, "What are you two doing here? Who do you know? Don't take this the wrong way, we're glad to see you, but please explain how in the hell you happen to be here."

Melissa's mother, Sandra, answered, "Mary, I can't tell you how thrilled I am to see you and Jones," as she hugged them. "There is actually a fairly logical explanation. During their freshman year at Chapel Hill, Melissa's Dad and Surry were roommates and fraternity brothers. We've been coming to Sugar Hollow for the Storytelling Festival for years."

Then there was more hugging and handshaking and catching up, not to mention all the news about Melissa. It was difficult to determine which couple was more surprised to see the other. This was a divine reunion for sure. It had been a little over a year since they had seen each other at Melissa's wedding. Pretty soon there was lots of conversation, many drinks being poured, and a very busy kitchen in total disarray. This was going to be one fine evening. Jones could feel it in his bones. Mary had decided she must be in heaven.

At dinner, Jones and Mary sat across the table from the doctor from Durham and his lady friend. When Jones was formally introduced to Surry, Jones gave Surry the secret DKE handshake. Surry let out a delighted yell. "Jones, my brother," the doctor exclaimed, "What brought you to Tennessee, and more specifically, to Sugar Hollow?"

Jones said, "It all started with a trip to Nashville to investigate the possible acquisition of the Fifth Third Bank in Nashville. Unfortunately for my bank, that investigation ended abruptly because the Fifth Third Bank, via its merger with SunTrust Bank, was buying CCB." The doctor could barely contain his laughter.

What's so damn funny about that? Jones wondered.

Then Surry told Jones, "I was born and reared in a home in Durham across the street from the family that was behind CCB. That family was best friends with my family. I've watched that bank grow all these years."

What a small world it really is when you think about it, Jones thought.

"Doc, to further answer your question," Jones added, "I saw a Sugar Hollow ad in a corporate magazine that came to the Bank, and I decided to call for a reservation. I had also heard that an older DKE brother owned the place. The rest is history, as they say."

After dinner, Jones and Mary had another surprise coming. All those guys there from Portland, Oregon, were in a band known as the Sons of Our Fathers, and played regularly at a club in downtown Portland. They had gone to the trouble and expense of bringing their instruments to Sugar Hollow. They were going to entertain the guests until everybody got sleepy and went to bed. They played and sang some bluegrass, country, pop, a little jazz, and even some gospel. Naturally, the band was incredibly good and very smooth. Some guests were taking photos, and others were videoing the group. They kept everyone entertained until well after midnight and even sold a few CDs. It was more than anyone had expected and then some. Jones and Mary were overwhelmed. When had they ever had such a great time with so many warm, interesting people. Sugar Hollow had turned out to be just what Jones had hoped and a truly sweet experience for each of them.

Before going to bed, Mary suggested they sit on the back porch overlooking the meadow. On the way they grabbed a couple of cups of coffee from the kitchen. The night was quiet and very dark. They wouldn't be seeing any wild turkeys or deer tonight, even if there were some grazing close by.

"You know, a lot of the couples we've met here have been married longer than we've been alive," Jones remarked. "That's amazing to me. Don't you think it's amazing?"

"Hell, my parents have been married that long or longer. Some couples just work harder to make their relationships work. Most honest married people will tell you that it takes hard work and understanding to make a marriage last," Mary said.

"You think our relationship could last that long? I mean, if we had one."

"I don't think our relationship could last forty plus years if we weren't married."

"Wait a minute. You know what I mean, don't you?"

"Yes I do, but did you understand my terms?" she said.

"Should I say I do?"

"Let's talk about something else."

"Let's go do something else."

They went back inside and jumped into bed.

In the morning, Jones and Mary were the first ones in the kitchen. They were still hyped from the night before as they made the coffee, put the pastries in the oven, and poured some juice. They were ready to chat up all of these people one more time before they left. This weekend had been so fantastic. They did not want to leave, but they knew they had to get back to work.

Parting is such sweet sorrow. Mr. Jones did not get his bank deal, but he and Mary had made some great new friends.

Chapter 32
THE SORROW

In August 2001, Jones got a call from his grandmother, Brenda Cain. She was sobbing. Jones calmly asked her what was wrong.

Between sobs, his grandmother managed to get out her news. "Your grandfather EC has died. He was eighty-four."

It made no sense to Jones why his grandmother should be so distraught about this man's death. EC had violated so many people, so many laws, and done it so many times – he certainly would not be getting any sympathy from Jones. He deserved all the bad things that had come his way, and more. In fact, because of the many terrible things EC had done, Jones had always felt that EC had gotten off way too easy. He marveled that someone as evil as EC was, could have even lived as long as he did.

Jones asked his grandmother, "Do you want to attend the funeral? If you want to go, I will send the plane to Tennessee for you. I have no plans of attending any service for EC, but I'll make all the arrangements for you to go, if that's what you want."

Brenda, still crying, said, "Jones, thank you so much for your offer, but I just wouldn't feel comfortable attending EC's funeral under the circumstances. Plus I wouldn't know anyone there. So I'll just stay right here and have my own little mourning session."

It was just fine with Jones that Brenda declined his offer. He didn't think EC deserved a decent funeral, and he was happy not to be spending any effort sending her.

Jones had always wondered why Brenda had never remarried after EC divorced her and ran her out of town. She was an attractive lady and had grown into a very loving and socially graceful woman. She had worked her way into a very good management position in the textile industry. She had a nice home in Oak Ridge and travelled abroad most every year. He did remember that his Mom had once told him that his grandmother had a traveling companion, but that was about all he'd ever heard about a man being in her life. Jones did not know if she ever had another boyfriend after divorcing EC. He thought he probably should have paid more attention to his grandmother. He regretted that he had not taken the time to see that she was doing okay. After his mother was killed, he was just too busy to spend any time with Brenda. He really felt sad about that now.

What Jones did not know about Brenda, now about eighty years old, was that she had sold her home in Oak Ridge and moved into an independent living facility. She enjoyed her life there and loved socializing with the other residents. Overall she was in pretty good health and had stayed fairly active as she grew older, which had been good for her. Her later years had been fairly kind to her, but there was not a day that went by when she didn't think about and miss her daughter Anna, Jones's mother. Jones would have liked knowing that.

Jones had spent years trying to erase his horrible mental images of how his Mom had been killed. It was such a terrible way for her to die. He refused to think about that tragic day at the bank. In fact, he was adamantly opposed to talking about that day and his mother's death. Many of his friends had suggested that he get professional assistance to help him handle this trauma, but he chose from the get-go to work through it on his own – and he did. He later learned that it was a great deal more difficult than he'd imagined, and it took longer than he thought. Through all this, Jones had a very deep, warm spot in his heart set aside for his Mother. He loved and missed her terribly.

According to EC's daughter Elaine, EC was buried at the Memorial Gardens cemetery just outside of New Ferry. His grave site was next to Edward (Will) Cain, Jr.'s plot who died in 1984. Although EC had outlived many of his friends and business associates, there was still a good crowd in attendance for his funeral – more than expected. Some came to pay their respects. Others came out of curiosity. A few came to make sure he was, in fact, dead. EC was gone for sure, but he had left an amazing trail that had affected so many different people. Some in good ways, others, not so much.

––––––

On September 11, 2001, the world fell apart in New York City and in Washington, DC, as hijacked planes crashed into the Twin Towers of the World Trade Center and into the Pentagon. Thousands of innocent people, mostly Americans, were killed as the two buildings caught fire and later came tumbling down in horrendous bursts of flame and twisted metal and concrete. It was the most horrible thing that had hit this country since World War II.

These terrorist acts spread fear from the east coast to the west coast. The entire country shut down as millions of Americans watched these horrible developments unfold on TV. Flights were grounded and the airports closed. All in-flight planes were forced to land. Trains stopped running. Thousands of businesses closed. Worldwide, the US military went on full scale alert. The nation was under attack. The US had been blindsided. It was like Pearl Harbor all over again, maybe even worse.

First responders in both cities rushed to try to save the thousands of people that so desperately needed help. Courageous acts of heroism occurred everywhere. Americans were standing up everywhere. Aboard the hijacked plane, United Flight 93, passengers stood up and yelled, "let's roll." These Americans forced the plane to crash in a Pennsylvania field rather than in DC. President Bush, on Air Force One, was taken to a safe haven in the Midwest.

People all across the country were reaching out to family members to see if they were okay and safe. It was no different for Jones and Mary. Jones was safely tucked away in his apartment in New York's Upper East Side. Mary, thankfully, had not yet left for work when the planes struck. Jones told her to come to his place for the weekend. She said she would once she was satisfied that all of her family members were safe, and thankfully they were.

Both Mary and Jones lost close friends and business associates that weekend; so many of the victims were lawyers, bankers, and financial people. So many people suffered tragic losses that day. The wound to the U.S. was deep and lasting.

Mary and Jones could not stop talking about the first responders; the firemen, the policemen, the EMTs and ordinary citizens. What courage. What bravery. What unbelievable displays of intestinal fortitude. What amazing acts of heroism. They wondered what the mindset was of those men and women as they ran into those buildings, those burning infernos. What were they thinking knowing each step they took up those stairways into the towers diminished their own chances of getting out alive. Talk about total unselfishness. These vicious and cowardly terrorist attacks would never be forgotten, or forgiven. All American people were demanding some serious payback to the bastards that did this to their country and to their brothers and sisters. Rightly or wrongly, payback came in the form of "Shock and Awe" with the war in Iraq.

In December of the same year, Jones was spending the holidays with Mary. They were celebrating Christmas in New York. On the day after Christmas they got the call from California. The one they both knew they'd get one day. It was more sad news. God needed an incredible, one of a kind, abstract artist in Heaven. So He called Melissa, "that bright star in the palm of the sky," home. What He got was exactly what He had asked for, and much, much more.

Jones and Mary flew to San Francisco and attended Melissa's memorial service. It was held at the very lovely, quaint San Francisco Swedenborgian Church. Inside there was standing room only, and outside an overflow crowd of friends. Hundreds of Melissa's friends, family, and associates had come from all around the country to honor and celebrate her life. They honored Melissa with dignity and grace. It was an amazing service. The world had lost a remarkable young woman. She had touched a lot of lives. Mary had lost her best friend.

Although saddened, Jones and Mary celebrated New Year's Eve in New York at his apartment on the Upper East Side with a small gathering of their friends and family. It was a quiet but nice evening as they watched the celebrations from around the world on TV. Most of their guests left just after midnight. It was a time for reflection. The 9/11 terrorist attack had left its mark on Americans everywhere.

Chapter 33
THE HOME STRETCH

It had been a very busy and exciting year for both Mary and Jones. With the emerging financial crisis, they both had much more work and pressure than usual. Mary's legal clients were more demanding because so many of them were up to their necks in what was currently going on in the financial world. Some were seeing signs of serious trouble and desperately needed legal advice about what to do and how to proceed in the coming year.

Mary's billings had increased with her workload. She was raking in some serious money, and that made a lot of difference to her. She did not exactly know where she stood with Jones as far as the long term went, but then again, she did not know if he was what she wanted long term. So it was important to her that she build a lasting and successful career through her legal practice so she would always be self-sufficient and financially independent. She was feeling better about that now.

Because they had been dating for over three years, Jones, on the other hand, thought it was a foregone conclusion. He assumed that when things settled down in a few years, the time would be right for him to ask Mary if she might be ready to settle down and marry him. His heart told him she would probably agree – that is if nothing intervened in the interim, and if the next few years did not become so many that they were almost middle-aged.

Over the next couple of years, Jones spent a lot of time in New York. He was there not only because of his banking business, but mainly because he wanted to spend more time with Mary, and he did, after all, have a penthouse there. With all the financial crises that seemed to pop up every other day, Jones was expected to attend meeting after meeting for the Bank in the Big Apple almost every week. This arrangement suited them both. At least Jones found out about Mary's gourmet cooking expertise. Wow, was she ever a great cook.

In 2003, Mary and Jones got on a serious culture kick and began to attend art museums, Broadway plays, concerts, and lectures. Almost once a week for many months in a row, they went somewhere to see or hear some cultural event. That usually meant a very fine dining experience as well. There was no better place than New York City to enjoy all of that. In the fall they went to see the World Series, only to watch the New York Yankees lose to the Florida Marlins in six games. How disappointing, especially for Jones, a lifetime Yankees fan. As a child he used to watch the Yankees play in spring training camp in Florida.

Jones decided that he and Mary should spend more time in the Caymans and make use of the villa he had purchased there. The one she had furnished so elegantly, yet so simply. They agreed to allocate more of their time to being there. Now they just had to figure out a time that would be suitable for both of them to take several weeks off from their demanding schedules.

As the relationship between Jones and Mary continued to develop, their bond became stronger and stronger. Realizing this, Jones began a conversation with himself about if and when he should come clean and tell Mary the truth about his past with the counterfeit money scam. With the upheaval in the banking industry growing, he was certain he'd rather Mary hear the potentially bad news from him than find out about it in the media. He wondered if he should tell her where he came from and exactly who he was as a person. He was having a difficult time deciding how much he should tell Mary about his position at the Bank. He wasn't sure he needed to go into detail with her about the counterfeit money. He wasn't sure Mary would understand his justification for doing all he did relative to the bogus money and the Federal Reserve's Burn Program. He thought being a lawyer might cloud her understanding. Would she buy into the idea that he had done most of the illegal stuff for his Mom. Probably not. *No need to insult her intelligence. May as well tell her the truth.*

These thoughts were constantly bouncing around in his mind. He knew he had to figure out what he would be comfortable sharing with Mary. He worried about how much of this information would be enough. Could he get by keeping some of the really bad stuff to himself?

He was about to find out.

The time finally came when Jones and Mary could get away together and head for the Caymans. Jones knew there would be plenty of opportunity while they were there for them to talk. He also knew there would probably never be a better time or place to discuss his very personal background details with Mary. They could talk about them on the beach, on the sailboat, at dinner, and even in bed. They would have plenty of time and privacy to discuss everything. Jones thought Mary had the right to know about him, but not necessarily everything there *was* to know. Jones was starting to feel better about these looming conversations.

Once Mary and Jones arrived in the Caymans and got settled into his lovely villa, they went shopping for groceries, stocked up on their favorite libations, and picked up some fresh flowers. As soon as they returned home they started making dinner reservations for most every night of the week. They were set to experience some great island cuisine in the coming days. Now they were ready to relax, rest, and enjoy doing nothing at all.

After they had been there a few days and while they were taking a morning walk on the beach, enjoying the sun and the cool breeze, he broached the subject. "Mary, have you ever wondered where I came from or what I was like as a child? Would you like to hear some things about the darker side of my life?"

"I figured you'd tell me one day, whenever you got ready," Mary replied. "I'd love to hear every single detail you want me to know about your life. Anything you want to share, I'd like to hear it."

Mary was making it easy for Jones. She started by telling Jones some things about her earlier years. "My sister and I grew up in Summit, New

Jersey, where we attended the City Day School. Our parents shipped us off to prep school when we reached high school age. I went to Phillips Academy in Andover, Massachusetts, north of Boston. My sister went to Madeira in Washington. After graduating from Andover, I went to Dartmouth College. After graduation I took a year off and travelled around the country before I enrolled in Yale law School. Now you know all my secrets."

"I doubt that. Talk about being over-educated. No wonder you're so damn smart. That's an unbelievable CV. How'd you like Andover?"

"It was tough academically, but it was a great place to go to high school. The campus was a miniature Chapel Hill, like the 'northern part of heaven.' There were lots of Federal style brick buildings for classrooms and dorms nestled among elegant looking trees. The town was like a small college town. Most of the students really loved Andover. Hell, George W. Bush and John Kennedy, Jr. went there. Need I say more?"

"I bet you graduated at the top of your class."

"Not even close to the top."

The stage had been set, and now it was time to talk about Jones' past. Over the next several days there were a lot of times when Mary just listened while Jones told her in detail about his childhood, his teenage years, and his high school and college days. She listened intently as if she were committing everything he said to memory. They talked about his past as they walked on the beach and over dinner. When they went sailing, their conversation took a break because Jones was busy handling the sails and because the wind noise made talking difficult, but he certainly impressed Mary with his nautical skills.

They found that conversations about the more serious aspects of his past were easier when they were in bed. The night Jones told Mary about his mother, Mary had a hard time holding back her tears. She felt such compassion for him. How was he able to survive such tragic experiences. She just wanted to hold him close until they fell asleep.

About a week later while they were sitting in a beachside bar enjoying rum and punch drinks, Jones brought up the touchy subject of the Bank and how and why he became involved with it. After his second drink, Jones was getting a little loose. He began to tell Mary why he joined the Bank.

Mary jumped in. "I don't think revenge is a justifiable motive for doing anything. It usually comes back to bite you in the ass."

Jones, slightly annoyed, said, "Please wait until you've heard all of the evidence, counselor, before you pass judgment!"

Mary, amused, jumped off of her stool, grabbed him by the arm, and said, "Let's go finish this conversation in bed."

The next morning over breakfast there were lots of questions and answers exchanged about all that Jones had revealed of his past. After a couple of hours of give and take, he was satisfied that Mary had been told enough, but not all, about his background. Jones told Mary how the Bank was involved with the counterfeit money early on. He didn't tell her about the safe deposit boxes filled with bogus bills and how much they contributed to his income over and above his bank salary. Nor did he tell her about his end game plan. That would have to wait until another time. The good news was she seemed to take it all in stride, and she showed no detectable signs of any diminished feelings for him because of what she had learned. Actually, the vibes Jones was getting from Mary made him feel their relationship had become even stronger. The next several days were most enjoyable for both of them.

From their base in the villa, they decided to do some exploring. They made several excursions to other islands, and then they got very adventurous and traveled to South America. First they spent a weekend in Rio. They both loved the carnival-like atmosphere everywhere they went. Jones could not get over the incredible number of gorgeous women he saw everywhere. He had to be reminded a couple of times that he already had a date. Smartly, he resumed his gentlemanly behavior.

Neither of them spoke fluent Spanish or Portuguese, but that did not keep them from enjoying an elegant dining experience at the Olympe restaurant. The South American wine selection was outstanding. What surprised and upset both of them was the desperate and ubiquitous poverty they saw.

They spent a great weekend in Buenos Aires where they discovered the La Cabrera. They swore they had the finest steak there they had ever eaten anywhere. This city was one of their favorites; cleaner, fresher, and more urban. It fit their personalities better. Mary did not want to leave. She was fascinated by the Gauchos they saw every day.

One morning Mary woke Jones up with a great idea. "I've made us reservations for a four day weekend at Dos Lunas."

Yawning, Jones asked, "What the hell is Dos Lunas? "

Mary responded with a twinkle in her eyes, "It's an estancia, a 3,000 acre cattle ranch, in Córdoba. We've got to go. We can ride horses, help brand cattle, participate in a barbecue, and rest. It'll be so exciting."

Mr. Jones jumped out of bed headed toward the bathroom and shouted, "By all means, let's pack up now and hit the road."

"You're too romantic," she said as she threw him a kiss.

They had a fantastic time at Dos Lunas and neither of them wanted to leave. They also journeyed to Caracas, where they found the La Isabella in an old colonial house, and fell in love with the chef, not to mention his entrees. Their love of every type of cuisine kept them searching for the next best thing and led them to many delightful discoveries in the process.

The night before they were scheduled to leave, Mary perked up and asked, "Can't we stay one more day and night, please?"

Jones answered jokingly, "Yes, but I'm ready to leave."

Mary declared, "We need to go back one more time for one more dinner at La Isabella."

They stayed over another night and dined again with their new best friend, the chef. He prepared a seafood combination dish just for them that included every type of fresh seafood imaginable. They'd be talking about that dining experience for years to come.

They had caught the travel bug and were spreading their wings.

Later they spent a weekend on a bareboat cruise out of Cancun. Jones got a great charge out of this sailing adventure. He took care of all of the sailing chores himself. Mary handled the cuisine. She not only liked the intimacy of it all, she instigated most of it. Like the skinny dipping and the lovemaking on the beach at night. Jones loved spooning with her in the hammock.

The following week, out of nowhere, Jones surprised Mary by taking her to Paris for her birthday. This was the big "40" for Mary.

The very first morning in Paris, Mary was up and dressed at sunrise and woke Jones up saying, "Get up, sleepy head. It's time to go to the Eiffel Tower. I've wanted to do this my whole life. I'm going to send everyone I know in the whole world an Eiffel Tower postcard."

"I'll take a quick shower, dress and meet you in the dining room in twenty minutes. Order me some coffee and a croissant. Maybe two. I'm hungry."

Mary nodded and said, "I'll be waiting. Hurry up, please."

In the City of Lights they indulged in fabulous food in the most elegant dining rooms in the city. Then they were off on a trip to the Louvre. The next day they took the train to Normandy. What they saw there made an impression that would last their lifetimes.

On their last evening in France, Jones told Mary, "We're going to Rome tomorrow so you can toss some coins in the Trevi Fountain and make a wish."

Mary said, "Great. I'll make a wish about us, you and me, and tomorrow."

"Somehow, I knew you'd say that."

After an overnight in Rome, they flew back to New York. Hell, they needed a vacation to get some rest before they went back to work. Jones' bank account needed some well-deserved rest as well.

They spent a quiet weekend doing absolutely nothing. Both knew that come Monday they each had a great number of issues to handle. They'd had a wonderful time in their travels and with each other, but now it was time to get back to work and to get serious.

Chapter 34
THE TURNING POINT

In the first two or three years of the 21st century, things were beginning to change in the banking industry. Actually, things were changing across all financial markets. Some peripheral lenders had started offering home loans to low income or even no income borrowers. These loans were extremely high risk, and they took advantage of people who could not afford conventional financing. The fees and interest factors were excessive, resulting in early refinancing or even foreclosure against these unqualified borrowers. It was the beginning of some very serious predatory lending practices by these lenders. Why did they do this? They did it because it was so very profitable, plain and simple.

It was so profitable that many regular mortgage companies and mortgage brokers decided to get involved. This was a new way of making mortgage loans to people who had previously been excluded from the realm of home ownership. By 2005 these new loans were popping up everywhere.

Over his years with the Bank, Jones worked very hard, and he played hard. He had never failed to keep an ear close to the ground as to what was going on in the banking industry and more specifically, with his Bank. Because of his position with the Bank, he had access to information available only to Bank upper senior management. He got his information either through direct contact with top bank officials, in weekly meetings, or via internal memos. So in a word, Jones knew what the hell was going on.

He had heard the concerns, the cautious conversations, and the criticism of this new subprime mortgage phenomenon sweeping through the financial markets countrywide. He had also heard how enormously profitable these new financial instruments had become, but Jones had his own ideas about them.

What he did not yet fully realize was that because of his position at the Bank and what he had done for the Bank over the past few years, he was now personally recognized as a major force in the banking industry, by both his banking rivals and by the Administration. Some of his competitors feared him. Others wished he'd retire. Jones had unintentionally managed to reach the radar screens of way too many potential enemies. One group actually ordered surveillance on him, both audio and visual. What was their end game. Time would probably tell.

Jones decided it was time to do some banking on his own. He started selling his stocks, a thousand shares of this and a thousand shares of that. He had the funds deposited into his checking account. He did this over the next several months. His actions were not simply based on his intuition. They were also based on an inside tip from the Federal Reserve.

What Jones knew was based on some highly secretive snooping he conducted over a several month period. Thanks to an inside tip, he had uncovered a Bank computer file that listed many of the top Bank executives' Bank stock holdings. It also listed the Bank's top 25 largest shareholders. When he saw that most of these shareholders were dumping their Bank stocks, it caught his attention. This was some serious selling of his Bank's stock by insiders, and it didn't take a rocket scientist to figure out what was going on. Mr. Jones knew it was time to divest, not invest. It was time for him to get liquid, and the sooner the better.

After about nine months of selling small blocks of his stocks, he had built up some serious balances in his bank accounts. He did not want these large bank balances to alert any inquirers, so he began systematically withdrawing a few thousand dollars each week from the different branches he frequented around the country. Then he would wire these funds to his offshore account in the Caymans. He had set up this account on one of his many vacation trips to the islands with Mary. Maybe he was thinking ahead. Yes, he was thinking ahead, and he had made up his mind.

Over the last several years bank lobbyists had been able to coerce or bribe enough congressmen to reduce the bank loan regulations. The consensus thinking on this was that it all started when President Bill Clinton twisted the arms of enough congressmen to repeal the Glass-Stegall Banking Act. That made it extremely easy for most anyone seeking a loan, qualified or not, to purchase a car or home.

The loans were there for the asking, and ask they did. Millions of Americans bought houses and cars as if there was no tomorrow. People who could not afford to buy a motorcycle were buying Mercedes. People, who could not afford a double-wide mobile home, were buying mansions. This was happening all across the nation. Financial companies were actually running ads on TV, radio, in print, and online that said, "No Job, No Money, No Credit, No Problem." Folks were signing up by the thousands for these easy to get loans, knowing full well they had absolutely no way of paying the money back.

So in the booming housing industry these sub-prime mortgages were beginning to add up. The brainiacs at the non-banks on Wall Street began bundling and packaging these troubling financial instruments and selling them to unsuspecting investors worldwide. They were mortgage-backed assets and insured financial instruments. What could be better than that. The Wall Street firms were selling them like hot cakes, and the securities rating agencies went along to get along. They were all making millions, and the bubble began to grow.

The first warning came in 2007 from Ms. Bran at the FDIC. Few people at the other government agencies agreed with her concerns, and they did not heed her advice. So the Monopoly game continued.

Mr. Jones began to hear some reports that deeply concerned him and the top guys at the Bank. He phoned a friend at the Fed, as well as a friend at Treasury and expressed his concerns, but he received strong denials that anything was wrong with the banking industry's financial health.

Maybe it was because this new product was mostly being marketed by non-banks. Both the Treasury and Fed heads continued to publicly assure everyone that all was well. All the players just kept on doing what they were doing and piling up the profits. Jones knew two things for sure. One, if the government said no, the correct answer had to be yes. Two, that it would not take long before regular banks and other financial institutions jumped on this new profit-making scheme; it was just too damn good to leave alone.

Conversations began to surface among some concerned regulatory officials. They began to ask questions about the capital reserve requirements that the Federal Reserve Bank imposed on all real banks. The Feds were not sure the requirements were high enough. They worried that lobbyists had convinced Congress to dilute the regulations to the extent that, if a financial crisis did occur, the banks and the US financial system might not survive. Many people thought so. These concerned souls knew that if something went wrong, the deal was so pervasive that it would bring down a variety of companies, including investment houses, non-banks, real banks, securities firms, insurance companies, and bond holders. They knew it could be catastrophic.

Bad news about these mortgage-backed securities started to surface only a couple of years after these financial instruments hit the market. Investor losses began to occur as more and more of the mortgage holders defaulted on their high risk loans. This was not a surprise.

One day the Federal Reserve got a call from Bear Sterns, a Wall Street investment company that had sold large numbers of these asset-based financial instruments. They needed a seriously large loan to keep their doors open. It was a secret and the Feds wanted to keep it that way. They asked the New York Federal Reserve Bank to secretly help arrange the financing to save this deeply troubled company from collapse. Ted Gomer, the New York Fed chairman, was right in the thick of things. They tried desperately to make it work, but they could not save the firm, even with an emergency loan.

What a dose of bad news for Harry Peters at Treasury. Something had to be done now. They simply could not let this company go broke and fail. The obvious answer was to get another solvent company to buy and absorb Bear Sterns. They found a taker in J P Morgan, and what a deal that company received.

By now the word about Bear Sterns was on the street. Bear Sterns was just "too big to fail." This was a statement that would be repeated over and over again in the coming months. The question became could a financial downturn be avoided. Systemic cracks in the banking industry were showing up in many other places.

Bill Baker, Harry Peters, and Ted Gomer met continually, trying to determine ways to avert a meltdown and to solicit financial assistance from other government agencies like the FDIC. They also asked for private sector aid. They had to find a way to get rid of all those toxic assets. Finding an entity they could either get or force to assume them, or to whom they could sell them, became a very difficult proposition.

One day out of the blue, Jones got a very strange call from the head of a major California subprime mortgage company. The mortgage company president asked Jones, "Can you meet me this afternoon at Union Square Cafe around six pm?"

"What are we going to talk about?" Jones wanted to know.

The caller replied, "To see if your American Bank Corporation would like to buy my mortgage company. I thought it might be timely if we discussed some type of merger or outright sale. I think it would be a perfect match."

Jones sighed heavily and said, "Bring current, audited financials. Also, I must have an audited updated balance sheet along with an Executive Summary. Most important, I need a written proposal outlining exactly what you will agree to in price and terms, signed by you. Don't bring any 'cooked books' type of bullshit or the game's over. Understood?"

The mortgage guy eagerly agreed. "Of course, I understand. I would not even consider trying to bullshit you or your Bank. I'll bring all the documents you asked for and I'll see you at six."

How fortuitous, Mr. Jones thought.

The two men met privately. They had a couple of drinks, exchanged some ideas, and threw out some numbers. Jones stood up, ready to leave, and said, "I'll agree to present the possible acquisition deal to the right people with the Bank. However, I want you to know up front that I don't like you, I don't like your deal, but I will see to it that my folks take a look at what you are proposing. As you know, there are no guarantees. I'll get back with you in two weeks."

The mortgage company president was ecstatic, and he had a hard time hiding his delight in what Jones had just said. "Mr. Jones, I really appreciate your time and candor. I've never found it necessary to like someone in order to do a deal. So let's all move forward in good faith and see what happens. Thanks for meeting with me."

The men shook hands and went their separate ways.

Jones was very adept at recognizing an opportunity when he saw one. He would spend some serious time on this project for sure.

The following week, Jones got another call from his friend at the Fed who told him, "Jones, I've got more bad news. Urban Bank & Trust had to have a bailout loan or it would have folded. The Fed didn't have a choice but to pony up millions of dollars just to save Urban Bank & Trust. Again, the word came down, it was the 'too big to fail' Can you believe that shit?"

Jones, in shock, said, "What the hell is going on? What's the problem with the big banks? How can we stop this madness?"

His friend at the Fed said, "Doesn't look like anyone around here has the slightest clue about how to correct this mounting financial problem. Nobody here knows shit!"

"Please keep me posted about any new developments, good or bad," Jones said.

"Roger, will do."

Bill, Ted, Harry, and even Sheila, the head of the FDIC, were wringing their hands in desperation. Out of all of this desperation, the Troubled Assets Relief Program (TARP) was born. The program was designed to provide money to purchase hundreds of billions of dollars of toxic assets from the troubled banks, thereby freeing the burdened financial companies so they could continue operating. Additionally, the top tier banks were called in and told they would have to take the money the Fed was offering, whether they thought they needed it or not. Some of the larger banks that did not need the money objected, but were finally convinced by Harry Peters to take the money. The smaller banks got very limited amounts of this money. This was not really a surprise.

The reasoning behind insisting that all banks must come forth and receive some amount of "bail out" money, regardless of their individual needs, came from Bill Baker at the Federal Reserve Bank. He wanted to make sure that all banks participated so that the more troubled banks would not be singled out and damaged. Harry Peters went along with this idea, but he fully realized there were few secrets in the banking industry, especially news about any bank that had fallen on hard times.

The top tier banks yelled and screamed about not needing the money, while they gleefully accepted hundreds of millions of dollars that they stashed in their vaults. Jointly, they decided they would not take any risks with this new found cash, so they decided to buy government bonds and reap the less than illustrious interest being paid on those bonds. The banks refused to put the money into play in the economy in the form of loans to qualified borrowers as the Feds had hoped they would do in an effort to jump start a failing market. The banks thought that was just too risky.

The major mistake the Feds made with TARP was not requiring the receiving banks to invest that money into the struggling economy. The country paid a heavy, heavy price for the Feds' lax judgment with a multitude of their policy decisions.

Chapter 35
THE DOWNFALL

Then the other shoe dropped. The proposed deal to save Lehman Brothers by helping Barclays assume ownership of the failing entity fell apart. The Feds ran out of time, and in late 2008 Lehman Brothers collapsed and went out of business. There was hell to pay. Investors were screaming about why Lehman Brothers was not "too big to fail." The financial crisis had begun in earnest. The US financial system was under full assault.

Early one Tuesday morning, Mr. Jones's phone woke him up. It was Kurt Lane, the new American Bank Corporation CEO, who had replaced Harold McNair when he retired from the Bank. Jones jumped out of bed, grabbed his phone, and ran to the kitchen so he could make coffee.

"Good Morning, sir. What can I do for you today?" Jones said.

Lane responded abruptly, "Meet me today at the Federal Reserve Building at thirty-three Liberty Street at one p.m. sharp. We're going to meet with Bill Baker, Ted Gomer, and Harry Peters. They're going to explain exactly what the hell is going on. Be there on time."

Jones chuckled to himself and said, "I'm going on the record right now as saying they don't have a frigging clue about what's going on with this financial collapse. I'll be there at one."

Mr. Jones accompanied the American Bank Corporation's new CEO to this high level meeting in New York with the Treasury and the Federal Reserve. They got a firsthand look at how these decisions were being made. One of the biggest shocks of Jones' life was when he heard Harry Peters instruct Ted Gomer to make arrangements to save NIG, the largest insurance underwriter in the US which was in major financial trouble. NIG needed $125 billion in order to survive. There were no objections. Peters just told Gomer to do it, and it happened. Mr. Jones and Kurt Lane were dumbfounded. It was plain to see that the US financial structure was crumbling, and solutions were becoming very difficult and quite expensive to find.

For the first forty-five minutes of the meeting, Harry Peters and Bill Baker explained in detail how the TARP deal was going to save the country's financial system. To Lane and Jones it seemed as if it were a massive government money giveaway to failing banks, with the government getting a massive amount of worthless paper in return. Ted Gomer said very little.

For the last fifteen minutes of the meeting, the CEO of the American Bank Corporation, Kurt Lane, asked innumerable questions. Finally, he slowly stood and told those same gentlemen, "Take your TARP program and shove it up your ass! My Bank is not having any part of this scam." The meeting ended abruptly.

Can you believe this? Jones thought. *What the hell is going on? Have Harry Peters and Bill Baker and Ted Gomer gone frigging mad?*

Later, Mr. Lane and his bank would suffer dearly for his outburst.

Next, billions more dollars went overseas to unnamed companies. The Feds refused to disclose how much money went to what company or country. Better yet, many individuals stocked their bank accounts with untold millions. This was a total bailout of Wall Street and the hell with Main Street. This truly was the biggest rip off, actually the biggest financial heist, of the US Treasury that had ever been executed in the history of the country. Jones had had enough. He did not like what he was hearing.

What Bill Baker, Harry Peters, and Ted Gomer were doing to the country was one thing. What they were doing for themselves and their buddies was another. It was nothing short of criminal. Bailing out irresponsible financial institutions because they were "too big to fail" certainly was not in the best interest of the USA. Moving billions of dollars out of the Treasury to who the hell knew where was subject to some serious fraud and thievery charges, especially when the Feds refused to say where it went and who got what amounts. That smelled to high heaven. The sad fact is that there would never be any accounting for all that money. These three men and others would never have to answer for what they allowed to happen, much less their actual participation in so many questionable actions. To Jones, that just didn't seem right.

The very next day Jones did two things. First, he went on a full court press at his Bank to convince his bosses to meet with the subprime mortgage company from California. He showed the American Bank Corporation CEO a strategy to acquire this company that would make the Bank millions. He sold the idea of getting in on this major cash cow gravy train. It took next to no arm twisting to convince the fairly new Bank head, Kurt Lane, to agree to the deal. Jones had it all worked out with the selling company CEO. Although Jones despised the man, he had planned on using him all along, for his own benefit.

The second thing Mr. Jones did was call his broker in the Caymans. That broker was managing all that cash Jones had wired down there over the last year. He said, "Richard, I want you to put in a short sell order for me."

"Whatever you say, bossman," Richard replied. "Just give me the details, and I will take care of it immediately."

"I want it put in a 'street name'. I want to short a very large block of my bank stock. It is important that you get this done today. Understand?"

"You might want to give me the name of the bank stock. Okay?"

"Okay smart ass. It's the American Bank Corporation stock. Get it done before the stock price falls even lower. Can I count on that?"

"Bossman, you know that I'll do whatever you ask of me just as soon as possible. Not to worry, consider it done. Gotta go. Goodbye."

Ten minutes later his broker called back and asked Jones, "Are you sure you want to do this? It's your own Bank's stock, bossman. This is crazy."

Annoyed, Jones said, "Richard, just place the goddamn order. Today. Just do it. *Now!*"

He hung up the phone.

It was the stock of the very Bank Mr. Jones had worked for for the last thirty years. It was time for Jones to cash in big time. He had burned his bridges with his Bank for sure.

Then, in late 2008, as Jones had proposed, the American Bank Corporation did a very stupid thing. They bought WideCountry, the largest sub-prime mortgage company in the country. The Bank paid way too much for this company which was nothing more than a trainload of sub-prime mortgages, many already in default. Jones had pushed for this acquisition because he thought it would further cripple his bank and the industry as well. The CEO of the selling company failed to disclose all of the minute distasteful details about his company. The buying American Bank Corporation CEO, Kurt Lane, who really trusted Jones's advice, never bothered to do his due diligence to protect his Bank from acquiring bad assets. They both wanted the deal too badly. The bubble was getting bigger.

The market was beginning to show some concern from both institutional traders and private investors. From one day to the next, one never knew whether to buy or sell. The stock market was like a yo-yo on steroids. It was overcome by short selling one day and everyone scrambling to buy everything in sight the next. The volatility index was moving like a rollercoaster on Coney Island. Lots of people were getting quite nervous.

Then, to make matters worse for the American Bank Corporation, amidst all of the financial chaos, they bought Murray-Lane Securities. What were they thinking? They bought this company one day before it collapsed. It was in the same position as the other investment house that had collapsed on the Street the week before. The truth is the Bank had actually tried to buy the Lehman Brothers that had just collapsed. Again, the Bank's CEO was too anxious. The Feds forced him into an untenable situation that he had a very hard time explaining later. He was forced to make misrepresentations about the final terms of the deal, and that eventually led to his downfall.

There were a lot of things going on at the American Bank Corporation at this time of the crisis. There were lots of meetings and lots of finger pointing. A very disgruntled board began publicizing their concerns. It seemed as if, all of a sudden, the Bank had run afoul of the Feds. They were getting legal threats from all sides; shareholders, investors, bond holders, the Feds, and the Treasury. What looked like great opportunities in the acquisitions of these two failing enterprises resulted in a number of lost jobs. The Bank went through two or three CEOs before you could say jack rabbit, and law suits began to flow like water. What followed over the ensuing years was billions upon billions of settlement expenses and fines for the Bank. The American Bank Corporation had become a Bad News Bank.

The Bank was trying to expand its involvement into the investment business while the regulations were relaxed for most banks. They just picked the wrong time. Then it happened. The bottom fell out of the economy. The market was in free fall, and all hell broke loose for all banks, but this Bank in particular. Its stock price plummeted. Heads rolled. The chairman was forced out along with many of his close advisors. Other banks hit the skids as well. The stock market lost more points in a day – and for several days on end – than it often gained in a year. A new Great Depression had set in on America. The smile on Mr. Jones' face was unending. Much of his dirty work had gone unnoticed.

In late 2008, to add insult to injury, the Madoff scandal broke wide open. For decades this guy had been swindling his investors via a very complex type of Ponzi scheme. Jones thanked his lucky stars that he hadn't gotten sucked in by Bernie. He actually attended two opportunity meetings that Madoff chaired. He remembered what his Mom had beaten into him as a kid, that when something seemed too good to be true, it probably was a situation to avoid. Jones could never understand how Madoff could pay his investors such high returns on their money even when the market was falling. It made no sense to him, so he did not fall prey to Bernie. During those years, thousands of mostly smart, rich folks had been plying Madoff with millions upon millions of their fortunes so they could participate in his incredible ability to pay them fabulous returns on their investments, even when the market and other financial firms were losing money. It was quite a trick, but Madoff got away with doing it for over thirty years. The end result was Madoff bilked his clients for about $65 billion. Yes, billion with a B. Thousands of families were wiped out and destroyed. This was just another example of devastating greed. Obviously, it was running rampant in the financial world.

One thing that concerned Mr. Jones a great deal was the tip he'd gotten from his friend at Treasury a few days earlier. His friend, the informant, told him, "I just recently saw an 'EYES ONLY' memo in Harry Peters's office that outlined a series of secret meetings that are scheduled to occur over several weekend intervals at some of the most luxurious resorts in the country. Places like The Mountain Lodge in Breckenridge, Colorado, the White Elephant on Nantucket, the Greenbrier in West Virginia, the Mission Inn in northern California's Napa Valley, the Cloister at Sea Island, Georgia, the Stowe Mountain Lodge in Vermont, and the Wyndham La Belle Mansion in New Orleans."

"Why are meetings being planned at these places?"

The informant responded, "According to the memo, large numbers of corporate jets seen on tarmacs at airports where these resorts are located would not draw any special attention, because there are normally many private jets on those tarmacs on any given weekend."

"Okay, who is in this secret group that will be attending these secret meetings?" Jones asked.

"According to the document, the meetings will be attended by many of the wealthiest and most powerful men and women in America. The list includes the Who's Who of American business and finance. They truly are the elite of the elite. They represent most every industry in the US., from Silicon Valley to Wall Street. These billionaires plan to meet and lay out a comprehensive plan that will put a national structure in place, including a monetary system with its own currency that will be activated immediately if the US banking system collapses. Basically, they're talking about a takeover of the entire financial industry."

"The hell you say," Jones said.

His friend at Treasury continued, "The plan also outlines details of many new policies that will be put in place overnight, not only to secure the country's domestic position, but also policies that will determine the country's overall foreign policy. Additionally, the military complex will be completely overhauled and controlled by these people."

What the informant told Jones next was mind boggling and very frightening.

"These folks know about everything. They know what is wrong with our financial system and why. They know more than most of the top CEOs at the major banks know. They know more than the Titans of corporate America. They know more than the heads of all of our governmental financial agencies combined. They've got the total picture."

Jones began yelling into his phone, "Tell me what the hell you are talking about. Explain it to me so I can understand what all of this shit means. Go ahead, tell me now."

"These people recognized that there was a real physical cash shortage crisis when it first started a year or so ago, because they, along with other billionaires and major global financial houses, were part of the problem. They were, in fact, the ones that began hoarding stockpiles of actual cash just a couple of years ago. You do know that the 'big boys' are the first ones to take their money and run when they smell a problem. When you hear that there are millions, if not billions, of cash dollars sitting on the sidelines, this is what they're talking about; except it's billions upon billions of dollars on the sidelines."

"They also know that the Fed has poured trillions of dollars into the US money supply since the crisis began just to replace all the cash that just keeps disappearing from the US cash currency inventory. How long they can continue to do this is a frightening unknown."

"This secret group knows that the ability to use cash to pay bills, get cash from banks, or to do most anything that requires cash, is becoming more restrictive every day. Soon it will be totally replaced with our credit system, which is already near the top end of its capabilities. In other words, real cash is being replaced by paper, just plain digital paper credit, not real legal tender. Real cash dollars are disappearing globally. The secret group knows we are heading for a major CREDIT COLLAPSE right here in America."

He continued, "They also know that if the time comes when all the American debt; personal, business, and government combined (over 50 trillion dollars) has to be paid, there will be a problem. It will be impossible to pay because there are less than $300 billion actual cash dollars available in our American currency system today. What happens to the credit lines across America when the lenders become fearful that the debtors no longer have the ability to pay off the loans. The answer; financial disaster, total collapse."

"They also know that the Federal Reserve must keep the interest level at or near zero so huge amounts of debt can still be afforded by so many huge lenders. And they know that the Treasury is having a difficult time raising the inflation rate to even a 2-3% level. They are also aware of the many huge withdrawal amounts that have already been demanded from some banks, and the chaos it's causing. This secret group is preparing to correct these problems and avoid a total financial meltdown in the US before it is too late."

Jones answered, almost screaming, "Jesus Christ, these are some very serious charges. If enacted over the next couple of months, they could drastically change the total dynamic of America, without any knowledge of or participation by the American citizenry. What an outrageous idea. Can Treasury stop these crazy bastards?"

His friend did not respond.

Jones pressured him. "You got to tell me the names of the people in this secret group." His friend relayed all the names to Jones.

Jones said, "Thanks for the heads up."

Jones was stunned to hear the names of several men and women he had been in contact with over the years. It was unbelievable to him that these people would go to these lengths to basically remake America. He was shocked to learn that some of these folks would actually participate in this bizarre scheme. Who the hell did they think they were? What the hell were they thinking? Some of the participants were infamous international financiers who were not even American citizens. One was a foreign born, self-avowed, destructive, leftist demagogue; a man, in fact, who had had major financial influence on one of the country's major political parties for years. This was becoming very serious.

Jones was sweating profusely.

This was shocking. It was dangerous. It was horrifying that this was actually happening in the USA. It meant that the banking industry was in even worse shape than Jones knew. He wanted to know how this debacle was going to evolve. He had lots of questions he wanted to ask, but he did not want any record showing that he knew anything about this new secret development. He wondered if the Bank knew. Then he decided it was not his responsibility to tell anyone. So, for the time being, he let it slide.

As Jones' Cessna Citation X jet began its descent into Teterboro Airport in New Jersey, he decided he should take Mary out for dinner. He called the River Cafe on Water Street in Brooklyn and made reservations for eight o'clock. This would be a great time for them to discuss things they could do, plans they should probably make, and decisions they might want to take in light of all the bad financial news he was now privy to. He did not want to frighten Mary, but he thought she deserved to have some input as to what they should at least consider under the circumstances.

Mary was completely taken aback after hearing what Jones had to tell her about what the elites had planned for America, if the banking system failed and collapsed. Mary's first remarks were, "I can't believe what the hell is going on, and how the hell did you get this information. Has it been verified? I wonder who else knows about this." Then she took a deep breath and sipped her Margarita. Jones was drinking Jack Daniels on the rocks. It had been a tough day.

Mary thought it was a horrifying notion for anyone to consider doing this in the US. Once she calmed down, they began laying out possibilities about their futures. Jones suggested they meet for lunch the next day to see if they could get on the same page about what they needed to do, and when they should do it. It seemed as if their futures were headed down the same path, maybe even a trip to the altar.

The next day Mary and Jones met for lunch at the 21 Club on west 52nd street and started writing out their combined plan of action. Mary was quick to say, "We both have to get out of debt, become debt free. It is imperative that we reduce our outstanding debt as soon as possible."

Jones agreed and said, "Let's get rid of our mortgages and any other long term financial obligations we have. I paid most of mine off last year."

Jones suggested, "We both need to get our respective apartments appraised immediately, so when we decide to put them on the market for sale, we will be ready and able to justify our asking prices."

Mary agreed. She said, "I will put together a proposal for any of my law partners that may be willing to buy my interest in the firm. If I'm leaving, I plan to leave it all. I also think we need to convert all our assets to cash or gold now, before the values of our holdings drop even more." They also agreed that they should keep their plan secret. No need to alarm anyone needlessly.

Jones did make one more suggestion, "It may be prudent for us to keep our ears close to the ground, so that if and when a deal pops up in the stock market or in the real estate market over the next several months, we will be in a position to take advantage of a bargain." Mary had no problem with that idea.

One thing that went unsaid, but seemed to be a foregone conclusion, was that they were comfortable with the idea that they would be riding out this national financial crisis together in his villa in the Caymans. There could be worse punishment. They also agreed on a timeline of no more than six months for them to get this done.

Jones' hunch of several months earlier had been right on. The pieces of the puzzle he had been able to connect, by putting all the dots in place, had provided him with the vision and understanding of what was coming, regardless of what anybody at the Fed or the Treasury could possibly enact.

The dye had been cast and it was very red. It was time for Jones to make his move. He did what he had to do. It was payback time.

More bad banking news spewed from the TV newscasts. The Winston Corporation was being absorbed by that other west coast bank, CFC.. It had been wrestled away from Urban Bank & Trust by California Financial Corp, who had only paid a token price per share to take over this merged entity of the aggressive First State and the staid Winston banks. Shareholders were screaming bloody murder as they saw their lifetime earnings disappear. This was highway robbery without a gun. Wasn't there something someone could do? Sadly, the answer was a resounding "No."

Their bank's stock took a beating. Every day it reached a new low. The share price fell below $2. Shareholders who had lived off of their dividends from this stock for years were now clamoring for cash flow. Month after month things got worse. First came the stock sell off to stop the bleeding at tremendous losses. Then came the foreclosures. That bank's stock value continued to decline. The shareholders were furious and wanted answers. It seemed this disaster would never stop. When it ended how would there be any value left. Not many people thought so. Some very bad things were happening in America. Lots of Americans would never recover.

Two days after the Winston Corporation was folded into California Financial Corp, the secret group called an emergency meeting. They did this via secured Skype lines in a GoToMeeting setup. Each participant called in with a secret dial-in number and password. Once everyone logged on, the meeting began.

First they elected officers. They discussed who would be president or chairman, vice-president, secretary of state, secretary of treasury, attorney general, and head of Homeland Security. They were setting up a proposed management structure for "The New America." They were organizing nothing short of a coup.

The next item of business was to establish a timeline to launch what they considered "The New America" with its new domestic laws, rules, currency, foreign policy, and military. When all of this was in order, they would convert the US financial system to their newly designed financial framework. They were dead serious, and they planned to move on this in a few days.

What most Americans never knew, and that is probably a blessing, was that on one Friday, late in September 2008, the Dow dropped almost 800 points. When the market's value decreased by more than a trillion dollars, this secret group went into emergency mode. They called for a mandatory meeting the following Tuesday, September 30, at of all places, the Greenbrier in West Virginia.

That same Tuesday morning Jones got another call from his friend at Treasury. The informant told Jones, "The secret group is on the move. They've called a mandatory meeting for tonight at the Greenbrier. Thought you might want to know."

"Damn right, I want to know," Jones answered. "I'll see what I can find out and get back to you. Thanks." Jones hung up and dialed Mary.

"Grab some fancy clothes and lots of jewelry. I'll send my car for you in an hour. We're flying to the Greenbrier this afternoon," Jones told her.

"Slow down, Jones. You're going too fast. Why are we going to the Greenbrier now? What's going on?"

"We're going to play 'Big Time.' Just get ready, please. I'll explain later."

Once Mary and Jones were on his Citation X headed to White Sulphur Springs, Jones explained the situation to Mary. "The secret group I told you about is planning to take over our country if our financial system fails. They have called a mandatory meeting for all its members tonight after dinner in the bunker at the Greenbrier."

Mary asked, "I suppose we're going to attend, although we have not been invited. Are you crazy?"

"Sure, we'll get all dressed up, mingle with the elite folks at dinner, and just slip right into the meeting when it starts. Arriving on this big bird will be all the credibility we'll need to fit right in."

"Why is it so important that you crash their meeting? What's it to you anyway?"

"It's about the future of our country. That's why it's so important that I hear their plan, so I can convey it to those who matter. Understood."

"If you say so. What happens if they ask you for your membership card? What then?"

"I'll cross that bridge when I get there, Miss Doubting Thomas."

The reason it was so unusual for the secret group to meet at the Greenbrier was that under this facility, some 720 feet into the side of the mountain, was a bunker accommodation for Members of Congress in the event of a nuclear or a terrorist attack on America. The facility had over 100,000 square feet of space and was equipped to provide for most any type of amenities that any congressmen or dignitary would ever need.

On that Tuesday morning and throughout the day, a good number of corporate jets invaded the airspace over White Sulphur Springs and subsequently dotted the tarmac everywhere. These elite citizens had come here, to this emergency meeting, to implement their plan for "The New America."

Jones' Citation X touched down sometime after lunch. He and Mary, dressed to the nines, and all the other elite members met for drinks and dinner, and then they moved downstairs to the bunker for their meeting. Mary and Jones mixed in easily.

It was a really scary meeting. What the secret group wanted for America was so foreign to the Constitution and to the Bill of Rights that the average American citizen would have never condoned their proposed actions. The secret group had voted unanimously to implement their "New America" plan immediately. This would definitely cause a serious outbreak of real class warfare in the country, not to mention all the other damage their agenda might cause.

After the meeting, Jones and Mary went straight to his plane. Once aboard, Jones dialed up his friend at Treasury and relayed everything he had heard at the meeting: facts, dates, names, plans, and details. He had done all he could do. It was up to Treasury to stop this madness.

Mary sat there in total disbelief about what she had just seen and heard. It was beyond amazing. She couldn't imagine what was going to happen next.

Fortunately, Harry Peters at Treasury knew about the secret group and had learned about their Greenbrier meeting while it was in session. From a mole in the meeting, he also learned about their outrageous plans for the country. It was a godsend that the mole conveyed the entire substance of the meeting to Treasury, because Treasury had actually underestimated the broad scope of the secret group's agenda. Harry Peters decided it was time for some serious action. He went directly to the White House for assistance. Together the Treasury Secretary and the President decided to confront the secret group head on. They demanded that the group's primary players come to the White House.

Two days later several members of the secret group were ushered into the Oval Office. They were quite surprised to see Mr. Jones sitting there with the President and Harry Peters. They probably realized then that the jig was up.

Harry Peters and the President put their demands on the table. They threatened to publicly expose to the nation every participant in the group to the American public. They threatened each individual with tough sanctions not only on their businesses and personal holdings, but on their foundations.

The group's contingency spokesperson initially pushed back hard. "We have all made sizable, personal financial contributions to the party, the President, Congress, and to an array of favorite political causes," he said. "We believe it is time for our group to take control because the current people in power have failed so miserably. We are adamant and steadfast about moving forward with our plan. It's what America needs."

The President, rising from behind his desk, made certain they understood the possible repercussions of their actions when he told them,

"My final demand is that a Cease and Desist order will be issued for each participant in your 'secret group.' If any one of your members fail to comply with the order, they will be arrested immediately and charged with treason. I'm sure you know the penalty for treason."

This got the secret group's attention. The uprising was squelched in a matter of days. A national disaster had been avoided. It was the first good news in almost a year, but the concerns that the secret group had raised about the country's financial future still existed, and that was not good news.

Several days later, Jones was relaxing in his penthouse when the doorman rang. Jones was a bit surprised as he was not expecting any company, and Mary was at work. He answered cheerfully, "Good Morning, may I help you?"

The doorman said very politely, "Mr. Jones, you have a visitor."

"Put him on, please."

A very stern voice spoke, "Are you the Mr. Jones that works in the banking industry?"

"Yes, I'm the banker. Who wants to know?"

"Mr. Jones, I am a US Federal Marshal. I have subpoena documents that I need to serve on you this morning. May I come up?"

"Subpoena for what?"

"The congressional hearings," the marshal said.

"Hell, come on up."

The visitor rode the elevator up to Mr. Jones's penthouse floor. When he stepped inside he explained, "Mr. Jones, this subpoena I'm serving on you compels you to appear before the Senate congressional hearings in Washington next Wednesday at ten a.m. sharp. You are allowed an attorney, if you would like to have one. If you elect to bring an attorney, you are required to provide the attorney's name and address to the Chairman of the hearings twenty-four hours prior to the day you testify. Do you have any questions?"

Jones thumbed through the subpoena documents, looked up at the marshal and replied, "Sir, I appreciate your time and trouble. I think I understand the drill. I don't have any questions. I'll be there with bells on. You can count on it. I'm looking forward to getting a few things off my chest."

The marshal extended his hand to Jones and said, "I hope you have a nice day, sir. Thanks for your cooperation. Good afternoon." He turned, stepped into the elevator and left.

When Jones met Mary for dinner later that evening at Aureole on 42nd Street near the theater district, he immediately told her about his visit from the marshal and his subpoena to appear before Congress.

Mary said, "What's this all about? Why do they want to talk to you? What do you know that they don't already know?"

Jones said, "What's the deal with all these questions? I'm just going there to tell the truth, the whole truth, nothing more. I have nothing to hide." He changed the subject by asking Mary, "How was your day? Any luck with your law partners buying your interest in the firm?"

She squirmed slightly and replied, "Maybe. The senior partner in the firm basically agreed to pay me a fair amount for my interest. That makes me happy, but the great news is that my sister called and said one of her husband's employees wants to buy my apartment. I'm having a good weekend."

Then she got real serious as she leaned across the table and whispered, "I think I'm ready to go to the Caymans now. It's time to get the hell out of the city. Now!"

Although a little surprised, Jones shook his head and said, "Certainly, you can go anytime you like, but I have to stay until after I testify at the hearings." They talked about this as they ate their dinner. Then Jones suggested, "Gather up some things, jump on the Citation, and go on ahead of me. I'll come on down the minute the hearings are over. I'll let you know when to pick me up at the airport."

Mary smiled and agreed. "Don't worry about that. I'll be waiting for you. Don't forget your briefcase."

"Don't worry. Never leave home without it."

Over the next several days Mary wasted little time in finishing up some last minute details and tying up some loose ends so she could leave the city for the islands. She settled all of her legal matters with her law partners. She visited with her sister and filled her in with the details about moving to the Caymans. She left all the necessary information about her apartment with her sister, so she could pass it on to the new owner. She visited by phone with her parents and brought them up to speed on her new plans. They were not too thrilled to get the news that their daughter was leaving the US, but they understood that love conquers all.

Mary planned to leave New York on Monday before the congressional hearings began on Wednesday. Jones planned to leave for Washington on Tuesday morning. Everything was set. They were ready to embark on their new journey. They were very pleased that things were working out without any hitches.

Chapter 36
THE CONGRESSIONAL HEARINGS

The congressional hearings began shortly after the DOW Jones Industrial Average dropped below 6,000.

The first to testify was former head of WideCountry. He was followed by the head of Murray-Lane Securities. These were the heads of the companies that sold the Bank their bad deals. They were testifying, but they were saying very little. Then came the congressional mandate that required all fourteen CEOs from the top banks to appear for questioning. What a site that was when they all stood up, hands on Bibles and were sworn to tell the truth, nothing but the truth, so help them God. What a farce, what a joke that turned out to be. Their combined testimony was one big fat lie. It was total bullshit, with one big stonewall all across the board. The banking lobbyists were noticeably absent. They should have been subpoenaed as well. Congress was still having trouble getting things right. Lots of trouble for sure.

On the last day, the Senate congressional hearing Chairman called one last person to testify. They called Mr. Jones. It was Mr. Jones' turn in the barrel, and what a splash he made.

As his Citation X jet screamed down the runway at Dulles International Airport later that September afternoon, Jones sipped his coffee as he looked out the window as the lights of the capitol city began to glow. His attaché case lay open on the seat beside him. Files of deposit slips and wire transfer notices peeked out from within. *Something seemed strange; there was something wrong with this picture*. At two hundred miles an hour, the jet lifted off the tarmac into the sky headed for the Caymans.

Jones reflected back on what he had done that day.

He had arrived at the Senate hearings precisely at 10 am, signed in, and had taken a seat at the witness table. He stated to the Chairman that he did not have nor did he need an attorney. He was looking confident and suave in his new dark Baroni pinstripe suit. He had purchased it just last month in New York. His omnipresent red tie was perfectly knotted. He stood to be sworn in. The moment he was seated again, a barrage of questions came from all sides. One senator after another shouted out questions and clamored for his attention. Mr. Jones said nothing. He answered no questions, not one. For about ten minutes this chaos prevailed. After the Chairman regained order, Mr. Jones stood up. He raised his hands for calm. He looked right into the eyes of the Chairman. Quiet fell over the Senate chamber. Mr. Jones began his testimony, at his own speed and on his own terms.

"Mr. Chairman and distinguished Senators.....

"I lost my father in a work-related accident in 1961 when I was only three years old. Not long after that my Mom and I moved to Florida. We lived in a mobile home for years before my Mom could afford a decent apartment. She worked initially as a bank teller, just to get us by. Then she worked her way up and became a loan officer at a bank in Melbourne. She made sure that I was never hungry. She saw to it that I always wore clean clothes. She taught me how to read and write. She took me with her to church and Sunday school every week. She taught me how to respect others, as well as respect what others had. She disciplined me each time I stepped out of line. I really loved and adored my Mother. She even helped pay for part of my early college education. She set me up to get a great job and grow into a fine and prosperous young man.

"Then one day, on my nineteenth birthday, just three weeks after I had returned to Chapel Hill to begin my junior semester, I received the terrible news that she had been murdered in a bank robbery in Florida. Three armed druggies crashed into the bank lobby from three different entrances. One of the robbers got spooked when a teller behind the window reached for her phone. He unloaded his weapon in that direction. My Mom was just an innocent bank employee standing in line at that teller station waiting to buy a $500 money order to send me for my birthday. She died where she fell. She lay there for the next thirty-six hours as a bank hostage stand-off situation ensued. At midnight the following night, the FBI SWAT team stormed the bank and killed all three robbers. Two more bank employees and another customer were also killed. It was a tragic nightmare. There was no rhyme nor reason for any of this to happen. They were just three thugs looking to take some money so they could buy more drugs. But what they took was my Mom. They took the most important person in my life. It was so unfair. I was devastated. I was overcome with grief. I blamed the bank for not having enough security to protect its employees and customers. I declared that very day I would get even, if it took me forever.

"Several weeks after my Mom was buried, I returned to college with plans to finish and get my degree. After I had gotten my thoughts halfway organized enough to move forward, I made a plan. I would find a job in the banking industry somewhere, somehow. A position that would give me a steady income, but more importantly, a job that would put me in the right place to pay back the industry that had taken my Mother from me.

"Later that year I was in the university library researching several in-state banks, where I just happened to read an old archived state newspaper article. It was about a person, Pete Hamilton, who had convinced a major in-state banking company to pay him a commission for causing large amounts of money to be deposited in their coffers. He had a signed commission letter from the president of that bank, and the letter was printed in the paper alongside the article. I decided immediately that I would pursue that same course. I knew that I could do the same thing.

"I contacted the man in the newspaper article and met with him two weeks later. He and I had some very serious conversations. Actually, we bonded once we leveled with each other as to who we really were, and where we had been.

"What that man told me changed the entire course of my life. What he told me in absolute secrecy put me on a pathway that brought me here today. He told me that some banks would pay an individual for doing certain 'off the record' jobs for their bank. He also told me how and why they would do this. He convinced me that I could do the same thing and make lots of money.

"But the most important thing he told me was that he was an ex-felon. He also told me that in the early 1960s he had spent some hard time in the Atlanta prison for several counts of financial trickery with other people's money. Furthermore, he told me his cell mate was a man named Edward Cain, known as EC, the counterfeit money man who ran ahead of the Secret Service for years before they got a conviction. The pieces of my plan were falling into place.

"Then he told me what I could do to get the Bank to pay me lots of money or give me lots of bank stock each time I increased the Bank's value. This was just what I was waiting for, a chance to get involved with the Bank. I was looking a bank job that would provide the pathway for me to pay back the bastards who let my Mom die in a bank heist that had gone very, very wrong. I knew right then that my college days were numbered.

"The rest of Pete Hamilton's story was very interesting. While he was in prison and sharing a cell with EC, EC told Pete all about his counterfeit money scam. EC told Pete how he made the counterfeit money, where he got the plates and the paper, and how he ran it through the 'Old Money' burn program at the Federal Reserve. EC explained how they got good money back and deposited it in the new Bank. Then he related how he got caught with the counterfeit money the first time, and how he got off because of a legal technicality regarding the search warrant. EC described how within a few months of being freed, he had cranked the counterfeit deal back up again. He also described how much better the counterfeit twenty dollar bills looked the second time. EC also said that many hundreds of thousands of counterfeit twenties were printed before he was caught for the second time four years later.

"EC told Pete exactly where millions of dollars of the bogus twenties were hidden – all that counterfeit money that was never found by the Federal agents. He told Pete how to access that bogus money, and then told Pete what to do with it once he got it. It was amazing. These were facts about the counterfeit scheme that hundreds of people had wanted to know for so many years.

"What EC told Pete was that millions of dollars of the bogus twenty dollar bills were stashed away in separate safe deposit boxes in almost every branch bank across the southeastern and southwestern US. EC said that every time they cranked out $100,000 in counterfeit twenties, they packaged them in a box. A box of bogus money fit perfectly in an ordinary black briefcase. EC then said he would get one of his appropriately dressed 'boys' to take the briefcase of counterfeit money to a specific bank. There he would place the money in a safe deposit box, collect the access information, and report back to EC. EC logged the information in his ledger for each batch that had been placed in a safe deposit box in these bank branches all over the southeast and southwest. Did you hear that? He hid the bogus money in safe deposit boxes in hundreds of banks across the southeast and southwest. This happened over and over again in most all branch banks that offered safe deposit boxes, in almost every Southern state. Millions of dollars of the counterfeit money was already hiding, legally, in the banks for safe keeping, in plain sight.

"Then Pete Hamilton instructed me to call the president of this Bank and arrange a meeting. I was to tell him who I was and what I wanted. Pete convinced me that I'd get the job. He told me that once I was hired, I was to return to Virginia Beach to see him.

"I called the Bank president immediately, and he agreed to meet with me right away. We had a productive meeting, and I immediately got the job. I left that meeting and drove straight back to see Pete, my new mentor. Pete told me that he'd been struggling financially for the past few years.

He wanted me to cut him in for $5,000 for each safe deposit box that was redeemed. He had them all listed in the ledger that he'd gotten from EC. It only took me two seconds to say, 'Hell yes!'

"Then Pete Hamilton gave me these instructions:

"He told me to get into the Bank's expansion division. That would give me access to the information about where the Bank was going, and what banks they were planning to buy or merge. Once I had that information, I was to contact the target bank first and speak directly with the CEO or the chairman, no one else. I was to tell them that I knew all about the counterfeit money. Pete warned me they would deny any knowledge of the counterfeit money. He said to let the bank official know that I knew about the money they still had in their safe deposit boxes. Also tell them that I could identify specific boxes and how the counterfeit money got there. If the banker still resisted, I should then threaten to expose their counterfeit money deposits. Once the banker acquiesced, then I would layout the plan..

"The target bank, in order to insure it would be purchased or merged with the Bank, had to agree to take the money out of the safe deposit boxes and slowly send it to the Federal Reserve via the 'Old Money' burn program. Once all the counterfeit money had been replaced with good money, they were to deposit $50,000 in my bank account and $5,000 in an account of my designation. The cooperating bank would keep $45,000 of each safe deposit box they emptied. The plan was going to be like taking candy from a baby, without the screaming. It was that simple. Then Pete handed me a copy of EC's ledger book, but he reminded me that he kept a copy to keep me honest.

"According to Pete, EC told him that this had all started in the late 1950s. He said each time a bank that had some of EC's bogus money in its safe deposit boxes was acquired, the Federal Reserve old 'Money to Burn' program went into effect. According to Pete, they continued this expansion model under Horace Felton, the new CEO who took over after Michael Banks died in 1972. It was still going on when I arrived in 1977. This bogus money helped prop up the Bank during some of its most difficult times. It was simply ingenious. No, it was outrageously clever.

"So in 1982, when the Bank began its incredible acquisition run, I decided it was the right time to burn some bogus bills again. I re-introduced the Fed's old 'Money to Burn' program with many of those banks in almost every southeastern and southwestern state. It was too easy. During the times when these banks were having problems, they would do almost anything to survive. So they all did as I asked, and there were very few questions asked. It was incredible.

"Now think about it. Who is going to turn down this deal that no one else will ever know about? Ever. And in the meantime, their bank deal goes through. The answer is no one, and over thirty some years, no one ever did. Not one single bank ever pushed back to any serious degree.

"Over the thirty some years I worked for the Bank, to the best of my knowledge and understanding of information I retrieved from EC's ledger book, there were nine hundred and sixty safe deposit boxes filled with EC's counterfeit money. Over the years, all of this counterfeit money was sent to the Federal Reserve Burn Center and burned. As I have already explained to you, a like sum of 'good money' was returned to the participating banks. That equates to an amount close to $100,000,000 dollars.

"So, you see, thanks to your selling out to the special interest groups that wanted total bank deregulation, we now have a banking industry that was partially financed and expanded by millions of dollars of counterfeit money. Additionally, your banking system was supported by all of those billions of worthless dollars the Fed printed. You can add to that the greed, dishonesty, deceit, bank fraud, and coercion that was allowed to grow and prosper with the subprime mortgages fiasco. Don't let me fail to mention the asset backed securities and credit swaps that were falsely rated by the corrupt rating agencies and sold to unknowing investors worldwide. Because of all that, today you have a banking industry that is on its knees.

"All of you, every one of you, with all of your self-serving actions, have allowed our country to fall to such depths of financial despair that a secret group made up of the elite of the elite, mostly billionaires, was just uncovered and disrupted. This secret group came damn close to taking over our country, our nation, our political structure, our domestic and foreign policy, our financial structure and currency, and our military complex

– all for their own benefit. Thankfully, their actions were thwarted by the highest power in our land. However, the major concern that this secret group had about our country, like the imminent Credit Collapse, still exists today. Consider yourselves forewarned. Maybe you should be a little more concerned about these very real dangers.

"And here is what you greedy bastards have left our country with:
"The banking industry has lost trillions.
"The bank shareholders have lost billions.
"America has suffered irreparable harm, at home and abroad.
"Had it not been for the billions of taxpayer bailout dollars from the Feds to all those 'too big to fail' banks, the banking industry would have collapsed.
"Hell, they gave my Bank $40 billion, and they guaranteed another $100 plus billion in assets!
"I suggest today that your billion dollar bank giveaways have come home to roost.
"I would further suggest that many of you, as well as many of the banking officials, should be indicted.
"Have a good day.
"Like grandfather, like grandson."
"I am...Edward Earl Cain, III......aka Mr. Jones."

And with that, Mr. Jones gave the Chairman a nod, straightened his red tie, and started to walk out of the Senate hearing room. But not before the Chairman of the Senate Committee on Banking, Cliff Dowd, the distinguished Senator from Connecticut, gaveled the noisy hearing room to order and exclaimed, "Mr. Jones, I mean EC III, uh..., I mean Mr. Cain, or whatever your damn name is, please take your seat."

Mr. Jones, slightly startled, spun around and faced the Chairman and said, "Yes Sir. What can I do for you, Senator Dowd?" Then he sat down.

The Chairman began, "Mr. Jones, the Committee really appreciates your time and testimony here today. However, what you have just done is totally unprecedented. To my knowledge this has never occurred before. I know that I personally have never seen this happen in the thirty years of my Senatorial career."

"Today, by your own admission while under oath, you gave sworn testimony that unveiled a cornucopia of Federal crimes that staggers the imagination. You sat right there and not only incriminated yourself, but you also implicated many of your colleagues, not to mention the dozens of banking and financial institutions across America. This is a monumental development to say the least. There have to be some consequences."

"There is no doubt that the Committee will insist on a complete examination and review of your most incredible testimony. This Committee will have to determine what steps, if any, legal or otherwise, that may be necessary in light of the sobering content of the information you presented before this hearing."

"Mr. Jones, do you have anything more to say?"

"I did what I had to do," Jones said. "I have no regrets. I wanted to get this off of my chest. I wanted everyone to know exactly what actually happened. I feel like I just gave my confessional. Do whatever you have to do. I'm done."

The Chairman cleared his raspy voice and continued, "Mr. Jones, with the power that this Committee has vested in me, Congress remands you to limit your travel to the continental United States. Additionally, within the next forty-eight hours you must surrender your passport, and you'll be required to sign a written affidavit acknowledging your testimony as factual and true."

As Mr. Jones stood and headed to the exit, the Senate Sergeant at Arms moved to block his path. The Chairman nodded to the Sergeant at Arms as if to say it was okay for Mr. Jones to leave.

Mr. Jones walked briskly out of the building while whispering to himself, "By the hairs of your chinny chin chin." He was anxious to get to the Caymans and tell Mary all about his day.

Chapter 37
THE CONFRONTATION

Jones knew deep down that EC would have been proud of him today. He also knew that EC would be spinning in his grave if he knew what he had done with the Bank and with all that counterfeit money over his thirty year career. He could not help thinking back to a few years earlier when he had decided to go see his grandfather, EC, for the first time. Jones was deep in thought about that face to face meeting as his plane climbed higher into the sky and headed south.

In 1997, Jones decided it was time for a face to face showdown with the man he had heard about all his life, but had never met. On EC's 80th birthday, Jones' jet flew into the New Ferry airport, which was about ten miles from town. He rented a car and drove to the Fork to the ongoing birthday celebration. No one knew he was coming, and no one knew who he was when he arrived.

Jones grabbed a soda from the iced-down tub of drinks and sat down to observe the ceremonies. There were lots of folks standing around talking about what a great guy the birthday boy was, and how they all loved him so much.

What total bullshit, Jones thought.

There was lots of food like fried chicken, barbecue, baked beans, slaw, hush puppies, sweet iced tea, banana pudding, and a giant three-tiered chocolate birthday cake, EC's favorite. Soon lines formed and the guests began digging into the buffet. It all smelled really good, and their plates were piled high. Jones decided he would eat after he took care of some business, or maybe not at all. Once the guests cleared out a bit, as they usually tended to eat and leave at functions like this, then he might grab a chicken wing.

He chatted with a couple of folks, who were curious enough to approach him and ask his name. He had no problem giving that up, but little else. One guy asked him if he was a relative and Jones's answer was, "I'm not sure." The guy, confused, turned and walked away.

Jones studied EC intently while he waited for the crowd to thin out. What he saw was an old, bald stooped-shouldered man, with fading, almost dead eyes, a wrinkled brow, and sagging jowls. EC, however, did manage a smile when talking with the few children that were there. Even then, it was sad. He was a fallen and beaten man, who was just waiting in the checkout line – that much was evident.

Jones thought, *he's my grandfather! Should I tell him that or not? Maybe? Maybe not. Should I be confrontational or reserved? Should I yell and scream or speak very softly? Should I spill the beans or be elusive?*

Deep down, Jones wanted to unload on EC. He wanted to berate him for everything he had done to his grandmother Brenda and to his mother, Anna, EC's own daughter. He also wanted to ask him about what he had *not* done for Brenda and her daughter. Jones wanted EC to know that he knew how poorly he had treated them both, and how heartless he had been with both women.

One thing Jones decided for sure, this would be his first, last, and only visit with EC. So whatever needed saying, he'd better get it said today. He decided to wait a few more minutes before he approached EC. He had noticed EC looking inquisitively his way a couple of times. It was about time to have that conversation.

Jones said, "EC, got a minute?" He reached to shake EC's hand, and at the same time pulled him up from his chair. "Happy Birthday, EC. Let's go for a walk." EC did not resist. Jones started slowly and EC followed. When they were safely out of earshot of the guests, Jones turned and faced

EC. He was right in EC's face. EC flinched slightly. Then Jones started his diatribe: softly, smoothly, concisely, and matter-of-factly.

Jones put his arm around EC's shoulders and quietly asked, "Why were you so damn mean and heartless to your first wife, Brenda?"

EC pulled back in dismay and said, "What the hell do you know about my first wife?"

Jones squeezed EC's arm and said, "Why did you never, ever recognize Anna, your first born?" Boy, did that hit home. EC was heating up.

Then EC started asking the questions. "Who the hell are you? You got a name? Why are you here? You got some damn nerve coming here."

Jones blew him off by scoffing at EC's inquiries and said, "Just shut the fuck up and listen to what I have to say, old man."

EC pulled back in disbelief. Jones took a deep breath and resumed talking, "EC, you bastard, everyone knows you killed Clara Mercer! I know it. I expect your daughter, Elaine thinks you killed her Mother. You're a fucking murderer! You went to prison for counterfeit money, not once, but twice. You're a felon. You had people burn down buildings. You're an arsonist. You were in the moonshine bootleg business. You married a sixteen year old child. You're a pedophile. Jesus Christ, you basically abandoned Elaine. You were never there for Will in his formative years, your only son and namesake. What kind of fucking father is that, EC? Tell me! You have yet to show any signs of remorse for any of these horrible actions. What do you have to say about that? You just don't give a happy goddamn about anybody, do you, EC?"

Surprised and stunned, EC slumped over, as if he might fall. Jones steadied EC as EC looked up, so frail and so vulnerable, and asked, "Are you from Melbourne?"

Jones knew that if he said 'yes,' EC would have it all figured out. So he lied through his teeth. Big time lies. Jones told EC, "I'm a well-known movie producer from LA, and I'm interested in doing a movie about your life. I have been gathering all kinds of info about you for over ten years. I have a file on you that's bigger than the one they have at Treasury. It includes everything you've done since 1934, including everything you've done since you were paroled from prison in 1967. There ain't nothing about you that I don't know. I also know that most of the people involved in your illegal activities are dead. I know that now is the perfect time to put your story on the big screen."

EC lit up like a Christmas tree. "You mean a movie about my life?" EC whispered.

Jones could barely contain his laughter as he nodded, "Yes."

Then Jones told EC the conditions of the movie deal. Jones said, "EC, you have to provide me with the details of where all the bogus twenties are hidden. I need to know about all those other folks you took the fall for, all of them, like who they were and why."

EC said, "You got a tape recorder?"

Jones replied, "That'll come later."

EC nodded as if he understood and agreed.

Jones continued, "This movie about you is going to be a smash hit. It'll be a 'tell all' movie about the life and times of Edward Earl Cain. It has all of the ingredients of a blockbuster film. You'll probably become a folk hero, and the residuals will be tremendous." He was really stroking EC's ego now, in a way it had not been stroked in a very long time. He was setting EC up for a big fall. EC was finally going to leave a legacy, or so he thought.

Talk about pulling the wool over an old man's eyes, Jones told EC, "My attorneys will be in touch with you soon by mail to wrap up the legal work. Then an all-out effort will begin to pull all this together for the movie. Maybe even a cameo role for you, EC." EC gleamed with pride.

Then Mr. Jones leaned over to EC and quietly whispered, "There was so much fuckin' money to burn, I kept the Feds' fires burning day and night." Then he turned abruptly, got in his rental car, and sped away. He had lost his appetite.

EC was left standing all alone with a look of total bewilderment. *Happy Birthday?* EC thought.

And that's just the way Jones wanted EC to live out the remainder of his life – alone, bewildered, and totally confused, anxiously waiting for something wonderful that would never happen.

Chapter 38
THE TRIP HOME

As his jet soared along the coastline flying almost due south at 25,000 feet, Jones could only smile thinking about how he had finally avenged his mother's senseless death. He was proud that over the years he had played a very significant part in orchestrating an ongoing assault on the banking industry. He had been complicit in infusing tens of millions in counterfeit money into the system. He had convinced the Bank to buy WideCountry, a massive failure. By taking advantage of insider information about the tumbling value of the Bank's stock, he had perpetrated a huge and successful short sell order of his American Bank Corporation stock.

Jones was glad he had confronted his grandfather. He was pleased that he had told EC explicitly how awful and evil a man he was in the eyes of all human and decent people. He chuckled at the thought of EC longing to hear from the man that was going to do a movie about his life that may include a cameo role for him. Got mail?

During all this, with all of his wheeling and dealing, Jones had amassed over $50 million in cash in an offshore Cayman bank account. The fact that he had sold his New York penthouse for twice what he paid for it, validated his business acumen in his own mind. He was very proud of that deal.

When Jones hacked into the banker's account, who had his apartment searched, he was getting even. He emptied over a quarter of a million dollars from that banker's account into his own favorite charity's account. It felt like an *Ocean's Eleven* kind of heist. That maneuver had definitely been top drawer Jones thought.

On a more personal level, he was thrilled that he now owned a beautiful, newly decorated and furnished villa in the Cayman Islands, not to mention his own personal Cessna Citation X jet. These two assets alone could enhance his transition into a totally different lifestyle, one without the stress of the daily grind of a senior management banking official. Let bygones be bygones, he mused.

But most important to Jones now was Mary, the love of his life. She had spent so many days and nights waiting for him while he flew around the country pursuing his dreams. He knew she would be waiting to pick him up when he touched down. It was going to be a wonderful homecoming.

Jones was thankful that he had taken the time to visit with his New York attorney, and had enough forethought to re-write his will. In his mind, sharing his wealth with Mary was the fair and honorable thing to do. She had been so supportive for so long. She deserved security. He could not wait to tell Mary that he had modified his will to include her.

Mostly, Jones knew the smartest thing he'd done was stop by Harry Winston's Jewelry on Fifth Ave. It was even more satisfying that he could afford the diamond ring he had seen Mary admire so many times over the years. He could not wait to give her that large, sparkling diamond, if only she would agree to marry him. More than anything else, he couldn't wait to see her reaction to these two revelations.

Finally, he thought about the possibility of the two of them having so much time to spend together, alone. There were going to be many happy days ahead.

He was thinking.... *life is good. Yes, life is really good!*

As Mr. Jones reached for his IPhone to tell Mary he was airborne, he glanced again at his brief case and saw what his subconscious had already recorded. There, lying among the wire transfer receipts and bank deposit slips, was a plain white sealed envelope. On the mailing label he saw his name "Mr. Jones," nothing else. No address, no return address, no postage stamp. *What the hell is this, and how the hell did it get in my attaché case?*

Jones opened the envelope. Inside was a plain white piece of typing paper. Glued to the paper were words that had been cut from a magazine. The words were all in red letters.

Mr. Jones, did you really think we'd let you get away with this?

At the bottom of the page was a distinctly recognizable logo.

Mr. Jones looked up from the letter and saw black smoke billowing from the left engine of his jet.

The last thing Jones heard over his plane's intercom was, " May Day! May Day! May Day!"

TO BE CONTINUED.......